Population studies, No. 39

# Demographic consequences of economic transition in countries of central and eastern Europe

Dimiter Philipov and Jürgen Dorbritz

Directorate General III – Social Cohesion

Council of Europe Publishing

The views expressed in this study are those of the authors and
do not reflect necessarily those of the Council of Europe.

Council of Europe Publishing
F-67075 Strasbourg Cedex

ISBN 92-871-5172-5
© Council of Europe, May 2003
Printed at the Council of Europe

# Introduction

The Council of Europe has a long tradition of producing population studies and the work of the European Population Committee contributes to the understanding of the relationship between social policy and demographic issues in Europe. The findings of this work are published in the series Population Studies where topics covered include migration flows, national minorities, demographic changes and the labour market, the ageing of European populations and the demographic consequences of economic transition. These publications provide the essential background information for the implementation of the Council of Europe's strategy for social cohesion: an integrated policy approach aimed at combating poverty and social exclusion through the promotion of access to social rights in areas such as employment and training, health, social protection, housing, education and social services.

The social, political and economic transformations experienced by the formerly socialist countries of central and eastern Europe since the beginning of the 1990s have resulted in abrupt shifts in demographic trends, whose consequences on nuptiality, fertility, mortality and migration will be significant and irreversible. The present study analyses and offers explanations about this process and compares these developments with the demographic changes that occurred earlier in Western Europe. A thorough knowledge of these demographic trends offers an essential tool for social policy-makers and researchers and the comparative approach of the study furthers our understanding of the underlying processes taking place in all European countries. The authors also make suggestions for further demographic research.

I should like to take this opportunity of thanking the authors, Dimiter Philipov and Jürgen Dorbritz, for their work which has resulted in the comprehensive and thorough study contained in this volume. My sincere thanks go also to the European Population Committee and its Group of Specialists whose careful discussion of successive drafts has guaranteed the high quality of the final result.

*Gabriella Battaini-Dragoni*
*Director General of Social Cohesion*

# Table of contents

## Chapter 3

## Chapter 4

# Foreword

*Zdenek Pavlik*

Noteworthy changes in demographic processes have taken place in central and eastern Europe since the fall of the communist regimes. Questions arise as to what extent they are due to the economic, social and political transition in these countries and/or to changes similar to those which occurred in more demographically developed western European countries a few decades ago. Understanding demographic processes plays a key role in political decision-making concerning economic development, social and health policies, education and regional and local planning.

The region of central and eastern Europe is demographically heterogeneous viewed separately, but is at the same time homogeneous within Europe as a whole and even more within the world context. The demographic revolution universal process had already started in some countries of this region in the first half of the 19th century and ended in the 1960s (with the exception of Albania, where it only recently ended). Exact time limits cannot be precisely set; data for a whole country are always an average of different regional or social groups of inhabitants.

The demographic position of eastern and central Europe at the beginning of 1990s was very specific. According to the level of mortality measured by male and female life expectation at birth, Europe was clearly divided into two parts. All central and eastern European countries had a male life expectation lower than 71 years of age and lower than 78 years of age for females; the western part of Europe had a longer life expectation (Ireland, Portugal, the former Czechoslovakia and Slovenia being border line). The position of central and eastern Europe according to its fertility rate was less clear; several countries in this region had already approached the western European situation.

In the 1990s changes in mortality and fertility rates as well as in marriage and divorce rates were drastic and unexpected. With this in mind, the European Population Committee of the Council of Europe approved the project "Demographic consequences of economic transition in countries of central and eastern Europe" at its 23rd meeting in June 1998. A group of specialists (PO-S-TEC) from ten Council of Europe member states (see membership in Appendix) was set up to assist the consultants and discuss the results of the research work. Dr Jürgen Dorbritz from the Federal Institute for Population

Research in Wiesbaden and Dr Dimiter Philipov from the Max-Planck Institute for Demographic Research in Rostock were appointed as consultants.

The research work was carried out over a period of three years starting from 1999 and finalized in 2002. The main burden of work was undertaken by the consultants. I would like to express my gratitude to both of them for successfully achieving interesting results. At the same time I would like to voice my thanks to all the group members for their comments and the support and data they gave the consultants.

The consultants have divided their work into four chapters. The executive summary presents an overview of the main findings. The present study does not merely show what we know about demographic changes in central and eastern Europe over the past ten years, but it also makes suggestions for further demographic research. I would like to mention at least one question concerning future fertility trends. Could we accept as an explanation of very low fertility levels in many central and eastern European countries a possible follow-up of the so-called second demographic transition or should we put more weight on birth timing (linked to questions concerning maternal age shifting, brides and grooms, marriage stability etc.)? However, both these explanations are not contradictory but are complementary. Our knowledge is always incomplete and any opening on to new problems is as important as presenting partial answers.

# Executive summary

*Dimiter Philipov*

The ex-socialist countries from central and eastern Europe experienced abrupt demographic changes since the beginning of the 1990s. Nuptiality and fertility dropped to unprecedented low levels; extra-marital cohabitation and the share of extra-marital births increased tremendously; rapid postponement of these events took place; migration increased significantly. All these new demographic trends were observed in all countries although at a different pace. Mortality was more divergent: it increased in some countries and remained about constant or decreased in others.

## 1. Social, political, and economic transformation

These trends were conditioned by a rapidly changing political, social, and economic environment. The starting point of the latter was the socialist state with its totalitarian social order, centrally planned economy dominated by politics, restriction on individual rights, limited rule of law. Politically, one party dominated in society and imposed its ideology in a totalitarian way. Economically, the situation towards the end of the 80s can be characterized as follows: an oversized industry had been formed dominated by large state-own firms; inconvertible currencies and underdeveloped financial market; closed markets with fixed prices, separated from the world market; dominance of capital investment.

The transition began in the end of 1989 and in the ex-USSR countries with its collapse in the end of 1992. Basic economic and social macro-level indicators describe vividly the transition process. The gross domestic product dropped suddenly and significantly during the first couple of years after the start of the transition. Its 1989 level was first recovered in Poland only in 1996, followed towards 2000 by Albania, Hungary, Slovenia, the Slovak Republic, followed closely by the Czech Republic. Everywhere else the gross domestic product (GDP) in 2000 was considerably below that observed in 1989, in some Commonwealth of Independent States (CIS) countries as low as under 50%. Unemployment changed in the reverse direction: a significant increase was observed in most of the countries. It remained low only in a few CIS countries, such as Belarus and Ukraine. The inflation rate reached high peaks in some countries, for example as high as 578 per cent in Bulgaria and 152 in Romania in 1997, and 251 per cent in Belarus in 1999.

The transition period can be divided into five phases: pre-transformation; collapse of the political system; structural caesura; consolidation; sustained upswing. The pre-transformation was described above. This was the time of rising unrest and dissatisfaction among the people with respect to the functioning of "real socialism". The "perestroika" came out as a result and it was the background of all further changes.

The collapse of the political system is the real start of the transition. It happened suddenly with the removal of the leading role of the communist party and the birth of a multi-party system. Civil society was rooted and its development initiated. The structural caesura is the period when the socialist economy was demolished, but a market economy was still not fully functioning. This was the period of economic shock, created by liberalization of prices, opening of new markets, restriction of subsidies to state enterprises. Uncertainty in the future and impoverishment spread among large groups of the population. The social security system is being reorganized.

During the consolidation phase the political system stabilized. Market economy prevailed through ongoing privatization. Large-scale state enterprises were restructured. Some countries witnessed significant growth of foreign investment and integration into world trade. Society is polarized into winners and losers of the transition, social exclusion of impoverished and unemployed people rose as a significant feature of social life.

Sustained upswing is the phase when the political system is integrated into the European scene, and the market economy prevails and is firmly established. The social security system is improved and becomes reliable.

The diverse countries from the region pass at a different pace through these five phases. Some of them are near the completion of the sustained upswing, others are still far from entering into it. A general assessment of their paths of changes allows for the following grouping:

• Economically successful countries at an advanced stage of a transition: Croatia, Czech Republic, Hungary, Poland, Slovak Republic, Slovenia, Estonia, Latvia, Lithuania.

• Countries at a medium state of a reform: Albania, Armenia, Bulgaria, Georgia, Kazakhstan, Kyrgyzstan, "the former Yugoslav Republic of Macedonia", Moldova, Romania, the Russian Federation, Ukraine and Uzbekistan.

• Countries at an early stage of transition: Azerbaijan, Belarus, Tadjikistan, Turkmenistan.

This complex and sudden political and economic transformation had significant social consequences. The rise of unemployment and impoverishment was marked briefly above. It should be added that income dropped significantly during the structural caesura. Income increased to very high levels in the economically successful countries. In the other countries the pre-transition level of (real) income was reached only towards the end of the 90s.

The fall in income was accompanied by a widening wage gap. In addition, restructuring of property led to the creation of a small group of rich individuals ("nouveaux riches"), an unscrupulous illegitimate new money elite. Society was thus polarized. Middle classes (doctors, teachers, scientists, specialist workers) experienced social decline, and the economically lower classes (pensioners, unemployed, agricultural workers) were impoverished. Self-destruction, criminal behavior, alcoholism rose. It has so far been impossible to alleviate the main social problems - poverty, unemployment, social injustice, social exclusion. The economic growth, even though positive during the most recent years, is still insufficient to fight these negative aspects of social life. Hence even the economically successful countries experience a significant gap in the standard of living as compared to western standards.

The overall political, economic, and social transformation is thus sudden, deep, and irreversible. It is hardly any surprise that it caused significant demographic changes. It is to be noted though that a simple correlation between demographic change and macro-economic change cannot be found. A correlation between the total fertility rate on one side and the GDP, or level of unemployment, on the other, is poor; the latter explain insufficiently the fertility changes.

## 2. Changes in demographic trends

*Marriages and divorces*

Where first marriages are considered, the data indicates that during the pre-transition period both level and timing of marriage were stable over a long period, covering some two to three decades. Some moderate and temporary changes towards younger age at marriage were due mainly to the effect of the pronatal policies that were introduced in most of the countries in the region. The total first-marriage rates (TFMR) were high, around 0.9 or higher, thus indicating the prevalence of nearly universal entry into marriage. Exceptions were observed in the western Balkan countries where the level of TFMR was around 0.8, and this is about the rate observed in western Europe. The mean age at first marriage was very low in all central and eastern European countries, and this level was considerably lower than the one observed in western Europe. Thus in the central and eastern European countries a pattern of early and nearly universal entry into marriage dominated. This is a pattern describing a traditional marital behavior that has been observed for many decades.

After the start of the transition this pattern began changing. The TFMR dropped abruptly during the first half of the 90s, while during the next 5 years its decrease was smoother. This change was observed in all central and eastern European countries, except in the western Balkans, where the decrease was smooth all throughout the 90s. Towards the end of the 90s the TFMR was considerably lower than 0.9. This fall indicates a loss of the universality of marriage all over the eastern part of Europe. The mean age at first marriage (MAFM) exhibited an abrupt increase during the transition of nearly 2-3 years. The highest rises were observed in Slovenia (3 years) and the Czech Republic (2.9) years. Therefore the 90s marked the rise of a new aspect in marital behavior: entry into marriage into later years in life.

Thus the 90s established new trends in marriage that were observed earlier in western European countries. These trends, of decrease in the TFMR and increase in the MAFM, were continuously running in western Europe too, and therefore it is hard to notice any trend of convergence in the two geographical parts of Europe. The changes depicted here were smoother where cohorts are considered. The cohort equivalents of the period TFMR and MAFM changed only slightly. For example, the MAFM did not rise above 23 years for cohorts born before 1968. Data on extra-marital unions (cohabitation) in the central and eastern European countries are scarce. Information derived from the European values surveys for 1995-97 reveal that the highest level of cohabitation among respondents aged 20-29 was observed in Estonia (26%) and Slovenia (17%). In several other countries where data were available it was below 10%. Fertility and Family Surveys (FFS) data show that younger cohorts have higher levels of cohabitation. Both sets of data indicate that during the 90s cohabitation spread rapidly as a new behavior. It complements the behavioral marital changes described above into a general picture typical for the changes observed earlier in western Europe.

Data on remarriages are also scanty. They reveal that the overall pattern of change in remarriages is similar to that of first marriages, where level of marriage is considered. That is, a significant decrease in remarriages was observed during the 90s. Second marriages comprise the bulk of remarriages; higher-order marriages were exceptional, and there was hardly any change in this pattern during the 90s. Both occurrence and registration of divorces are subject to the legal system. Modifications in the latter may provoke considerable variation in the level of divorces, measured for example with the total divorce rate (TDR). This was often the case during the 90s. An explicit example is the ex-GDR where the legal divorce system of the FRG replaced the previous one after the reunification. Before the start of the transition the TDR marked a steady and moderate increase in nearly all countries in the region. Its level was very high in the ex-GDR, the Czech and Slovak Republics, Hungary and particularly high in Estonia and Latvia. The TDR was around 03-05 in these countries. Similar high levels were observed in a few countries in western Europe. In the other central and eastern European countries the TDR was considerably lower. Thus it ranged from as low as 0.05 to as high as 0.5. The transition did not bring any particular changes in the level of divorces, except for variations caused by law modifications. These variations were extremely strong and could be either towards a fall or rise, depending on whether the legal amendments were towards restriction or liberalization. They lasted usually 1-2 years only. In general the level of the TDR remained high, around the values observed towards the end of the 80s.

*Fertility*

During the last 1-2 decades before the start of the transition the TFR was around replacement level, 2.1, in most of the central and eastern European countries. Significant fluctuations were noticed as a result of the introduction of pronatal policy instruments in most of the countries in the region. During the 90s the TFR was slightly below replacement level, and there was a soft tendency of its further decrease, observed most clearly in Bulgaria, the Czech Republic, and Hungary. Fertility in the western Balkan states and particularly Slovenia was considerably lower, and it was low for more than a decade. This low level was characteristic for most of the western European countries at that time.

A value around 2 of TFR corresponds to the prevalence of a two-child family model. This model was observed in most of the countries in the region. The first-order TFR was close to 1. Since this value was observed for a long period of time it indicates the universality of the birth of at least one child. That is, nearly every woman would have been a mother at least once in her life. This pattern was a traditional one and it was not common at that time in the western European countries. Hungary and the ex-GDR are important exceptions, in that the first-order TFR was lower than 0.9 during the 80s and towards 1989 it was below 0.8. Hence the break of the traditional pattern of universality of births has been initiated before the start of the transition, at least in a few countries. The second-order TFR was also very high in the region as compared to western countries.

The mean age at birth of the first child (MAFB) was low, similarly to the low mean age at first marriage. The value of 23.5 was like a demarcation line between east and west of Europe where MAFM is considered. A value for MAFB a little higher divides the same two parts of Europe too. It can be generalized that the start of family formation takes place at an earlier age in the east as compared to the west. The narrow age schedule of births is another characteristic of births in the east. This clustering of births in a narrow age interval is the result of both early start and early stopping of childbearing.

Extra-marital births before the transition were rare, analogously to the rare extra-marital cohabitation. Marital fertility dominated with few exceptions, namely ex-GDR and Slovenia, and to some extent Hungary. In the ex-GDR it was the pronatal that encouraged couples to have extra-marital births, but the outbreak of a new behavior due to ideational shifts was also present.

The start of the transition brought about significant changes in all these trends. First, the TFR dropped abruptly to unprecedented levels. This drop occurred with the onset of the transition, and towards the second half of the 90s the TFR dropped down to levels as low as 1.2 and was only rarely higher than 1.5. The ex-GDR experienced a tremendous drop during the first years after reunification, when the TFR decreased down to 0.88; a slow recovery was observed later. Towards 2000 the TFR seems to have remained around constant at the low levels reached earlier, and there are some indications that a moderate increase may follow.

The age span of births began to widen during the years of the transition. This reflects a divergence of fertility behavior among the population. The MAFB experienced a considerable rise, as a result of postponement of births to later years of life. Order-specific fertility changed considerably too. First births decreased considerably and therefore the universality of births is expected to remain in the past. The two-child model was broken, because of the speedy decrease of second-order births. Births of third or higher order became rare and were observed mainly among some ethnic groups.

A drastic change was observed in the share of extra-marital births. In 2000 it rose to levels as high as 54 per 1000 live births in Estonia, 40 in Latvia, 38 in Bulgaria. These high levels indicate a sudden expansion of non-marital cohabitation. The rise of extra-marital births in some countries could be the result of the drop in legal marriages, although the factual marriage is carried out according to prevailing customs and traditions.

Thus the transition brought about a salient behavioral modification. In brief, it is a break from traditional behavior and spread of a new one that is close to that observed in western Europe. The major components of this modification are:

• Traditional universality of marriages and births remained in the past. Remaining single and voluntary infertility is accepted by society and it extended analogously to its proliferation in western European countries, observed 1-2 decades earlier.

• Early start of family formation remained also in the past. Entry into marriage and having a first child were postponed to later ages.

• New family forms appeared. Non-marital cohabitaton was replacing marriage. Extra-marital births increased considerably, usually within a non-marital union.

- The level of marriages and particularly of fertility decreased considerably.

Family planning changed considerably during the years of transition. Induced abortion, a traditional means of birth control, decreased and the usage of modern contraceptives extended impressively. A negative trend was observed with the worsening of reproductive health.

## Mortality

A recent extended study of mortality in Europe was issued by the Council of Europe and therefore the discussion here gives only a general outline. Demographic research has outlined two major periods in the change in life expectancy during the couple of decades preceding the transition. Until the mid 60s it marked a rapid increase, primarily due to the drop in morbidity due to contagious diseases. Since then and until the end of the 80s the increase was only moderate in some countries and disappeared in others. Life expectancy for males even marked a decrease during this period. This stagnation covers significant changes in the causes of mortality. While mortality due to contagious diseases as well as infant mortality dropped, a marked increase took place due to the rise in heart and cerebro-vascular diseases as well as malignant neoplasms.

The transition brought about a new phase in the change in life expectancy. Life expectancy for males residing in central European countries was increasing during the 90s, after the previous period of stagnation. The female life expectancy increased even faster. Changes in life expectancy in the ex-USSR countries are peculiar. For example, during the first half of the 90s there was an abrupt drop down to around 58 years for the males in the Russian Federation. Female life expectancy also decreased. During the second half of the 90s life expectancy marked certain fluctuations. In general, these drops are considered to be the result of the anti-alcohol campaign carried out during the years of *perestroika*. Its effect was similar to a postponement of the event with several years. The countries in the western Balkans experienced a smooth and moderate rise in life expectancy. Infant mortality decreased continuously in the countries of central Europe, with the partial exception of Bulgaria where its level remained about constant during the 90s.

There is hardly any other demographic process where changes are as smooth both before and during the transition. Infant mortality rose in the ex-USSR countries during the first years after the transition, but during the second half of the 90s its drop was recovered. Note should be taken that the definition of infant mortality in some of the ex-USSR countries and in Bulgaria has still not changed to international standards. Adult mortality (observed for the age interval 35-54) was unusually high during the period preceding the transition. It remained high during the 90s; in fact its high level was the main cause for the drop in life expectancy during the first half of the 90s in the ex-USSR countries.

The high level of deaths due to cardiovascular diseases and injuries had the greatest impact on the slowdown of mortality. Deaths due to malignant neoplasms remained relatively high during the 90s too.

In general, mortality in the central and eastern European countries remains high when compared to western Europe. There are diverse reasons for this unfavorable difference. Unhealthy diet dominates in many central and eastern European populations. High consumption of alcohol and smoking are observed too. Lifestyle and deficiency of physical exercises in particular have also their contribution.

The impact of the transition on mortality is far from being uniform among the central and eastern European countries. Those populations that suffer most from the transition are also those most affected by the rise in mortality. They are the people with lower income, lower education, as well as the unemployed. Social exclusion in this respect marks an extreme.

## 3. Possible explanations of the demographic changes in the central and eastern European countries

The patterns in nuptiality and fertility that prevailed before the transition have been explained by demographers along the following lines. First, these patterns were the continuation of long-lasting cultural traditions, characterized by early in life family formation. In some countries the cultural patterns were dissimilar though. Second, population policies favored early entry into family life. Third, and perhaps the most powerful explanations, are social and economic ones. They refer to matters such as high female labor-force participation rate compensated by the state-based childcare system, shortage of housing, rising direct costs of children relatively to a moderate increase in income. Other explanations refer to the character of the totalitarian regime: lack of freedom means restricted set of alternatives in life and therefore the choice of family formation gets a relatively higher probability than in democratic societies of the western European type. The Marxist ideology had also its significance through the meaning of family as the basic cell in society.

The start of the transition swept away all this possible explanations. They were either invalidated or their relevance dropped down. New explanations became more relevant, and they are the ones that refer to the western European countries. There are two major, grand, theoretical approaches: the economic one and that of ideational shifts.

The economic approach emphasizes the proliferation of unemployment, impoverishment, and a general decrease in income. Their effect is in the rise of direct costs of children. According to "new home economics" this implies a decrease in natality. Opportunity costs increased too, even though income decreased, because the latter dropped too low and the time a woman needs to get some income becomes valuable for her own survival. Economic uncertainty increased significantly. During uncertainty people would postpone and even reject irreversible and crucial events such as marriage or a birth. Less crucial events can be used as substitutes, for example non-marital cohabitation is less binding than a marriage. Ideational shifts are considered as an important reason for changes in nuptiality and fertility in western Europe. They refer to long-term secularization, rise in self autonomy, individuation, and similar value shifts. One can reason that the collapse of the totalitarian regime has opened the way to similar value shifts in the central and eastern European countries. The description above indicated that some demographic changes observed during the end of the 80s were similar to those observed in western Europe. Hence ideational shifts might have been rooted before the start of the transition. The latter has only accelerated their impact.

Both grand approaches provide insufficient explanations to the demographic changes. The validity of the economic approach would require that better-off countries or regions within countries, or population subgroups like that of the "winners", would have higher fertility. This is not observed. It is hard to explain the rise of ideational shifts within a totalitarian regime; it is even more difficult to understand how ideational shifts could have invoked the observed sudden swift changes in nuptiality and fertility.

These issues can be clarified by considering the essence of the transition. The transition is a time of discontinuation, when one civil regime is suddenly broken down but a new one is still not firmly grounded. This period of hiatus is characterized by disorderliness and anomie. Old norms and values are broken and time is necessary for the establishment of new ones. Hence the guiding role of norms is broken. Such a period creates a high general uncertainty in the future whose impact on individual decision-taking is similar to economic uncertainty. This situation looks like ideational change but is different from it. For example, disorderliness forces individuals to be autonomous but this is not the rise of individual autonomy observed in the west.

## 4. Population change

Before the start of the transition nearly all populations in the region had a positive rate of population growth. Towards 2000 only seven populations had a positive growth, while 15 other populations had a negative growth. The population growth turned negative with the recent abrupt fall in fertility while mortality remained about constant. In most of the cases negative growth has been observed earlier only in times of war or famine. International migration was very low and virtually inexistent during the socialist times. With the start of the transition it boosted up for a few years. Most of the countries experienced an initially strong outmigration flow. Later this flow decreased and some countries began to accept immigrants. The impact of migration on population change is diverse. In Bulgaria and Hungary recent population censuses reveal that their populations have decreased by more than half a million because of emigration. In other countries emigration was either lower or was compensated by return migration or immigration.

Population ageing was a strong process during the 90s. Towards 2000 the share of the elderly population (aged 60+) was around 20% with the highest value being observed in Bulgaria, 21.75. This share was lower than 15% in few populations, and the lowest number was observed in Albania, 9.0%. Ageing was caused by the fall in the birth rates that made the population pyramid thinner at the bottom. Ageing in the east is not as advanced as it is in the west towards 2000, but it is an inevitable process that will continue in the future. Population projections show that ageing will accelerate towards 2050. The elderly population will grow considerably relatively to the young and adult population, and towards 2000 it will be as high as 24.6% in Albania and 42% in Slovenia.

# Chapter 1

## Social, political and economic transformation

*Jürgen Dorbritz*

### 1.1 The political history

When Mikhail Gorbachev took on the Chairmanship of the Communist Party of the Soviet Union in 1985, he saw in the USSR as it existed at that time, and not only in that country, a system that was economically stagnant and calcified politically in Stalinist structures. It was obvious that the reform process was in a rut, and that this obstacle had first of all to be removed by means of democratic renewal within the framework of the Socialist system (*Glasnost, Perestroika*). It was this path taken by Gorbachev that ultimately developed from the minor reforms into a complete transformation of the system.

The end of Socialism was at that time closely linked with the situation in Hungary and in the former GDR. In both countries, diverging political developments occurred during the eighties. *Realsozialismus* collapsed in Hungary in 1989. The Communists had indicated their willingness to hold elections at a very early stage, and thus facilitated a change in the political system. A consequence of the political freedom thereby gained was the opening of the Hungarian border to Austria on 11 September 1989. A completely different situation applied in the former GDR. Society was politically comparatively stable in the GDR until well into 1989. There was a lack of practice in resistance on the part of both the Government and of the resistance movement itself (Meuschel, 1990: 563).

Society was virtually unprepared for a transformation process, so that it appeared to be only logical that the system change should be introduced by means of a spontaneous outbreak. Because of the increased discontent over the lack of reforms and of basic democratic rights, anger over rigged elections and monitoring by the state security service, a lack of understanding regarding the failure of the planned economy or the incipient ecological catastrophe, in 1989 a broader opposition was able to form by means of which the problems were brought to the attention of the public (Häder and Häder; 1995: 24). An unwillingness on the part of the Party and state leadership to reform, coupled with political discontent on the part of the population, combined with the willingness of west Germany to accept mass immigration over the Hungarian-Austrian border or by occupying west German embassies in other countries. This set in motion the first 'demographic shock' – the exodus from the former GDR - caused by the social, political and economic change in the reforming states of central and eastern Europe. The state and Party leadership of the GDR increasingly started to lose control of the situation, which led to the fall of the Berlin Wall on 9 November 1989, and hence to the end of the GDR on 3 October 1990, with accession to the Federal Republic of Germany.

November 9, 1989 has come to be regarded as the start of the central and eastern European reform process. Subsequently, between 1989 and 1991 the Socialist state structures collapsed, a process climaxing in the more or less peaceful dissolution of the Soviet Union. Violent solutions as in the former Yugoslavia or the Caucasus Region remained the exception. These 'revolutions' of the political system which took place in 1989/1991 facilitated broad economic, political and social change. In the initial phase of the transformation process, only the political power situation – more or less consistent and rapid in the individual countries – changed. The restructuring of the entire economic and social system had yet to occur.

## 1.2 The starting conditions and the elements of the transformation process

The end of Socialism came unexpectedly, but was ultimately inevitable. Pallinger (1997: 13) put forward the following arguments in explaining the collapse of the system, without exclusively addressing the economic situation: The legitimation of modern states is based on various elements such as democracy, the rule of law, welfare or self-determination. The Socialist states did not have such a variety of legitimation factors, and since a system of domination cannot be based on coercion and ideology in the long term, a social system must provide reasons for its legitimation. These consist of consumption and social security, intended to replace democracy, the rule of law and political freedoms. "Because of the inadequate mix of legitimation factors, economic success was indispensable for Socialism" (Dahrendorf, 1990: 81). And this was impossible to achieve in a continuing comparison with western democracies because of the construction of the Socialist domination system.

The economy was dominated by politics, which meant that it was prevented from following its own development logic. Centralist planning and the prevalence of social ownership, the decisive construction elements of Socialist societies, must lead in highly-complex and differentiated structured industrialised societies to laborious control mechanisms preventing innovation and efficiency. "The combination of a dictatorship and a planned economy formed an eternal circle. Because all the sub-systems were interlinked, in other words were not autonomous, disturbances in the individual sub-areas tended to expand, becoming crises in the overall system. Because of their excessively political nature, the Socialist states had no way of carrying out effective correction. The tools of crisis management turned out to be dysfunctional because they were unable to remedy the causes of the problems, namely the primacy of politics, without questioning the dominance of the one Party itself" (Pallinger, 1997: 13). Because of the inherent design fault, the load-bearing legitimating pillar, namely the economy, was ultimately able to destabilise the whole system. This was the situation that had been reached by the end of the eighties. However, it was not only the unstoppable decline in the performance of the system which led by itself to the collapse (Höhmann, 1995: 189). There were three other factors:

- With its increasing inability to structure the planned economy, the Communist party had lost authority;

- The Soviet *Perestroika* and the lack of democracy and the rule of law had given the populations a political awareness in the sense of rejecting the Communist ideology;

- It became more and more clear that in the competition between the systems the Socialist societies would lose in comparison with the democracies in the west.

The main course of the end of the socialism was the inability of the system to create innovative economic structures. In spite of the obvious need for action and the topicality of innovation strategies for innovative technologies and for modern forms of work and production systems, the Socialist economies remained in the traditional structures. In the seventies and especially the eighties, the international reproduction conditions underwent major changes. *Realsozialismus* was unable to follow these trends. "It was precisely the same production conditions which consolidated Realsozialismus in the first half of its existence and accelerated its dynamic development that then prevented its necessary innovative modernisation and hence led to its collapse" (Burchardt 1995: 119). The political collapse, in addition to the way in which political power was exercised centrally, also had an economic history demonstrating the inability over a period of 20 years to introduce modern production structures. This situation was characterised by the following:

*Structural changes which prevented investment.* The example of the Soviet Union: The investment share required to exploit raw materials and primary energy-carriers increased in the eighties to one-quarter of total investment in the industrial sector. At the same time, investment stagnated in leading innovative sectors such as mechanical and electrical engineering, as well as electronics. Also in countries with a different economic structure than the Soviet one, such as the GDR, similar trends towards intensifying extensive forms of production could be observed. The share of investments fell steadily as against national income from the beginning of the seventies, and onward into the mid-eighties. This policy led to increasing wear and tear, to an ageing of the capital stock and to a relative decrease in the use of modern technology. This orientation of economic policy had a real background. As stated in the introduction, social systems must provide proof of their legitimacy. Because of a lack of democracy, political freedoms and the rule of law, these consisted of consumption and social security. And these in turn were bought by using up the capital stock, plunging the social and economic systems into a Catch 22 situation which could not be solved.

The structural starting point of the economic transformation was therefore an *oversized state-owned industry* typified by a low degree of competition intensity, a weak orientation towards the world market and considerable demand surpluses (inadequate production) (Welfens, 1999: 62). This system was supplemented by a grey Socialist economy which for instance accounted for 10 – 25 % of the added-value in Poland at the end of the eighties. This led into a grey capitalist economy, which prevented the launch into the free market economy.

A *financial crisis* had come about in many Socialist countries in the eighties. All the countries had a major discrepancy between the official exchange rate and the black market rate of the currencies, which led to open inflation (Poland and Hungary). Amongst other things, there was "a reflex towards the soft budget restriction in state ownership of the means of production in the central administrative economy, and towards negative real interest rates and increasingly distorted calculation of resource allocation" (Welfens, 1999: 62). Added to this was the fact that by virtue of the increasing subsidies, considerable budget deficits had arisen in Poland, Hungary and Bulgaria, as well as much foreign debt.

The *lack of the rule of law* prevented a new economic start. State arbitrariness, a lack of ownership rights and duties to publish for enterprises are incompatible with a free market economy.

At the end of the eighties, the social economic situation of the former Socialist countries can be summarised in the following terms: An oversized industry had been formed, dominated by major state-owned firms which could be centrally steered; the currencies were not convertible, economic development was not linked to the world market, prices were fixed by the state, there were faults in the structure of investments, some of the countries had major debts, budget deficits had been created and open inflation could be noticed. Because of their internal structures, the Socialist societies had revealed themselves to be incapable of reform. It therefore became a matter of necessity that they should come to an end!

The tasks of economic transformation can be derived from the inheritance of Socialism that is inherent to the system and the crisis-ridden situation (Brezinski,

1996: 134 / Welfens, 1999: 64/). Figure 1.1 contains in an overview the main reconstruction requirements which apply to the transformation of the state Socialist social systems into democratically-organised market economies.

**Fig. 1.1 – Elements of system transformation in the post-Socialist countries**

| Economic sector | Monetary sector | Political and social sectors |
|---|---|---|
| Privatisation of the state companies and reduction of the role of the state as a producer | Liberalisation of prices and reduction of price subsidies | Creation of the basis of political pluralism and the rule of law (statutes on the constitution, election and parties) |
| Creation of economic freedom and creation of the conditions for successful business start-ups | Dissolution of administrative forms of wage and price fixing | Reform of the social security systems |
| Removing enterprises from the sphere of state subsidy | Reform of the banking and credit system with the establishment of a two-tier banking system (central bank and private commercial banks) | Reorientation of foreign policy |
| Breaking up the network of economic structures built up in Socialism and the enterprises from the state economic bureaucracy | Removal of the state monopoly on foreign trade | Creation of a legal and administrative system |
| Formation of an economic system, industrial policy and creation of competition supervision | Creation of a framework for free trade in currency | Adjusting the educational system to the market economy |
| Creation of a functional labour market in the wake of the removal of state employment guarantees | Partial convertibility of the currency | |
| | Reformulation of fiscal policy | |

## 1.3 The economic and social transformation process

The following macroeconomic analyses are largely based on the data from the Economic Survey of Europe from 2001 (United Nations, Economic Survey of Europe) and the database of the Vienna Institute for International Economic Studies (WIIW). Reference is made in various estimates to previous issues.

In the economic surveys, the post-Socialist countries are sub-divided into three groups:

<u>Eastern Europe</u> (Albania, Bosnia and Herzegovina, Bulgaria, Croatia, Czech Republic, Hungary, Poland, Romania, Slovak Republic, Slovenia, "the former Yugoslav Republic of Macedonia", Federal Republic of Yugoslavia);

<u>Baltic states</u> (Estonia, Latvia, Lithuania);

Commonwealth of Independent States (Armenia, Azerbaijan, Belarus, Georgia, Kazakhstan, Kyrgyzstan, Republic of Moldova, the Russian Federation, Tadzhikistan, Ukraine and Uzbekistan). All the information below is based on these groups. With the exception of the Caucasus region, the Asian countries of the former Soviet Union are not included in detail in the analyses, and nor are they listed in the tables.

The transformation process is to be described using various indicators which when combined provide an overview of the economic situation. An analysis of the economic trends is carried out using economic growth, gross domestic product, gross industrial output, price trends and inflation, employment and unemployment, balance of trade, foreign investment, changes in the economic structures and labour productivity. The developments which have taken place are detailed below.

## 1.3.1 Economic growth

All post-Socialist countries had negative economic growth in 1990 and 1991, in each case in comparison to the previous year.

**Table 1.1 – Economy growth in the transition countries (compared with the year before, in %)**

| Countries | 1989 | 1990 | 1991 | 1992 | 1993 | 1994 | 1995 |
|---|---|---|---|---|---|---|---|
| Poland | 0.2 | -11.6 | -7.0 | 2.6 | 3.8 | 5.2 | 7.0 |
| Czech. Rep. | 1.4 | -1.2 | -11.6 | -0.5 | 0.1 | 2.2 | 5.9 |
| Slovak Rep. | 1.4 | -2.5 | -14.6 | -6.5 | -3.7 | 4.9 | 6.7 |
| Hungary | 0.7 | -3.5 | -11.9 | -3.1 | -0.6 | 2.9 | 1.5 |
| Slovenia | -1.8 | -4.7 | -8.9 | -5.5 | 2.8 | 5.3 | 4.1 |
| *East-Middle-Europe* | *0.4* | *-4.7* | *-10.8* | *-2.6* | *0.5* | *4.1* | *5.0* |
| Estonia | 8.1 | -6.5 | -13.6 | -14.2 | -9.0 | -2.0 | 4.3 |
| Latvia | 6.8 | 2.9 | -10.4 | -34.9 | -14.9 | 0.6 | 0.8 |
| Lithuania | 1.5 | -5.0 | -5.7 | -21.3 | -16.2 | -9.8 | 3.3 |
| *Baltic States* | *5.5* | *-2.9* | *-9.9* | *-23.5* | *-13.5* | *-3.7* | *2.3* |
| Albania | 9.8 | -10.0 | -28.0 | -7.2 | 9.6 | 8.3 | 13.3 |
| Bulgaria | 0.5 | -9.1 | -11.7 | -7.3 | -1.5 | 1.8 | 2.1 |
| Macedonia* | 0.9 | -9.9 | -7.0 | -8.0 | -9.1 | -1.8 | -1.2 |
| Romania | -5.8 | -5.6 | -12.9 | -8.8 | 1.5 | 3.9 | 7.1 |
| *South-East-Europe* | *1.4* | *-8.7* | *-14.9* | *-7.8* | *0.1* | *3.1* | *5.3* |
| *CIS* | *0.6* | *-3.7* | *-6.0* | *14.1* | *-9.3* | *-13.8* | *-5.2* |

| Countries | 1996 | 1997 | 1998 | 1999 | 2000 |
|---|---|---|---|---|---|
| Poland | 6.1 | 6.9 | 4.8 | 4.1 | 5.0 |
| Czech. Rep. | 4.8 | -1.0 | -2.2 | 0.2 | 2.0 |
| Slovak Rep. | 6.2 | 6.2 | 4.1 | 1.9 | 2.0 |
| Hungary | 1.3 | 4.6 | 4.9 | 4.5 | 6.0 |
| Slovenia | 3.5 | 4.6 | 3.8 | 4.9 | 5.1 |
| *East-Middle-Europe* | *4.4* | *4.3* | *3.1* | *3.0* | *4.0* |
| Estonia | 3.9 | 10.6 | 4.7 | -1.1 | 5.0 |
| Latvia | 3.3 | 8.6 | 3.9 | 0.1 | 4.5 |
| Lithuania | 4.7 | 7.3 | 5.1 | -4.2 | 2.2 |
| *Baltic States* | *4.0* | *8.8* | *4.6* | *-1.7* | *3.9* |
| Albania | 9.1 | -7.0 | 8.0 | 7.3 | 7.0 |
| Bulgaria | -10.9 | -6.9 | 3.5 | 2.4 | 4.0 |
| Macedonia* | 1.2 | 1.4 | 2.9 | 2.7 | 5.0 |
| Romania | 3.9 | -6.1 | -5.4 | -3.2 | 1.5 |
| *South-East-Europe* | *0.8* | *-4.7* | *2.3* | *2.3* | *4.4* |
| *CIS* | *-3.5* | *0.9* | *-3.5* | *2.8* | *5.9* |

Source: EBRD: Transition Report 2000, S. 65

* The use in the tables of the term "Macedonia" is for descriptive purposes and the convenience of the reader.

The decreases in 1991 ranged from – 5.7 % (Lithuania) to – 28.0 % (Albania). One can observe in general terms that the declines in economic development were most observable for between about one and two years following the initiation of the first reforms. Clear breaks in economic growth however also occurred in the countries which from today's point of view have overcome the transformation process relatively successfully (Poland -11.6 %, Hungary – 11.9 %, Czech Republic – 11.6 %). In 1992, one country – Poland – already had positive growth rates. The majority of other countries, in particular the Baltic States and the CIS countries, showed negative growth in the first half of the nineties. The trough of economic growth was not reached in the CIS states until 1994. From 1995 onwards, positive economic growth set in for the majority of the transformation countries. Bulgaria, Romania, "the former Yugoslav Republic of Macedonia" and the CIS states are still the exceptions. Clear progress can be seen for eastern Europe in particular. There were considerable drops once again in Bulgaria and Romania in the second half of the nineties. Without going into detail concerning the CIS states, there were only three countries still marked by negative economic growth in 1999 (Lithuania – 4.2 %, Romania – 3.2 %, Estonia – 1.1 %). A positive trend was visible for the whole economic area in 2000 – a sign that the change in the economic systems is taking a positive course. Albania recorded economic growth of 7.0 %, Hungary 6.0 % and the CIS states averaged growth of 5.9 %.

### 1.3.2 Gross domestic product

At the beginning of the nineties, trends in gross domestic product (Real GDP/NMP) took on a similar upwards trend to that of economic growth (in the portrayal selected in Table 2 and Figure 1.2 the year 1989 has been taken as 100 %). A gradually increasing trend in GDP can be observed in all transition countries during the 1980s. After that, the economic shocks are obvious. In eastern Europe as a whole in 1993, gross national product was only 77.9 % of the 1989 figure. After that an upward trend began which reached all eastern European countries and the Baltic states in 1994. By contrast, the majority of the CIS states did not reach the trough of the development of gross national product until 1995 and 1996, in some cases not until 1997. The differences in the reductions between the individual countries are massive here. With the exception of the Federal Republic of Yugoslavia, they were not too extreme in eastern Europe. Reductions to 85 % – 75 % have been recorded in the majority of cases. The Baltic Republics and the CIS states have been typified by considerable falls in GDP. In the best cases, it fell to approx. 60 % of the 1989 level. A fall to less than 50 % can however be observed in a large number of countries. The lowest value was reached in Georgia in 1994, namely 23.4 %. In this context, it can be ascertained that the end of the Soviet Union caused the clearest negative trends in 1992. In the second half of the nineties, apart from a few exceptions, all countries show a positive development trend in gross national product. Stagnating development can be found in Yugoslavia, Bulgaria, Romania, Moldova, Ukraine and Tadzhikistan. The post-Socialist countries have gone through the trough of their economic development, but only a small number of countries reached a higher gross national product in 2000 than in 1989. The most positive development took place in this sense in Poland, where an increase to 126.8 % took place. Positive developments can also be found in Slovenia (110.6 %), Hungary (104.5 %), Slovak Republic (102.7 %) and Albania (102.6 %). In this positive context, one should not overlook the fact that a large number of countries are still in a deep structural change crisis. In 2000 Georgia, for instance, only achieved 31.9 % of the gross national product of 1989. One finds similar situations in other countries (Moldova: 33.9 %, Ukraine: 41.6 %, the Federal Republic of Yugoslavia: 45.7 %). On an average of all post-Socialist countries, 70.2 % of the level of 1989 was achieved in 2000.

| Countries | 1980 | 1986 | 1987 | 1988 | 1989 | 1990 | 1991 | 1992 | 1993 | 1994 | 1995 | 1996 | 1997 | 1998 | 1999 | 2000 |
|---|---|---|---|---|---|---|---|---|---|---|---|---|---|---|---|---|
| Eastern Europe | 88.7 | 97.8 | 99.4 | 100.8 | 100.0 | 93.2 | 82.9 | 79.3 | 79.0 | 82.1 | 86.9 | 90.3 | 92.2 | 93.9 | 95.2 | 98.7 |
| Albania | 79.4 | 93.1 | 92.4 | 91.0 | 100.0 | 90.0 | 64.8 | 60.1 | 65.9 | 71.4 | 80.9 | 88.2 | 82.0 | 88.6 | 95.7 | 102.6 |
| Bosnia & Herzeg. | .. | .. | .. | .. | .. | .. | .. | .. | .. | .. | .. | .. | .. | .. | .. | .. |
| Bulgaria | 76.2 | 93.6 | 99.3 | 101.9 | 100.0 | 90.9 | 83.3 | 77.2 | 76.1 | 77.5 | 79.7 | 71.6 | 66.6 | 68.9 | 70.7 | 74.1 |
| Croatia[a] | 99.0 | 102.6 | 102.5 | 101.6 | 100.0 | 92.9 | 73.3 | 64.7 | 59.5 | 63.0 | 67.3 | 71.3 | 76.2 | 78.1 | 77.9 | 80.7 |
| Czech Republic | 86.3 | 95.5 | 99.4 | 99.3 | 100.0 | 96.5 | 85.0 | 82.4 | 81.9 | 84.4 | 85.6 | 86.8 | 90.7 | 95.5 | 95.3 | 97.7 |
| Hungary | 91.1 | 94.1 | 95.9 | 99.8 | 100.0 | 88.4 | 82.2 | 84.4 | 87.6 | 92.1 | 98.6 | 104.5 | 111.7 | 117.1 | 121.8 | 126.8 |
| Poland | 88.5 | 105.8 | 106.7 | 106.2 | 100.0 | 94.4 | 82.2 | 75.0 | 76.2 | 79.2 | 84.8 | 88.2 | 82.8 | 78.3 | 75.8 | 77.0 |
| Romania | .. | 94.8 | 97.1 | 99.0 | 100.0 | 97.5 | 83.3 | 77.9 | 75.1 | 78.7 | 84.2 | 89.7 | 95.6 | 99.8 | 101.7 | 102.7 |
| Slovak Republic | 98.9 | 104.1 | 103.5 | 100.5 | 100.0 | 91.9 | 83.7 | 79.1 | 81.4 | 85.7 | 89.3 | 92.4 | 96.6 | 100.4 | 105.3 | 110.6 |
| Slovenia | 93.3 | 102.7 | 101.4 | 98.1 | 100.0 | 89.8 | 84.3 | 78.7 | 72.8 | 71.6 | 70.8 | 71.6 | 72.6 | 74.8 | 76.8 | 80.7 |
| Macedonia | 95.7 | 101.4 | 100.2 | 98.8 | 100.0 | 92.1 | 81.4 | 58.7 | 40.6 | 41.7 | 44.2 | 46.8 | 50.3 | 51.5 | 41.6 | 45.7 |
| F.R.Yugoslavia[c] | 67.8 | 85.6 | 89.0 | 96.0 | 100.0 | 97.8 | 89.9 | 67.9 | 58.2 | 55.2 | 56.4 | 58.8 | 63.7 | 66.6 | 65.4 | 68.5 |
| Baltic states | 74.5 | 88.2 | 89.2 | 93.8 | 100.0 | 91.9 | 82.7 | 71.0 | 65.0 | 63.7 | 66.4 | 69.0 | 76.3 | 79.4 | 78.3 | 84.1 |
| Estonia | 68.5 | 85.1 | 89.0 | 93.6 | 100.0 | 102.9 | 92.2 | 71.0 | 60.1 | 51.5 | 51.0 | 52.7 | 57.3 | 59.5 | 59.6 | 64.1 |
| Latvia | 64.7 | 84.9 | 88.9 | 98.4 | 100.0 | 96.7 | 91.2 | 71.8 | 60.2 | 54.3 | 56.1 | 58.7 | 63.0 | 66.2 | 64.2 | 65.3 |
| Lithuania | 77.5 | 92.4 | 93.9 | 98.1 | 100.0 | 96.8 | 90.9 | 78.0 | 70.4 | 60.3 | 56.9 | 55.0 | 55.6 | 53.9 | 55.5 | 59.8 |
| CIS[bc] | 73.5 | 97.7 | 94.5 | 92.2 | 100.0 | 94.5 | 83.4 | 48.6 | 44.3 | 46.7 | 49.9 | 52.8 | 54.6 | 58.5 | 60.3 | 64.1 |
| Armenia | 79.6 | 100.6 | 105.1 | 109.7 | 100.0 | 88.3 | 87.7 | 67.9 | 52.2 | 41.9 | 37.0 | 37.4 | 39.6 | 43.6 | 46.8 | 52.1 |
| Azerbaijan | 65.7 | 88.9 | 91.3 | 92.4 | 100.0 | 98.1 | 96.9 | 87.6 | 81.0 | 70.8 | 63.4 | 65.2 | 72.6 | 78.7 | 81.4 | 86.1 |
| Belarus | 79.4 | 98.8 | 96.8 | 103.6 | 100.0 | 84.9 | 67.0 | 36.9 | 26.1 | 23.4 | 24.0 | 26.7 | 29.7 | 30.6 | 31.5 | 31.9 |
| Georgia | 72.1 | 89.2 | 90.3 | 91.9 | 100.0 | 97.6 | 80.5 | 57.2 | 56.5 | 39.0 | 38.3 | 35.3 | 35.9 | 32.8 | 31.3 | 33.9 |
| Republic of Moldova[d] | 78.1 | 92.9 | 94.2 | 98.4 | 100.0 | 97.0 | 92.2 | 78.8 | 71.9 | 62.8 | 60.2 | 58.2 | 58.7 | 55.8 | 57.6 | 62.2 |
| Russian Federation | 75.0 | 90.0 | 93.4 | 95.2 | 100.0 | 96.4 | 88.0 | 79.2 | 68.0 | 52.4 | 46.0 | 41.4 | 40.2 | 39.5 | 39.3 | 41.6 |
| Ukraine | 80.3 | 93.7 | 95.2 | 98.7 | 100.0 | 95.9 | 88,8 | 78.1 | 72.4 | 65.9 | 64.8 | 64.3 | 65.4 | 64.7 | 66.1 | 70.2 |
| Total above | 77.3 | 92.2 | 93.8 | 98.0 | 100.0 | 96.8 | 90.9 | 77.7 | 70.1 | 60.2 | 56.9 | 55.1 | 55.8 | 54.3 | 55.8 | 60.1 |
| *Memorandum items:* | | | | | | | | | | | | | | | | |
| Former Soviet Union[b] | 77.3 | 92.2 | 93.8 | 98.0 | 100.0 | 96.8 | 90.9 | 77.7 | 70.1 | 60.2 | 56.9 | 55.1 | 55.8 | 54.3 | 55.8 | 60.1 |
| Former GDR | .. | .. | .. | .. | 100.0 | 84.5 | 68.3 | 73.6 | 80.4 | 88.2 | 92.0 | 95.0 | 96.6 | 98.5 | .. | .. |

Source: UN/ECE Common Database, derived from national and CIS statistics.
Note: Data for the east European countries are based on a GDP measure, except where otherwise mentioned. For the countries of the former Soviet Union, NMP data for 1980-1990 were chain-linked to GDP data from 1990. Country indices were aggregated with previous year PPP-based weights obtained from the European Comparison Programme for 1996.
a Gross material product (1980-1989 for Croatia).
b Sum of individual country data for former members.
c Net material product for 1980-1990 (until 1992 in the case of Turkmenistan).
d Excluding Transdniestria since 1993.

**Figure 1.2 – Real GDP in the ECE transition economies, 1980-2000 (Indices, 1989 = 100 %)**

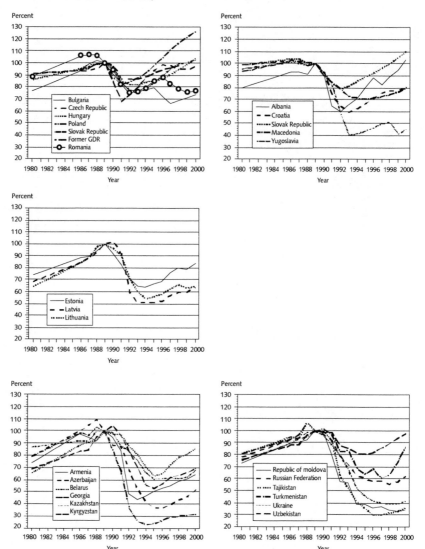

Source: UN/ECE Common Database, derived from national statistics.

### 1.3.3 Price development and inflation

The inflation rates were extremely high in all the post-Socialist countries at the start of the transformation phase. This is partly a result of their economic past since in the Socialist countries a considerable monetary overhang (a too high ratio of money to income) was created. For this reason, when price fixing was abolished in these countries there were in some cases enormous price increases. This process was still moderate in the leading eastern European transformation countries, being 35 % in Hungary in 1991, 56.7 % in the Czech Republic or 61.2 % in the Slovak Republic. In Poland the price increases had already reached a level of 585 % in 1990, which corresponds to a medium-level increase like that observed in Romania or Slovenia.

Table 1.3 – Consumer prices in eastern Europe, the Baltic states and the CIS, 1990-2000 (Annual average, percentage change over preceding year)

|  | 1990 | 1991 | 1992 | 1993 | 1994 | 1995 |
|---|---|---|---|---|---|---|
| Albania | .. | 35.5 | 193.1 | 85.0 | 21.5 | 8.0 |
| Bosnia and Herzegovina | 594.0 | 116.2 | 64218.3 | 38825.1 | 553.5 | -12.1 |
| Bulgaria | 23.8 | 338.5 | 91.3 | 72.9 | 96.2 | 62.1 |
| Croatia[a] | 609.5 | 123.0 | 663.6 | 1516.6 | 97.5 | 2.0 |
| Czech Republic | 9.9 | 56.7 | 11.1 | 20.8 | 10.0 | 9.1 |
| Hungary | 28.9 | 35.0 | 23.0 | 22.6 | 19.1 | 28.5 |
| Poland | 585.8 | 70.3 | 45.3 | 36.9 | 33.2 | 28.1 |
| Romania | 5.1 | 170.2 | 210.7 | 256.2 | 137.1 | 32.2 |
| SlovakRepublic | 10.4 | 61.2 | 10.2 | 23.1 | 13.4 | 10.0 |
| Slovenia | 5511.6 | 115.0 | 207.3 | 31.7 | 21.0 | 13.5 |
| Macedonia[a] | 608.4 | 114.9 | 1505.5 | 353.1 | 121.0 | 16.9 |
| F.R.Yugoslavia | 580.0 | 122.0 | 8926.0 | 2.2E+14 | 7.9E+10 | 71.8 |
| Estonia | 18.0 | 202.0 | 1078.2 | 89.6 | 47.9 | 28.9 |
| Latvia | 10.9 | 172.2 | 951.2 | 109.1 | 35.7 | 25.0 |
| Lithuania | 9.1 | 216.4 | 1020.5 | 410.1 | 72.0 | 39.5 |
| Armenia | 6.9 | 174.1 | 728.7 | 3731.8 | 4964.0 | 175.5 |
| Azerbaijan | 6.1 | 106.6 | 912.6 | 1129.7 | 1663.9 | 411.5 |
| Belarus | 4.7 | 94.1 | 971.2 | 1190.9 | 2219.6 | 709.3 |
| Georgia | 4.2 | 78.7 | 1176.9 | 4084.9 | 22286.1 | 261.4 |
| Republic of Moldova | 5.7 | 114.4 | 1308.0 | 1751.0 | 486.4 | 29.9 |
| Russian Federation | 5.2 | 160.0 | 1528.7 | 875.0 | 309.0 | 197.4 |
| Ukraine | 5.4 | 94.0 | 1485.8 | 4734.9 | 891.2 | 376.7 |

| | 1996 | 1997 | 1998 | 1999 | 2000 |
|---|---|---|---|---|---|
| Albania | 12.7 | 33.1 | 20.3 | -0.1 | - |
| Bosnia and Herzegovina | -21.2 | 11.8 | 4.9 | -0.6 | 1.7 |
| Bulgaria | 123.1 | 1082.6 | 22.2 | 0.4 | 10.0 |
| Croatia [a] | 3.6 | 3.7 | 5.9 | 4.3 | 6.4 |
| Czech Republic | 8.9 | 8.4 | 10.6 | 2.1 | 3.9 |
| Hungary | 23.6 | 18.4 | 14.2 | 10.1 | 9.9 |
| Poland | 19.8 | 15.1 | 11.7 | 7.4 | 10.2 |
| Romania | 38.8 | 154.9 | 59.3 | 45.9 | 45.7 |
| SlovakRepublic | 6.1 | 6.1 | 6.7 | 10.5 | 12.0 |
| Slovenia | 9.9 | 8.4 | 8.1 | 6.3 | 9.0 |
| Macedonia [a] | 4.1 | 3.8 | 1.1 | -1.4 | 10.1 |
| F.R.Yugoslavia | 90.5 | 23.2 | 30.4 | 44.1 | 77.9 |
| Estonia | 23.1 | 11.1 | 10.6 | 3.5 | 3.8 |
| Latvia | 17.7 | 8.5 | 4.7 | 2.4 | 2.8 |
| Lithuania | 24.7 | 8.8 | 5.1 | 0.8 | 1.0 |
| Armenia | 18.7 | 13.8 | 8.7 | 0.7 | -0.8 |
| Azerbaijan | 19.8 | 3.6 | -0.8 | -8.6 | 1.8 |
| Belarus | 52.7 | 63.9 | 73.2 | 293.7 | 168.9 |
| Georgia | 39.4 | 7.1 | 3.5 | 19.3 | 4.2 |
| Republic of Moldova | 23.5 | 11.8 | 7.7 | 39.3 | 31.3 |
| Russian Federation | 47.8 | 14.7 | 27.8 | 85.7 | 20.8 |
| Ukraine | 80.2 | 15.9 | 10.6 | 22.7 | 28.2 |

Source: UN/ECE Common Database, derived from national statistics.

Note: From 1992 onward indices derived from monthly data except for Armenia, Georgia, Hungary, Slovenia, the Federal Republic of Yugoslavia (from 1993); Turkmenistan (from 1995); Uzbekistan (from 1996). [a] Retail prices.

In contrast, in the CIS states increases occurred which were usually greater than 1000 % and which were exceeded by a multiple of this in the war-torn regions of the former Yugoslavia, as well as in Armenia or Georgia. After the relatively short price explosions caused by price liberalisation, the increase rates fell considerably, but remained at a relatively high level. In 2000 Belarus still registered the highest rate of increase, at 168.9 %. In only a small number of countries is it higher than 50 %, revolving at around 10 % in the majority of countries, still a relatively high level in comparison to western Europe. The cause of this is that difficult conditions exist for a stabilising monetary policy, especially in the CIS countries (Eger, 2000: 16). In spite of positive trends throughout the entire transition period, still stability has not been reached with regard to this item. "Inflationary pressures in the transition economies intensified in 2000. Under the impact of higher import prices for energy and related products in general and bad harvests in some, rates of consumer price inflation rates in 2000 were higher than in 1999 in most of the east European and Baltic countries" Economic Survey of Europe, 2001: 114).

Linked to the trends in prices, the inflation rate followed similar trends. Inflation rates are available from 1995 up to 2000. In the most of the countries the inflation rate in 1995 was higher than in 2000. But only some countries show a clearly decreasing trend. To this group belong the forerunners Hungary, Poland, the Baltic states and, more or less, Azerbaijan. A stable situation was found in Croatia, Slovenia and on a low level in the former GDR. The economies of these countries are more advanced in the reform process and in their capacities to handle external shocks.

**Table 1.4 – Inflation rate in the ECE transition economies, 1995-2000 (%, change from Dec. to Dec.)**

|  | 1995 | 1996 | 1997 | 1998 | 1999 | 2000 |
|---|---|---|---|---|---|---|
| Eastern Europe |  |  |  |  |  |  |
| Albania | 6.0 | 17.4 | 42.0 | 7.8 | -1 | 4.2 |
| Bosnia Herzegovina | -34.2 | 3.2 | 12.2 | 2.2 | -0.4 | 3.4 |
| Bulgaria | 33.0 | 311.1 | 578.7 | 0.9 | 6.2 | 11.2 |
| Croatia | 3.7 | 3.5 | 4.0 | 5.6 | 4.6 | 7.5 |
| Czech Republic | 7.9 | 8.7 | 9.9 | 6.7 | 2.5 | 4.1 |
| Hungary | 28.5 | 20.0 | 18.4 | 10.4 | 11.3 | 10.1 |
| Poland | 22.0 | 18.7 | 13.2 | 8.5 | 9.9 | 8.6 |
| Romania | 27.7 | 56.8 | 151.7 | 40.7 | 54.9 | 40.7 |
| Slovak Republic | 7.4 | 5.5 | 6.5 | 5.5 | 14.4 | 8.3 |
| Slovenia | 8.6 | 8.8 | 9.5 | 6.6 | 8.1 | 9.0 |
| Macedonia | 11.2 | 0.3 | 4.5 | -1.0 | 2.4 | 10.8 |
| F.R.Yugoslavia | 110.7 | 59.9 | 10.3 | 45.7 | 54.0 | 115.1 |
| Estonia | 28.8 | 14.9 | 12.3 | 6.8 | 3.9 | 4.9 |
| Latvia | 23.3 | 13.2 | 7.0 | 2.8 | 3.3 | 1.9 |
| Lithuania | 35.5 | 13.1 | 8.5 | 2.4 | 0.3 | 1.5 |
| Armenia | 32.0 | 5.6 | 21.8 | -1.2 | 2.1 | 0.4 |
| Azerbaijan | 84.5 | 6.8 | 0.3 | -7.6 | -0.5 | 2.1 |
| Belarus | 244.2 | 39.1 | 63.4 | 181.6 | 251.3 | 108.0 |
| Georgia | 57.4 | 13.6 | 7.3 | 10.8 | 11.1 | 4.6 |
| Republic of Moldova | 23.8 | 15.1 | 11.1 | 18.2 | 43.8 | 18.5 |
| Russian Federation | 131.4 | 21.8 | 11.0 | 84.5 | 36.7 | 20.1 |
| Ukraine | 181.7 | 39.7 | 10.1 | 20.0 | 19.2 | 25.8 |
| Former GDR | 2.6 | 1.6 | 2.3 | 1.1 | 0.2 | ... |

Source: UN/ECE Common Database, derived from national and CIS statistics

In most of the transition countries a deflation trend continued from 1995 to 1997. From 1997 to 1999 the process of steady deflation for several years was reversed and in the majority of transition economies price increased in 1998 up to 2000.

In 1997 the transition economies were generally favoured by external market conditions, not least by the stronger than expected growth in western Europe's import demand. There was a notable improvement in consumer confidence and the fall in wages inflation was accompanied by widespread improvements in productivity.

Mainly in the countries of the former Soviet Union the inflation rate grew from 1997 up to 1999. In general, the increased turbulences of 1998 and 1999, which combined an external demand shock with unexpected fluctuations in world commodity prices, was a major challenge and test for the stability of national economies. Especially the CIS countries were victims of the currency crises triggered by the devaluation of the rouble. However, inflation rates were also higher in other transition economies (Slovak Republic, Federal Republic of Yugoslavia, Romania, Slovenia, "the former Yugoslav Republic of Macedonia"), largely because of the sharp increase in the world price of crude oil and the appreciation of the dollar.

### 1.3.4 Employment and the unemployed

In the UN/ECE database used here, the proportions of employees, registered unemployed and beyond this the proportions of industrial employees are stated.

The data from Table 1.5 shows that the level of employment hardly increased in the second half of the eighties in almost all post-Socialist states. Full employment had almost been achieved. This is also confirmed by the proportions of unemployed at the start of the nineties, which were extremely low (Fig. 1.3). After 1989, the proportion of employed people started to fall, with a small number of exceptions. At first, they fall very quickly only in eastern Europe until 1992/1993. By 1993 the average proportion of employed people in eastern Europe had fallen to 82.6 %, after which this figure only decreased slightly. Exceptions are the Czech Republic, Romania and Poland, where these proportions remained higher than the eastern European average.

In the Baltic states, the employment rates remained high in 1990 and 1991, after which they also fell quickly to the eastern European level until 1994. In the CIS states, the employment rate fell very slowly until the mid-nineties, and also remained at a high level in the second half of the nineties. In some countries, the proportions indeed reach a level in excess of that of 1989.

Table 1.5 – Total employment in eastern Europe, the Baltic states and the CIS, 1980, 1987-2000 (Indices, 1989=100)

| | 1980 | 1987 | 1988 | 1989 | 1990 | 1991 | 1992 | 1993 | 1994 | 1995 | 1996 | 1997 | 1998 | 1999 | 2000 |
|---|---|---|---|---|---|---|---|---|---|---|---|---|---|---|---|
| **Eastern Europe** | 96.7 | 100.0 | 99.9 | 100.0 | 97.1 | 90.7 | 85.4 | 82.6 | 82.6 | 82.2 | 82.7 | 82.7 | 83.0 | 80.7 | .. |
| Albania | 77.9 | 95.9 | 97.6 | .. | 99.2 | 97.5 | 76.0 | 72.7 | 80.7 | 79.0 | 77.5 | 76.9 | 75.3 | 74.0 | .. |
| Bosnia Herzegovina | .. | .. | .. | 100.0 | 97.1 | 58.1 | 22.1 | 9.9 | 9.1 | 10.1 | 22.5 | 34.4 | 36.4 | 37.6 | 38.0 |
| Bulgaria | 100.0 | 102.8 | 102.4 | 100.0 | 93.9 | 81.6 | 75.0 | 73.8 | 74.3 | 75.2 | 75.3 | 72.3 | 72.2 | 70.4 | .. |
| Croatia | 87.4 | 100.6 | 100.4 | 100.0 | 97.1 | 89.2 | 79.3 | 76.6 | 74.8 | 73.9 | 74.5 | 73.9 | 78.8 | 78.5 | .. |
| Czech Republic | 95.3 | 98.9 | 99.4 | 100.0 | 99.1 | 93.6 | 91.2 | 89.7 | 90.4 | 92.8 | 93.4 | 91.6 | 90.1 | 86.9 | .. |
| Hungary [a] | 104.2 | 101.7 | 100.7 | 100.0 | 96.7 | 86.7 | 78.1 | 73.2 | 71.8 | 70.4 | 69.8 | 69.8 | 70.7 | 72.9 | 73.6 |
| Poland | 102.0 | 100.8 | 100.1 | 100.0 | 95.8 | 90.1 | 86.3 | 84.3 | 85.1 | 86.7 | 88.3 | 90.8 | 92.9 | 90.4 | .. |
| Romania [b] | 94.6 | 97.9 | 98.7 | 100.0 | 99.0 | 98.5 | 95.5 | 91.9 | 91.5 | 86.7 | 85.7 | 82.4 | 80.5 | 76.9 | .. |
| Slovak Republic [b] | 90.8 | 99.0 | 99.8 | 100.0 | 98.2 | 85.9 | 86.8 | 84.6 | 83.7 | 85.7 | 84.5 | 82.6 | 81.8 | 78.0 | .. |
| Slovenia [c] | 84.0 | 101.9 | 101.3 | 100.0 | 96.1 | 88.7 | 83.8 | 81.3 | 79.3 | 79.1 | 78.7 | 78.6 | 78.7 | 80.2 | 81.1 |
| Macedonia | 81.2 | 99.9 | 99.7 | 100.0 | 98.2 | 90.7 | 86.4 | 81.5 | 76.6 | 69.0 | 65.8 | 61.8 | 60.1 | 61.1 | 60.4 |
| F.R.Yugoslavia | 83.4 | 99.0 | 99.8 | 100.0 | 97.0 | 94.1 | 90.9 | 88.3 | 86.5 | 85.3 | 84.8 | 89.9 | 89.7 | 82.4 | .. |
| **Baltic states [d]** | 94.9 | 99.4 | 99.6 | 100.0 | 98.5 | 98.9 | 94.4 | 89.0 | 83.2 | 80.6 | 80.1 | 80.9 | 80.5 | 79.5 | .. |
| Estonia [c] | .. | 97.6 | 97.6 | 100.0 | 98.6 | 96.4 | 91.4 | 84.5 | 82.7 | 78.3 | 77.0 | 77.4 | 76.4 | 73.3 | 72.6 |
| Latvia | 97.0 | 100.4 | 100.5 | 100.0 | 100.1 | 99.3 | 92.0 | 85.6 | 77.0 | 74.3 | 72.3 | 73.7 | 74.1 | 73.8 | .. |
| Lithuania | 93.4 | 99.5 | 99.8 | 100.0 | 97.3 | 99.7 | 97.5 | 93.4 | 88.0 | 86.4 | 87.2 | 87.7 | 87.0 | 86.6 | .. |
| **CIS** | 93.8 | 98.4 | 98.8 | 100.0 | 100.2 | 98.9 | 96.6 | 94.2 | 91.4 | 90.5 | 89.8 | 88.5 | 87.5 | 87.2 | .. |
| Armenia | 86.6 | 99.5 | 101.4 | 100.0 | 102.4 | 105.0 | 99.2 | 97.0 | 93.5 | 92.8 | 90.2 | 86.2 | 84.0 | 81.6 | 80.6 |
| Azerbaijan | 62.7 | 74.7 | 75.2 | 100.0 | 100.9 | 101.7 | 101.4 | 101.2 | 98.9 | 98.4 | 100.5 | 100.7 | 100.9 | 100.9 | 100.9 |
| Belarus | 95.4 | 99.0 | 99.5 | 100.0 | 99.1 | 96.6 | 94.1 | 92.9 | 90.4 | 84.8 | 84.0 | 84.1 | 85.0 | 85.5 | 85.4 |
| Georgia | 92.7 | 101.0 | 101.1 | 100.0 | 102.3 | 93.3 | 73.5 | 66.4 | 64.8 | 79.0 | 79.1 | 82.7 | 84.6 | 77.0 | .. |
| Republic Moldova [e] | 97.3 | 99.7 | 98.9 | 100.0 | 99.1 | 99.0 | 98.0 | 80.7 | 80.4 | 80.0 | 79.4 | 78.7 | 78.5 | 71.5 | 72.0 |
| Russian Federation | 96.9 | 99.7 | 99.9 | 100.0 | 99.6 | 97.7 | 95.3 | 93.7 | 90.6 | 87.9 | 87.2 | 85.5 | 84.2 | 84.6 | 85.5 |
| Ukraine | 99.6 | 100.3 | 99.9 | 100.0 | 99.9 | 98.3 | 96.3 | 94.1 | 90.5 | 93.3 | 91.3 | 88.8 | 87.9 | 85.8 | 84.9 |
| **Total above** | 94.6 | 98.8 | 99.1 | 100.0 | 99.3 | 96.6 | 93.4 | 90.9 | 88.8 | 88.0 | 87.6 | 86.8 | 86.1 | 85.2 | .. |
| Memorandum items: | | | | | | | | | | | | | | | |
| Former Soviet Union | 93.8 | 98.4 | 98.8 | 100.0 | 100.2 | 98.9 | 96.5 | 94.0 | 91.2 | 90.2 | 89.5 | 88.3 | 87.3 | 87.0 | .. |

Source: UN/ECE Common Database, derived from national and CIS statistics. [a] End of year, up to 1992; since 1992, annual average, [b] End of year, [c] Self-employed excluded until 1987, [d] Excluding Estonia until 1985, [e] Excluding Transdniestria since 1993.

With the decline in employment rates, the proportions of the registered unemployed increased (see Table 1.6). In 1992, already 12.4 % of all employees are unemployed on an eastern European average. Particularly high values can be found in Albania, Croatia and Slovenia. Unemployment is relatively low only in the Czech Republic. However, this country also did some catching up in the second half of the nineties. It can be observed in general terms that the eastern European countries did not gain control of the problem of unemployment in the second half of the nineties.

On average, an upward trend began in this period. In 2000 in eastern Europe 15.1 % were unemployed. Only in Hungary was it possible to reduce somewhat the relatively high figures of the nineties. The highest figures can be observed in the countries of the former Yugoslavia as a result of the war. In the Baltic region and the CIS states, unemployment increased from a very low level in the first half of the nineties to a low level in the second half of the nineties. Exceptions are constituted only by the Russian Federation and Armenia. In both countries, unemployment in 2000 was approx. 10 %.

In general terms, since the restructuring of industry and agriculture and the establishment of new branches of the economy has not yet been completed, a fall in the unemployment rate can hardly be expected in the coming year. There might even be a further increase in unemployment if the structural change from labour-intensive to capital-intensive production accelerates.

force, end-of-period)

| | 1990 | 1991 | 1992 | 1993 | 1994 | 1995 | 1996 | 1997 | 1998 | 1999 | 2000 |
|---|---|---|---|---|---|---|---|---|---|---|---|
| **Eastern Europe** | .. | 9.6 | 12.4 | 14.0 | 13.6 | 12.5 | 11.7 | 11.9 | 12.6 | 14.6 | 15.1 |
| Albania | 9.5 | 9.2 | 27.0 | 22.0 | 18.0 | 12.9 | 12.3 | 14.9 | 17.6 | 18.2 | 16.9 |
| Bosnia and Herzegovina | .. | .. | .. | .. | .. | .. | .. | 39.0 | 38.7 | 39.0 | 39.4 |
| Bulgaria | 1.8 | 11.1 | 15.3 | 16.4 | 12.8 | 11.1 | 12.5 | 13.7 | 12.2 | 16.0 | 17.9 |
| Croatia | .. | 14.1 | 17.8 | 16.6 | 17.3 | 17.6 | 15.9 | 17.6 | 18.6 | 20.8 | 22.6 |
| Czech Republic | 0.7 | 4.1 | 2.6 | 3.5 | 3.2 | 2.9 | 3.5 | 5.2 | 7.5 | 9.4 | 8.8 |
| Hungary | 1.7 | 7.4 | 12.3 | 12.1 | 10.9 | 10.4 | 10.5 | 10.4 | 9.1 | 9.6 | 8.9 |
| Poland | 6.5 | 12.2 | 14.3 | 16.4 | 16.0 | 14.9 | 13.2 | 10.3 | 10.4 | 13.1 | 15.0 |
| Romania | 1.3 | 3.0 | 8.2 | 10.4 | 10.9 | 9.5 | 6.6 | 8.8 | 10.3 | 11.5 | 10.5 |
| Slovak Republic | 1.6 | 11.8 | 10.4 | 14.4 | 14.8 | 13.1 | 12.8 | 12.5 | 15.6 | 19.2 | 17.9 |
| Slovenia | .. | 10.1 | 13.3 | 15.5 | 14.2 | 14.5 | 14.4 | 14.8 | 14.6 | 13.0 | 12.0 |
| Macedonia [a] | .. | 24.5 | 26.2 | 27.7 | 30.0 | 36.6 | 38.8 | 41.7 | 41.4 | 43.8 | 44.9 |
| F.R.Yugoslavia [a b] | .. | 21.0 | 24.6 | 24.0 | 23.9 | 24.7 | 26.1 | 25.6 | 27.2 | 27.4 | 26.6 |
| **Baltic states** | .. | .. | 2.1 | 4.5 | 5.3 | 6.6 | 6.4 | 6.3 | 7.3 | 9.1 | 10.0 |
| Estonia [c] | .. | .. | 1.6 | 5.0 | 5.1 | 5.0 | 5.6 | 4.6 | 5.1 | 6.7 | 7.3 |
| Latvia | .. | .. | 2.3 | 5.8 | 6.5 | 6.6 | 7.2 | 7.0 | 9.2 | 9.1 | 7.8 |
| Lithuania | .. | .. | 3.5 | 3.4 | 4.5 | 7.3 | 6.2 | 6.7 | 6.9 | 10.0 | 12.6 |
| **CIS [a]** | .. | .. | 2.7 | 3.6 | 4.4 | 5.8 | 6.6 | 7.6 | 9.0 | 8.3 | 6.9 |
| Armenia | .. | .. | 3.5 | 6.3 | 6.0 | 8.1 | 9.7 | 11.0 | 8.9 | 11.5 | 10.9 |
| Azerbaijan | .. | .. | 0.2 | 0.7 | 0.9 | 1.1 | 1.1 | 1.3 | 1.4 | 1.2 | 1.2 |
| Belarus | .. | .. | 0.5 | 1.3 | 2.1 | 2.7 | 4.0 | 2.8 | 2.3 | 2.0 | 2.1 |
| Georgia | .. | .. | 0.3 | 2.0 | 3.8 | 3.4 | 3.2 | 8.0 | 4.2 | 5.6 | .. |
| Republic of Moldova | .. | .. | 0.7 | 0.7 | 1.0 | 1.4 | 1.5 | 1.7 | 1.9 | 2.1 | 1.8 |
| Russian Federation [d] | .. | .. | 5.2 | 6.1 | 7.8 | 9.0 | 10.0 | 11.2 | 13.3 | 12.2 | 9.6 |
| Ukraine | .. | .. | 0.3 | 0.4 | 0.3 | 0.6 | 1.5 | 2.8 | 4.3 | 4.3 | 4.2 |
| **Memorandum items:** | | | | | | | | | | | |
| Russian Federation [e] | .. | 0.1 | 0.8 | 1.1 | 2.1 | 3.2 | 3.4 | 2.8 | 2.7 | 1.7 | 1.4 |
| Former GDR | .. | .. | 13.5 | 15.4 | 13.5 | 14.9 | 15.9 | 19.4 | 17.4 | 17.7 | 17.2 |

Source: National statistics and direct communications from national statistical offices to UN/ECE secretariat.
[a] The data reported on employment cover only the social sector in agriculture, hence unemployment rates are biased upwards. [b] Since 1999, excluding Kosovo and Metohia. [c] Job seekers till 2000, [d] Based on the Russian Federation Goskomstat's monthly estimates according to the ILO definition, i.e. including all persons not having employment but actively seeking work, [e] Registered unemployment.

## Figure 1.3 – Registered unemployment in the ECE transition economies, 1990-2000 (percent of labour force)

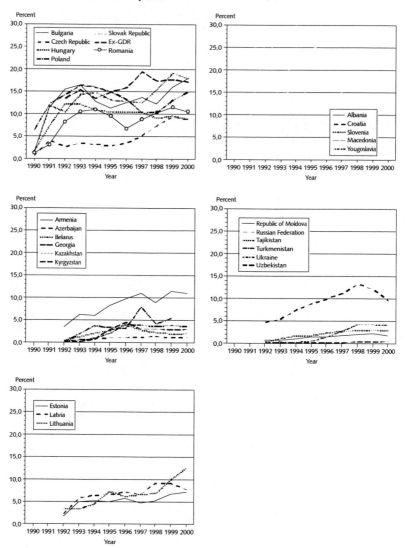

Source: UN/ECE Common Database, derived from national and CIS statistics,

### 1.3.5  Changing economic structures

The structural changes from large Socialist industry and the oversized agricultural sector to a private market economy system are regarded as one of the major tasks of the transition in the economic system. The following structural distortions had occurred:

- The industrial sector was oversized in comparison with the service sector.

- The consumer goods industry had been neglected in favour of heavy industry.

The extent to which this coming structural change has been successful can be read from the indicators 'industrial and agricultural workers', 'service workers' and 'private sector workers'.

The trend in the share of employees in industry in particular provides information on how successful the post-Socialist countries have been in restructuring their economies, since some of the Socialist inheritance consisted of forming an oversized industrial sector. This indicator also reveals the differing courses taken in the transition process. The number of industrial workers has fallen radically in eastern Europe, and in 1994 on average accounted for only 69.5 % of the level of 1989. In 1999, the level had fallen to 60.9 %. In some countries, such as Bosnia and Herzegovina, Bulgaria or Romania the share had more than halved. The trends in changes are similar in the Baltic Republics. Only 54.0 % of employees there worked in industry in 1999. In the average of the CIS states, this process of change started later, but in the second half of the nineties it reached similar dimensions to the other transformation states. The process of restructuring the old economic sector is not complete. The proportion of industrial workers is still higher than in the developed western countries.

The share accounted for by the private sector in gross domestic product in the eastern European and Baltic states reached values in excess of 50 % in 1999. The highest shares are achieved by the private sectors of the economy in the Czech Republic and Hungary with 80 % and in the Slovak Republic and Estonia, both with 75 %. The shares are still relatively low in Poland with 65 % and in Slovenia with 55 %. The data shows that the transformation process as a process of removal from the state system has already made considerable progress, at least in the leading transformation countries. This result at the end of the nineties is all the more remarkable, especially since the disentwining of state heavy industry in the first half of the nineties was started late and caused the countries massive problems. This task was made more difficult in the first half of the nineties, especially by the fact that the state companies were in a monopoly situation, the credit markets were not suited for disentwining and privatisation and no effective company monitoring was available (Eger, 2000: 5 et sqq.). Other questions that needed to be clarified were those of fairness in distribution, the approval of foreign investments and the evaluation of the enterprises, in other words sub-division into those that could be rescued and those to be closed.

Table 1.7 – Employment in industry in eastern Europe, the Baltic states and the CIS, 1989-2000 (Indices, 1989=100)

| | 1989 | 1990 | 1991 | 1992 | 1993 | 1994 | 1995 | 1996 | 1997 | 1998 | 1999 | 2000 |
|---|---|---|---|---|---|---|---|---|---|---|---|---|
| **Eastern Europe** [a] | 100.0 | 95.6 | 86.7 | 76.7 | 71.9 | 69.5 | 68.6 | 68.3 | 66.2 | 65.2 | 60.9 | : |
| Albania | 100.0 | : | : | : | : | : | : | : | : | : | : | : |
| Bosnia and Herzegovina | 100.0 | 98.3 | 60.3 | 23.3 | 8.3 | 9.2 | 18.7 | 22.0 | 26.8 | 28.9 | 28.9 | 28.4 |
| Bulgaria | 100.0 | 91.0 | 74.7 | 64.8 | 59.5 | 57.3 | 56.0 | 55.4 | 53.0 | 50.8 | 46.7 | : |
| Croatia | 100.0 | 102.4 | 84.8 | 70.3 | 70.4 | 67.3 | 59.5 | 59.0 | 56.6 | 60.0 | 58.3 | : |
| Czech Republic | 100.0 | 95.8 | 92.2 | 85.1 | 80.9 | 76.6 | 77.0 | 76.4 | 76.1 | 75.8 | 73.4 | : |
| Hungary | 100.0 | 97.0 | 85.4 | 77.3 | 69.1 | 66.0 | 62.5 | 61.9 | 63.0 | 65.9 | 66.4 | 65.6 |
| Poland | 100.0 | 93.7 | 86.1 | 76.7 | 74.4 | 73.8 | 76.2 | 75.6 | 75.8 | 75.0 | 69.5 | : |
| Romania [b] | 100.0 | 96.5 | 91.6 | 79.5 | 73.0 | 65.4 | 66.0 | 66.0 | 59.0 | 55.8 | 49.5 | : |
| SlovakRepublic | 100.0 | 95.7 | 88.2 | 78.7 | 74.0 | 71.7 | 71.6 | 71.6 | 70.2 | 67.3 | 65.4 | : |
| Slovenia | 100.0 | 95.1 | 85.2 | 84.6 | 78.1 | 75.1 | 72.2 | 71.5 | 68.5 | 67.8 | 66.7 | : |
| Macedonia | 100.0 | 95.3 | 87.3 | 81.6 | 77.5 | 72.9 | 63.1 | 59.0 | 54.4 | 52.5 | 55.4 | 52.9 |
| F.R.Yugoslavia | 100.0 | 100.9 | 92.1 | 87.2 | 85.0 | 82.7 | 80.6 | 78.8 | 76.3 | 74.2 | 65.3 | : |
| **Baltic states** | 100.0 | 96.8 | 95.5 | 87.0 | 74.2 | 63.0 | 60.8 | 58.0 | 57.7 | 55.8 | 54.0 | : |
| Estonia [c] | 100.0 | 96.9 | 93.0 | 85.8 | 73.6 | 70.7 | 76.4 | 73.0 | 68.8 | 67.5 | 63.6 | : |
| Latvia | 100.0 | 97.0 | 92.1 | 81.4 | 69.0 | 56.3 | 53.1 | 50.1 | 51.9 | 47.6 | 45.7 | . |
| Lithuania | 100.0 | 96.7 | 99.0 | 91.4 | 78.0 | 64.5 | 59.5 | 57.0 | 57.1 | 56.5 | 55.7 | . |
| **CIS** | 100.0 | 98.2 | 96.7 | 91.8 | 79.7 | 73.3 | 69.2 | 63.8 | 62.6 | | | |
| Armenia | 100.0 | 102.6 | 95.0 | 84.0 | 75.2 | 73.7 | 62.8 | 52.9 | 47.5 | 43.4 | 40.5 | 40.0 |
| Azerbaijan | 100.0 | 97.1 | 94.9 | 88.9 | 81.1 | 77.4 | 72.9 | 58.6 | 50.1 | 52.0 | 53.6 | 53.6 |
| Belarus | 100.0 | 98.6 | 96.9 | 92.1 | 88.5 | 84.4 | 75.2 | 74.4 | 74.5 | 75.5 | 76.2 | 75.9 |
| Georgia | 100.0 | 104.2 | 92.6 | 66.0 | 56.5 | 51.6 | 46.8 | 33.6 | 25.8 | 26.4 | : | : |
| Republic of Moldova [c] | 100.0 | 102.4 | 95.1 | 93.1 | 55.0 | 52.1 | 44.7 | 43.9 | 42.9 | 40.8 | 35.9 | 33.7 |
| Russian Federation | 100.0 | 97.7 | 96.1 | 91.3 | 89.8 | 80.7 | 74.1 | 70.4 | 64.5 | 63.0 | 62.6 | 64.0 |
| Ukraine | 100.0 | 98.1 | 97.3 | 92.7 | 87.9 | 78.3 | 72.2 | 66.8 | 61.2 | 59.3 | 54.4 | : |
| **Total above** [a] | 100.0 | 97.4 | 93.5 | 86.9 | 82.8 | 76.1 | 71.5 | 68.7 | 64.5 | 63.2 | : | : |
| Memorandum items: | | | | | | | | | | | | |
| Former Soviet Union | 100.0 | 98.2 | 96.7 | 91.6 | 87.9 | 79.2 | 72.9 | 68.9 | 63.6 | 62.3 | : | : |

Source: UN/ECE Common Database, derived from national and CIS statistics.
[a] Excluding Albania. [b] End of year. [c] Excluding Transdniestria since 1993.

If one considers the share of the popular economy in gross domestic product, contradictory trends can be observed. However, a radical structural change has not become visible in any of the transformation countries. As a trend, there has been a shift from industry and agriculture towards services, telecommunications and trade, although there are contrary examples. The relative stability of the sector shares over the nineties shows that the structural change is progressing slowly and has not yet been finished.

## 1.4 The phases of the transformation process

The transformation process can be divided into five phases:

- Pre-transformation
- Collapse of the political system
- Structural caesura
- Consolidation
- Sustained upswing

These phases have been developed based on publications by Merkel (1995: 32) and Höhmann (1997: 194). By using such phases it is possible to classify the countries and show the transformation stage of each country. An overview to the phase-level of social transformation is given in figure 1.4. The main characteristics of the transformation process are explained in the fields here; the vertical axis shows the structures and the horizontal axis, the phases. As to the structures of the processes, three levels are presumed: firstly, the transformation of the economic system (transition from a planned to a market economy); secondly, the transformation of the political system (transition from an authoritarian one-party system to democratic political structures) and thirdly, conversion of society (building up civil society, releasing people from the totalitarian structures of the Socialist social system). The course of the transformation process so far can be sub-divided into five phases: the pre-transformation phase; the phase of the collapse of the political system; the review or structural caesura phase; followed by the two consolidation sections.

**Figure 1.4 – Phase-level model of social transformation**

| Phases structures | Economy | Political system | Society |
|---|---|---|---|
| 1. Pre-transformation | Primacy of policy on the economy, centralist organised economy, losses of efficiency, inadequate crisis management, economy aimed at basic supply of the population | One-party system, reduction in the competence and authority of the Communist parties, lack of confidence among the population, formation of opposition | Increasing public political awareness and rejection of the prevailing ideology, in the final phase lack of confidence among the population, formation of opposition |
| 2. Collapse of the political system | Continuance of the traditional, state-centralist economic structures | Fall of the Iron Curtain, removal of power from the Communist parties, free elections, initial democratisation and establishment of a multi-party system | Many possible future development paths, a need for strategic decisions, uncertainty as to how things are to go on |
| 3. Structural caesura | Economic shocks, inflation, negative economic growth, increasing unemployment, low labour productivity, restricted subsidies for state enterprises, liberalisation of prices and markets | Establishment of democratic structures, frequent changes in power and conception, political instability, politically-ordered change in the economic system | Change in social institutions, uncertainty and impoverishment of large sections of the population, starting changes to the social security systems |
| 4. Consolidation | Economic structural change by reducing the oversized industry and agriculture, privatisation of the large enterprises, increase in foreign investment, integration into world trade | Stabilisation of the political system, elections no longer endanger the democratic and market economy reforms, creation of constitutions and party statutes | Polarisation into winners and losers of transformation, social exclusion through high unemployment, creation of new elites, unemployment still high, economic growth does not reduce unemployment |
| 5. Sustained upswing | Rapid economic growth beyond the level of 1989, beginning approximation to the countries of southern Europe | Integration into European political structures | Change in social structure, expansion of the social security systems, change in people's way of thinking and conduct |

### 1.4.1 Collapse of the political system

The actual transformation process starts with the collapse of the political system. This section can be referred to as the second phase, after the pre-transformation phase. The peaceful revolutions at the beginning of the nineties are only the end of the pre-transformation phase and the starting point of the actual transformation process. It was political changes that had decided the power question against the Communist parties (Nikolic, 1995: 9). This is covered under definition of the system change, in other words the change in the form of political dominance structure, the transition from an authoritarian to a liberal type of social system (O'Donnell, Schmitter, 1986: 6). The actual task, namely to implement democratic standards and to establish modern market economies, had not yet been put forward at this time. This is the task belonging to the second phase of social change, in which the framework was created for starting the transition of the entire economic and social system. This phase was largely completed in 1991. The main result was the removal of power from the Communist parties and the beginning of democratisation. The institutions of planned economies start to destruct (Höhmenn, 1997: 194). After initial orientation problems and discussions on reform plans and trends the post-Socialist countries have now created well-functioning democratic structures.

The fundamental problem of all post-Socialist states at the start of phase two consists of the lack of synchronicity between the completed change in the political system and the still unchanged basic economic and social structures. The transformation of the Socialist economy to become a market economy proved to be a complex, difficult task which was made even more difficult as a result of the inadequate political framework. A primary characteristic, and a particularity of the transition processes, is that both the political change, namely the transition from an authoritarian system to a democratic one, and the economic change, namely the transition from a planned economy to a market one, had to be completed at the same time. The state was therefore in an area of tension between the historical starting situation, market economy reorientation and the globalisation of economic relations. The state took on a prominent role in the framework of Socialist central administration. The change in the system leads to a fundamental reorientation in the role of the state which is reduced in the market economy. This reorientation must run in phases. Initially, an active role must be played by the state which is needed in order to overcome the Socialist shortcomings and to kick-start the transformation. This is needed since it was not yet possible for regulatory mechanisms to form within the economy in the first phase of the transformation process (Nikolic, 1995: 9). If this has been successful, one needs a state willing to retreat and set itself limits.

Phase two of the transformation process was however relatively short. In it the political preconditions are created for economic transformation.

### 1.4.2 Structural caesura

The phase of collapse of the political system is followed by the phase of structural caesura. In the third transition phase, a democratic political system is established and the traditional institutions of the economic system are dissolved, in particular the old centralist economic system. This section is also referred to as a phase of structural caesura or transition recession since it is accompanied by economic failures.

Entering the phase three of economic structural change - the so-called shock phase – of necessity started relatively quickly. It was necessary in the majority of post-Socialist countries to react to the spontaneous economic trends caused by the political collapse of Socialism and which had led to a decline in economic growth and high inflation rates. In a few countries, such as Poland, this situation had already occurred by the end of 1989. All reforms in this phase in the economic sphere were implemented initially with massive deployment of the state and in some cases using radical means. New monetary and financial policies were implemented as early as in 1990 (Breziniski,1996: 137 et sqq.). The central banks were separated from the state and first steps were taken towards creating financial and capital markets. Examples of this include the establishment of stock exchanges in Budapest (1990), Warsaw and Ljubljana (1991), Sofia (1992), Prague and Bratislava (1993). This was followed by the introduction of competition statutes and the creation of antimonopoly authorities. Relatively quickly, largely between 1990 and 1992, the state's foreign trade monopoly, typical of Socialist societies, was removed (Poland 1990, Hungary, former SSR, Romania, Bulgaria and Slovenia 1991). The fiscal and social security systems were adjusted with still relatively slight delays. These changes took place around 1993 and 1994.

The change in the ownership situation was much more difficult. In the initial phase, state-controlled privatisation was dominant, initially restricted to smaller enterprises. Roughly 90 % of small enterprises were privately-owned in the mid-nineties. However, the framework was missing for privatisation by means of start-ups since the financial and capital markets were not functioning and the enterprises could not be provided with the necessary capital. As to the privatisation of larger enterprises, the Czech Republic and Hungary are regarded as being the pioneers. At the end of 1994, 81 % of all state enterprises in the Czech Republic (Hungary 75 %) had been privatised or closed. In the case of the Czech Republic, however, one should point out that this was a privatisation which was not a privatisation. The Czech Republic chose to hand out ownership shares to citizens, thus impeding real privatisation.

In the other countries, this change was much slower. In Bulgaria at the same time, only 10 % had been privatised (Romania 13 %, Poland as many as 32 %). A special situation in the process of economic restructuring can be observed in the Russian Federation. With one exception, namely the privatisation of large companies, the market economy reforms were set in motion very late in the Russian Federation, not until the mid-nineties.

This starting phase of restructuring threw the young post-Socialist economies into a grave adjustment crisis (Kutz, 2001: 26). All economic indicators show steep downward trends. These declines have been much clearer than originally presumed (Lavigne, 1995: 121). It appears to be a natural law that the transition from a planned economy to a market economy leads to a temporary crisis which appears with hindsight to be unavoidable. As a rule, the crisis reached its peak roughly three years after the reforms had been initiated. It is caused by the indispensable structural change, and hence almost takes on the characteristics of a natural law. It appears that all transition countries need to go through this phase. The structural change - mainly consisting of the process of removing power over the economy from the state and of privatisation, redistributing employees between the sectors of industry, changing monetary and subsidy policy, creating economic legal security and then permitting foreign investment and regulating its influx - were tasks that were extremely complex and difficult to deal with which could not be handled without crises, failed developments, using inadequate concepts or creating chaotic situations. The goals pursued in the first half of the nineties were very difficult to attain. It initially appeared as if the radical changes, the so-called shock therapies, had missed their aim. Successful privatisation had initially proven to be difficult since parallel financial resources, markets and institutional carriers had to be created. The first steps towards reforms consequently led to a rapid decline in economic performance. The declines in economic growth, the falls in gross domestic product, are however unlikely to have been caused exclusively by the reforms that were set in motion in the first half of the nineties. The collapse of the Council for Mutual and Economic Cooperation (COMECON) and the unfavourable economic situation in the west amplified the extent of the economic collapse.

### 1.4.3 Consolidation and sustained upswing

The consolidation phase covers the economic upswing until the level of 1989 and the last phase entails rapid economic growth and integration into European political structures.

In the mid-nineties the first states started entering the consolidation phase. Economic growth, an increase in gross national product and labour productivity, the interest shown by foreign enterprises in direct investment, an initial structural change towards capital-intensive production or a progressing privatisation policy are a few characteristics of this section. However, the economic upswing starts at a very low level. In this phase of initial consolidation, the countries still do not achieve the gross national product they had in 1989. The starting economic upswing however does not lead to social improvements. Inflation rates and unemployment remain at a high level. What makes things even more difficult for the population is that the restructuring of the social security systems has not advanced so far that the high social costs to be paid for the economic change by the population can be cancelled out. All transformation countries are now in this phase. Some have already left it behind them. These countries show economic successes in 2000 in particular.

The consolidation successes can be summarised in three items:

*An institutional change has taken place.* The countries have created a stable foundation for democracy, plurality and legal certainty. They have created constitutions, adopted party statutes and built up a basic legal system. Economic and trade policy has been formulated. However, all the countries appear to find it difficult to transform the centralist administrative structures which persist strongly.

*The market economic reforms have progressed.* The privatisation and restructuring of the economy, limiting state subsidies, linking to world markets, have become the framework conditions of the economic upswing. Difficulties are still experienced in the privatisation of the large state enterprises, although the private and service sectors are starting to expand.

*Foreign policy reorientation has taken place.* Following the end of the Cold War, the post-Socialist transformation countries have turned towards the European Union and the North Atlantic Treaty Organisation.

A small number of countries have already managed to jump to the next phase of a sustained economic upswing. This only applies to the so-called forerunner countries of Hungary, Poland, the Czech Republic and Slovenia, which have been able to improve their economic situation in comparison to the last year of Socialism. In these countries the gross national product is already higher than the values reached in 1989. These countries are on a path towards the economic performance of the southern European countries. In addition to rapid economic growth, there is much that needs to be done in this phase; the expansion of the social security systems, a change in thinking and conduct towards becoming independent citizens and full integration into the political structures of Europe.

However, a rapid conclusion of the economic and social changes in the region of the post-Socialist states cannot be expected, even in the economically successful countries for two reasons. Firstly, it is a matter of country-specific differences which have started the transformation with different economic and political frameworks; some of the CIS states are only at the beginning of the economic structural change, and will still go through difficult economic and social phases for quite some time. Secondly, it is not only a matter of economic restructuring, but of the parallel exchange of the entire economic and social system, the economic, democratic and social transformation. New ways of thinking and acting, new social structures and social security systems must be established. This is a process which naturally takes longer and which even the forerunner countries still need to go through.

## 1.5 Differences and shared features – the integration of the countries into the phases of the transformation process

In the second half of the nineties, the post-Socialist countries are in general recorded as being successful in dealing with economic transition. This is the most important conclusion reached in the above analyses. With the exception of a few of the CIS states, all the economic indicators show a positive trend. Overall, the year 2000 was the most successful to date in terms of economic development following the political collapse of Socialism. The Economic Survey for Europe (2000: 9) states: "For the first time since the start of their economic and political transformation, the former centrally planned economies of eastern Europe and the former Soviet Union were all growing in 2000: their aggregate GDP increased by 6 per cent, significantly more than the world economy as a whole. This very high rate of economic growth was largely due to the unexpectedly strong recovery in the Russian Federation where GDP increased by 7.7 per cent, its highest growth rate in more than 30 years". This description of the situation by no means implies that the transition countries have traversed the economic trough into which they had fallen without exception at the start of the nineties. Now, in all post-Socialist countries far-reaching reforms have been set in motion which are reflected in economic successes.

However, these reforms are based on different starting conditions, have been implemented with differing degrees of consistency and have consequently led to different levels of success. The process of the economic transformation is also a process of economic differentiation between the countries.

The evaluation of the countries by the European Bank for Reconstruction and Development (EBRD) assists in classification. The countries are classified using four criteria: (i) company reforms; (ii) market reforms; (iii) financial reforms and (iv) reforms to investment law.

By looking at the course of structural change within the economy, the countries can be sub-divided into three groups; the economically successful eastern and central European countries, the Baltic countries with medium progress in transformation and the CIS states, which are still far behind in the transformation process.

### 1.5.1 The economically successful eastern and central European countries

These countries - Croatia, Czech Republic, Hungary, Poland, Slovak Republic, Slovenia, Estonia, Latvia, Lithuania are in an advanced state of transformation. The reforms started relatively quickly and relatively favourable starting conditions were found in the majority of these countries. On the whole, the so-called old burdens in these countries are still relatively small: In some cases, links were possible to previous reforms; there was a national consensus on the need to go through the transformation process; the political situation was relatively stable in spite of a few changes in governments and the west supported the reforms more intensively than in other regions of the post-Socialist states (Höhmann, 1995: 195). The dimensions of the adjustment crisis caused by the structural changes were therefore less grievous. Economic trends troughed relatively early in the first half of the nineties – in Poland as far back as in 1991, in the other countries in 1992 and 1993. Some of the countries of the former Yugoslavia do not belong to these groups because of the war.

The economic upswing in the group of eastern European countries started in the first half of the nineties and continued until 2000. All these countries have already left the phase of the structural caesura (phase 3, cf. Fig. 1.1) and are in different phases of the consolidation process. Here, it is possible to further sub-divide the countries in this group. The smaller section is still in the first consolidation phase, and in spite of a gross domestic product which has been increasing gradually they have not yet returned to the level of 1989 (Croatia, "the former Yugoslav Republic of Macedonia", the Federal Republic of Yugoslavia, Romania, Bulgaria, the Baltic States). Special situations can be found in Romania and Bulgaria. The economic upswing that started in the mid-nineties weakened once more in the second half of the nineties and did not recommence until 1998/99.

The majority of the group of eastern European countries has left consolidation phase one behind and gross national product has exceeded the values of 1989. These countries include Hungary, Poland, the Slovak Republic and Slovenia. The Czech Republic is about to cross this threshold. The Czech Republic, Poland, Hungary and Slovenia in particular radically pushed the reforms in the first half of the nineties. The result was that they initially fell into a deep adjustment crisis. It is however noticeable that in those countries which had set the transition process in motion first and most radically were also the first to stop the economic collapse, and then recorded the most successful economic trends. It is also decisive for the positive development that after the collapse of the Soviet Union traditional economic areas have been reactivated once again. "In summary, it can be stated that the reconstruction of the economy in the states of central and eastern Europe is successful in that they are wholly or partly in the zones of traditional, cultural and economic dynamics of central Europe. This is clearly the case of the Czech Republic, the Slovak Republic and Hungary which experience this dynamic in the broad region of the Viennese Basin, in other words with the region surrounding Bratislava and in western Hungary as far as Budapest. Slovenia has the proximity of Upper Italy and Vienna. The Polish situation with the western territories of Silesia, Poznan and the Region around Katowice and Cracow cannot be so clearly described for the reasons that have been stated, but here too the trend cannot be ignored, at least as regards the dominant role of Germany in foreign trade" (Kutz, 2001:30). The countries of the so-called Visegrád group (Poland, the Czech Republic, the Slovak Republic, Hungary) are in a solid economic condition a decade after the start of the structural change. Democracy, the rule of law, market economy, free competition and the trade links to the world market are the foundation for further restructuring and approximation to the western market economies.

### 1.5.2 The south eastern European countries

These countries – Albania, Armenia, Bulgaria, Georgia, Kazakhstan, Kyrgyzstan, "the former Yugoslav Republic of Macedonia", Moldova, Romania, the Russian Federation, Ukraine and Uzbekistan – are in a medium state of reform. In this group of countries, the trough of the economic shock phase was reached in about the mid-nineties. In contrast to the countries of central and eastern Europe, the economic collapse was deeper and the process of consolidation is much slower. None of the countries has so far achieved a gross national product corresponding to that of 1989. On the contrary, these countries are still relatively far from reaching phase two of consolidation.

Initial success can be attributed to privatisation. As to the financial reforms, supervision of enterprises and the investment statutes, a clear backlog can be seen as against the forerunner countries. In spite of the favourable trend in gross national product, Albania is still not among the group of countries where the economic reforms have progressed furthest because of the unfavourable starting position.

A relatively favourable situation has occurred in the Russian Federation, which however only constitutes a special case because of its size (Höhmann, 1995: 198). However, because of old burdens such as the unfavourable economic structure, the power situation and different political plans – which were still not clarified in the mid-nineties – the state, which was too weak in the starting phase for the initiation of reforms, hindered the economic transformations. This explains why the reforms were not initiated until later. This also applies to the majority of other CIS states, which are still further behind in the transformation process.

### 1.5.3 The Commonwealth of Independent States

These countries – Azerbaijan, Belarus, Tadzhikistan, Turkmenistan – are still in an early state of transformation and the reforms started very late. The low point in economic development was not reached until the second half of the nineties, in some cases not until 1999. The declines in the various economic indicators reached a worrying level, going down to one-third of the 1989 level. Progress has been achieved in liberalising the internal market and in privatisation. The states in the third group are hence only starting on the first consolidation phase. Reaching the 1989 level appears to be relatively distant.

Viewed in light of the situation in the states of the former Soviet Union, the economic successes in the states of central and eastern Europe are very worthy of observation. However, in spite of all the success reports, which do not always depict reality, and actual successes in the 'economic miracle' of eastern and central Europe, the transformation process is far from complete and is only starting in the states of the former Soviet Union. In none of the post-Socialist transformation countries, ultimately, has economic, political and social restructuring been an all-round success.

The transformation process will hence still continue – since privatisation of the oversized large state enterprises has not yet been completed. This will indeed take some time since the privatisation methods used to date have not proved to be entirely successful (Brusis, Ochmann, 1996: 21). The main problems that have emerged here are the high level of company debt, the still underdeveloped capital markets and the interdependence between enterprises and banks.

### 1.5.4 Differences between the transformation countries and the 15 EU States

Economic transformation is the main task, as well as being the starting point for a whole series of processes of extensive social change. The structural changes in the economy transfer to social structures. In the course of the transformation process, it was necessary for the social security systems to be changed. A change has taken place in the social structure. The political system had to become more stable and the Socialist past had to be dealt with in ideological terms. People had to find new identities. It is therefore not only necessary to ask about the state of the economic reforms, but to know how economic change impacts the demographic behavioural patterns, and what the consequences are for people in the post-Socialist transformation countries.

There remain differences between the transformation countries and the 15 EU States which indicate the considerable changes yet to be made in order to achieve approximation to these states. In spite of a majority of economic successes in the second half of the nineties, the gross national products show pronounced gaps between the transformation countries (the following are included in the analysis: Slovenia, the Czech Republic, Hungary, Poland, the Slovak Republic, Estonia, Lithuania, Latvia, Romania and Bulgaria) and the EU 15 countries (Piazolo, 2002: 14 et sqq.)

The gross domestic product per inhabitant (calculated using purchasing power) is still much lower than the EU average. The situation is favourable in Slovenia and in the Czech Republic, which reach 68 % and 60 % of the EU level respectively. Romania (27 %), Latvia (27 %) and Bulgaria (23 %), in contrast, only achieved extremely low values. The gap between these countries and the EU 15 States has widened since the start of the transformation process.

There is also a need to adjust the economic structures. A major part of gross domestic product is still achieved in the agricultural sector. A proportion of 2.3 % in the EU 15 is faced by 21.1 % in Bulgaria and 17.6 % in Romania. Oversized industrial sectors are to be found in the Czech Republic, Romania, Slovenia and Poland. The transformation states are however no longer purely industrial societies. This is shown by the high proportions in gross domestic product now accounted for by the service sector. Estonia, Latvia, the Slovak Republic and Hungary demonstrate similar proportions to the EU 15. These proportions are still much lower in the Czech Republic, Bulgaria and Romania.

The various data show that there is still a need to adjust, and that approximation to the situation in the EU 15 cannot be achieved in the short term, indeed, that specific problems exist in the individual transformation countries. Even the most successful transformation countries show some considerable differences as to their economic structures. The demographic transformation, which is anchored in social change, cannot therefore yet be considered complete.

## 1.6 The social consequences of transformation

In this section, the level of the individual is to be observed. Questions are asked as to the impact of macrostructural change for people in the post-Socialist countries.

The populations in the transition countries have had to pay a high social price for democracy, freedom and economic reforms. "It is an illusion to believe that the return to a capitalist market economy alone offers a solution to the economic problems. This return itself has still not happened in many not inconsiderable sections of these economies because the industrial policy inheritance of the Communist system cannot be overcome in the large, uneconomic industrial complexes without massive social shifts" (Kutz, 2001: 25). The phase of euphoria which was experienced in the short term with the collapse of the political system of Socialism gave way, from the point of view of the broad population, to a phase of sobering up and even disappointment. The individual consequences of the economic transformation became obvious in the phase of the structural caesura. Social structural caesuras lead to existential fear and insecurity for individuals. These have been transferred to people by means of the elements discussed below.

The growth rates in average gross monthly wages show pronounced falls during the phase of the structural caesura in all macro economies (Fig. 1.5). In the countries in which macroeconomic restructuring has progressed, such as the Czech Republic, Hungary, Poland and Slovenia, these falls were restricted to the beginning of the nineties. Thereafter, considerable increases once more led to increases in income. In the second half, the upward trend levelled somewhat, although the growth rates remained positive, with the exception of Poland. The trend in the Czech Republic has been positive since 1993, but such a trend did not start in Hungary until 1996. In the countries which are lagging behind in the transformation process, the structural caesura crisis did not reach its climax until the mid-nineties or later. This is the period of considerable reductions in gross real wages and is accompanied by considerable fluctuations. These crises are much stronger than they were in the forerunner countries. The situation here does not improve until the end of the nineties, whilst only a few countries show a stable, positive situation.

In parallel with this development, the standard of living indicators show changes in consumption habits. Foodstuffs consumption, observed by selected indicators (meat and meat products, milk, butter, vegetables) fell in the majority of countries observed (see Table 1.8). This should not be immediately interpreted as a symptom of crisis, in other words as a reduction in the standard of living. Such an evaluation is likely to apply accurately only to those countries which are making slower progress in the transformation process. A fall in, for instance, the per capita consumption of meat and meat products by 20 kg, 30 kg or 35 kg in Bulgaria, the Russian Federation or Ukraine between 1990 and 2000 can also be interpreted as indicating worsening living conditions, especially since consumption of other foodstuffs was also on the decline in these countries. The trend in the forerunner countries has been more towards a change in consumption habits. There is a slight fall in the consumption of meat, whilst fruit and vegetables have taken on greater significance as part of the general diet. At the same time, car and telephone ownership has clearly increased. The Czech Republic, Hungary and Poland are unmistakable examples of this trend. However, car and telephone ownership increased in all the countries observed here.

One may presume that economic change has influenced family formation in two ways. The economic structural caesuras and the consequent trans-formation crises have led on the one hand directly to a fall in the standard of living as expressed in falling incomes. On the other hand, a change in the supply structure is likely to have led to new consumption patterns. One may presume that both poverty and insecurity, as well as new goals regarding consumption, and the combination of these two factors, will have influenced decisions not to have children.

**Figure 1.5 – Average gross monthly wages, real growth rate in selected Transformation Countries, 1990-2000 (in %)**

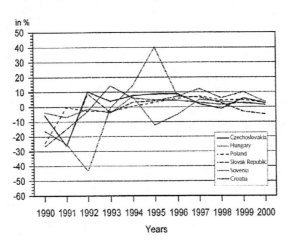

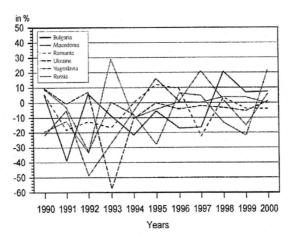

Source: WIIW, Handbook of Statistics

**Table 1.8 – Selected living standard indicators in former Socialist countries, 1990-2000**

| Countries | Indicators | Years | | | | |
|---|---|---|---|---|---|---|
| | | 1990 | 1995 | 1997 | 2000 | |
| Bulgaria | Food consumption: Meat and meat products (Kg) | 54.5 | 38.2 | 25.4 | 34.7 | |
| | Milk (litre) | 55.7 | 35.2 | 31.3 | 29.1 | |
| | Butter (kg) | 2.1 | 0.8 | 0.5 | 0.4 | |
| | Vegetables (kg) | 61.1 | 59.0 | 46.7 | 58.4 | |
| | Hospital beds (per ten thous. persons) | 104 | 106 | 105 | 66 | |
| | Motorcars in use (per thous. persons) | 147 | 187 | 209 | - | |
| | University students (per ten thous. persons) | 175 | 266 | 283 | 270 | |
| Croatia | Food consumption: Meat and meat products (Kg) | 49.5 | | | | |
| | Milk (litre) | 101.0 | | | | |
| | Butter (kg) | 0.6 | | | | |
| | Vegetables (kg) | 57.2 | | | | |
| | Hospital beds (per ten thous. persons) | 74 | 59 | 60 | | |
| | Motorcars in use (per thous. persons) | 167 | 152 | 204 | | |
| | University students (per ten thous. persons) | 148 | 167 | 195 | 212 | |
| Czech Republic | Food consumption: Meat and meat products (Kg) | 96.5 | 82.0 | 81.5 | | |
| | Milk (litre) | 91.5 | 64.6 | 57.7 | | |
| | Butter (kg) | 8.7 | 4.5 | 4.1 | | |
| | Vegetables (kg) | 66.6 | 78.0 | 81.1 | | |
| | Hospital beds (per ten thous. persons) | 131 | 114 | 109 | | |
| | Motorcars in use (per thous. persons) | 233 | 301 | 344 | | |
| | University students (per ten thous. persons) | 114 | 135 | 161 | | |

| Countries | Indicators | 1990 | 1995 | 1997 | 2000 |
|---|---|---|---|---|---|
| Hungary | Food consumption: Meat and meat products (Kg) | 73.1 | 63.1 | 58.9 | |
| | Milk (litre) | | | | |
| | Butter (kg) | 1.7 | 1.5 | 1.2 | |
| | Vegetables (kg) | 83.3 | 91.6 | 98.8 | |
| | Hospital beds (per ten thous. persons) | 102 | 91 | 82 | 83 |
| | Motorcars in use (per thous. persons) | 185 | 220 | 227 | 236 |
| | University students (per ten thous. persons) | 99 | 176 | 231 | 295 |
| Macedonia | Food consumption: Meat and meat products (Kg) | | 28.6 | 25.2 | |
| | Milk (litre) | | 62.7 | 64.8 | |
| | Butter (kg) | | | | |
| | Vegetables (kg) | | 70.2 | 74.5 | |
| | Hospital beds (per ten thous. persons) | 60 | 54 | 52 | |
| | Motorcars in use (per thous. persons) | 114 | 145 | 145 | |
| | University students (per ten thous. persons) | 123 | 143 | 161 | |
| Poland | Food consumption: Meat and meat products (Kg) | 68.6 | 63.4 | 61.7 | 65.2 |
| | Milk (litre) | | | | |
| | Butter (kg) | 7.8 | 3.7 | 4.3 | 4.2 |
| | Vegetables (kg) | 119.0 | 120.0 | 116.0 | 120.0 |
| | Hospital beds (per ten thous. persons) | 70 | 66 | 64 | 60 |
| | Motorcars in use (per thous. persons) | 138 | 195 | 221 | 259 |
| | University students (per ten thous. persons) | 105 | 204 | 279 | 408 |

| Countries | Indicators | Years | | | |
|---|---|---|---|---|---|
| | | 1990 | 1995 | 1997 | 2000 |
| Romania | Food consumption: Meat and meat products (Kg) | 61.0 | 51.2 | 48.5 | |
| | Milk (litre) | | | | |
| | Butter (kg) | | | | |
| | Vegetables (kg) | 110.8 | 140.4 | 135.9 | |
| | Hospital beds (per ten thous. persons) | 89 | 76 | 74 | |
| | Motorcars in use (per thous. persons) | 55 | 93 | 110 | |
| | University students (per ten thous. persons) | | | | |
| Russian Federation | Food consumption: Meat and meat products (Kg) | 75.0 | 55.0 | 50.0 | |
| | Milk (litre) | | | | |
| | Butter (kg) | | | | |
| | Vegetables (kg) | 89.0 | 76.0 | 79.0 | |
| | Hospital beds (per ten thous. persons) | 138 | 126 | 121 | 115 |
| | Motorcars in use (per thous. persons) | 59 | 93 | 114 | |
| | University students (per ten thous. persons) | 190 | 179 | 208 | 294 |
| Slovak Republic | Food consumption: Meat and meat products (Kg) | 84.0 | 63.7 | 66.1 | |
| | Milk (litre) | 107.6 | 72.0 | 73.6 | |
| | Butter (kg) | 6.4 | 2.5 | 2.3 | |
| | Vegetables (kg) | 70.8 | 79.5 | 80.7 | |
| | Hospital beds (per ten thous. persons) | 119 | 114 | 114 | |
| | Motorcars in use (per thous. persons) | 165 | 189 | 211 | |
| | University students (per ten thous. persons) | 120 | 158 | 189 | |

| Countries | Indicators | Years | | | |
|---|---|---|---|---|---|
| | | 1990 | 1995 | 1997 | 2000 |
| Slovenia | Food consumption: Meat and meat products (Kg) | 34.8 | 30.4 | 37.4 | |
| | Milk (litre) | 98.8 | 94.3 | 74.5 | |
| | Butter (kg) | 0.5 | 0.7 | 0.7 | |
| | Vegetables (kg) | 12.2 | 23.2 | 21.9 | |
| | Hospital beds (per ten thous. persons) | 59 | 57 | 57 | |
| | Motorcars in use (per thous. persons) | 289 | 351 | 385 | |
| | University students (per ten thous. persons) | 152 | 231 | 281 | |
| Ukraine | Food consumption: Meat and meat products (Kg) | 68.0 | 39.0 | 35.0 | 32.0 |
| | Milk (litre) | | | | |
| | Butter (kg) | | | | |
| | Vegetables (kg) | 102.0 | 97.0 | 91.0 | 101.0 |
| | Hospital beds (per ten thous. persons) | 136 | 125 | 100 | 95 |
| | Motorcars in use (per thous. persons) | 63 | 87 | 96 | |
| | University students (per ten thous. persons) | 171 | 180 | 219 | 258 |
| F.R. Yugoslavia | Food consumption: Meat and meat products (Kg) | 68.6 | 52.9 | 58.3 | |
| | Milk (litre) | 99.1 | 97.2 | 102.3 | |
| | Butter (kg) | 1.0 | 0.3 | 0.3 | |
| | Vegetables (kg) | 110.4 | 113.9 | 133.1 | |
| | Hospital beds (per ten thous. persons) | 59 | 53 | 55 | |
| | Motorcars in use (per thous. persons) | 134 | 152 | | |
| | University students (per ten thous. persons) | 149 | 151 | 178 | |

Source: WIIW, Handbook of Statistics

The change in the structure of society goes hand-in-hand with social shifts which are polarising the formerly homogeneous Socialist societies. This polarisation comprises elements of social injustice. The fall in incomes was accompanied by a widening of the wage gap. What arose in the transformation process was a smaller group of winners and a larger group of losers. The distribution of income from work to capital led to polarisation into a small group of rich individuals and the creation of a poor population which in some cases was many in number. A. Rothacher has stated the following on this matter: "Here, the societies are in a process of elementary restructuring and uncertainty which is difficult to understand in western Europe, being as it is saturated and resistant to adaptation, linked with mass impoverishment and the redefinition of all previous socially-dominant values.

The social decline of the middle classes (doctors, teachers, civil servants, specialist workers) and the impoverishment of the lower classes (pensioners, the unemployed, agricultural workers, gypsies) went hand-in-hand with the rise of a too frequently unscrupulous illegitimate new moneyed elite which took possession of the riches of society earmarked for redistribution by handing out political privileges and through corruption. Most people reacted to losing their jobs and status with passive survival strategies: self-help, gardens and bartering, illegal work, as well as increasingly with asocial (self)destruction: alcoholism, delinquency, drug consumption, vandalism, homelessness, suicide" (Rothacher, 1999: 9). The general trends in differentiation are supplemented by the rise of regional differences. The change in economic structures necessarily arising by virtue of the collapse of Socialist heavy industry led to regional deindustrialisation, accompanied by unemployment and impoverishment in these regions.

It has so far been impossible to alleviate the main social problems - poverty, inflation, unemployment, social injustice, social exclusion. Economic growth has so far only started to have a broad effect among the population (Lang, 2001: 19). A deep gap opens up between those who have benefited from transformation and those who have lost out. For instance, in the second half of the nineties, 30 % of Poles considered themselves poor, and this in the country with the highest growth rates, whilst 50 % considered their opportunities to be restricted (Golinowska, 1999). It has therefore not yet been possible to ease the main problems of poverty, inflation, unemployment and social exclusion even in the economically successful countries. The downsizing of workforces made necessary by structural change (reconstruction of an oversized industrial apparatus and of the agricultural sector) has not been compensated for by the creation of new jobs. The consequence is continuing high unemployment. And another effect can be observed. Where foreign direct investment flows in, an increase takes place in labour productivity, and as a consequence labour is released that is no longer needed. This leads to economic growth, but not necessarily to a fall in unemployment.

The gap in the standard of living in relation to the western nations is massive, even for the economically successful countries. In Table 1.9 the per capita purchasing power in the transformation countries is compared with the situation in Germany in 1998. It becomes clear for all countries that there is still a major gap in relation to western Europe. The differences between the individual post-Socialist countries are shown in turn. In Slovenia, the country with the greatest success in this respect, purchasing power is 67 % of the German level. The Czech Republic and Hungary reach 51 % and 47 % respectively. Purchasing power in the Slovak Republic is 60 % lower than in Germany. The states of the former Soviet Union can be found at the lower end of the scale. Purchasing power in these countries is less than 20 % of that in Germany.

**Table 1.9 – Per capita purchasing power in the transformation countries in comparison to Germany (Germany 1998 = 100 %), index values. 100 = per capita purchasing power in Germany 1998**

| Values % | Country | Values % | Country |
|---|---|---|---|
| 67 | Slovenia | 21 | Bulgaria |
| 51 | Czech Republic | 19 | Macedonia |
| 47 | Hungary | 19 | F.R.Yugoslavia |
| 40 | Slovak Republic | 18 | Russian Federation |
| 38 | Poland | 17 | Belarus |
| 29 | Lithuania | 14 | Bosnia and Herzegovina |
| 28 | Estonia | 12 | Ukraine |
| 28 | Croatia | 11 | Albania |
| 24 | Romania | 09 | Moldova |
| 22 | Latvia | | |

Source: GfK AG, Regionalforschung, (EBM 1998 - Europäische Basismarktdaten and OBM 1998 – Osteuropa-Basismarktdaten)

## 1.7 Thesis – fertility and economic development

Consequences for demographic change have been derived in this section on the basis of the course and dimensions of structural change. The connection between economic development, changes in circumstances and demographic trends can be described using four theories: euphoria theory, the theory of structural caesura, the thesis of value anomie and the adjustment theory.

### 1.7.1 The euphoria theory

With the exception of the former GDR, the phase of political collapse did not cause an immediate fall in the birth rate. In the former GDR this was caused by the consistent change of all the social institutions of Socialism. This led to a phase of short-lived euphoria in the time of the political collapse. In the other post-Socialist countries, this phase started later and the reforms took place more gradually. The euphoria of the new beginning lasted longer; the impact of the system transformation did not become visible to the population until later in the phase of the structural caesura in which consistent economic reforms were initiated. As a consequence of this situation, the Total Fertility Rate did not fall as rapidly as in the former GDR, but more gradually.

### 1.7.2 The theory of structural caesura

The population was made to feel the deep ruptures involved in structural change in the shape of inflation, unemployment, increasing poverty, the removal of women from the labour market, the collapse of the social security systems and the reduction of social benefits, political uncertainty and frequent changes of the political powers which led the transformation. The reduction in the level of social security, impoverishment of, in some cases, broad sections of the population, and thus existential fears, immediately led to the shelving of plans to form families where contraception was available. Furthermore, the economic structural caesuras also provide opportunities to start again in a manner that is capital intensive, so that social risks increase and have a negative impact on family formation.

### 1.7.3 The thesis of value anomie

The transformation process in the post-Socialist countries consists not only of economic structural change, but also covers society as a whole, and hence leads to a complete change of all social institutions. What ultimately takes place is a change from a closed society to an open society in which new economic structures and technologies are expanding. Changing political players enter the scene with competing ideas for social development and changes take place in the role of the mass media, which have to compete in disseminating new information and which propagate the new philosophies in which social models are exchanged and in which philosophical pluralism spreads. This change devalues the existing cultural traditions and standards. According to Höpflinger (1987: 43) such a situation has a variety of impacts on family formation which can be transferred to the post-Socialist transformation process.

Firstly, the dissolution of traditional values can be linked with increased individualism on the basis of which marriage and having children are given a different evaluation. The traditionally Socialist family orientations are replaced by values such as emancipation or self-realisation for which opportunities have become much greater and which make it less desirable to have children.

Secondly, the dissolution of traditional values goes hand-in-hand with the transfer of economic rationality to the family area. Value anomie leads to changes in individual circumstances directly impacting family formation since the balancing impact of traditions is removed. Having children is then regarded more from the point of view of the cost of having children, the risk to one's own standard of living, the cost of social security for the family, and the factors restricting one's mobility.

In the case of the post-Socialist countries, the impact of value anomie is amplified in two ways by the economic structural changes. On the one hand poverty and social insecurity strengthen the transfer of economic rationality to the area of family formation in the social groups which are the losers in the transformation process. On the other hand, economic rationality applies to the winners in transformation to the extent that economic and social new starts lead to social risks with a negative impact on the willingness to form families. Both situations lead to the same results – emotional uncertainty, fear of the future and the dominance of dealing with everyday worries cause broad sections of the population to distance themselves from binding long-term biographical decisions such as marriage or having children.

Thirdly, one can presume that social anomie has effects on family formation that differ greatly by age. For the older population, which has thoroughly internalised the traditional orientations, the family appears to be a stable unit which offers security and protection against rapid social change. Striving to preserve family stability is the dominant factor for this group. The young are likely to regard the family as posing an obstacle in the transformation process. At the same time, they start to accept the new pluralistic value system, to increasingly experience their family bonds in an open system with stronger leanings towards individualisation. The general rejection or postponement of family forming is to be expected as a consequence. It is therefore to be expected that those involved in family forming who are of different ages will react to the economic and social change with specific behavioural patterns. The growth in childlessness, a decline in the tendency to marry, and increasing age at marriage and at the birth of the first child are to be expected.

### 1.7.4 The adjustment theory

Even in those countries which are already in the final phase of the transformation process, no sustainable increase can be observed in the birth and marriage rates. Economic upswings do not lead directly to an improvement in people's circumstances. The transformation countries have not yet managed to install effective social security systems or to capably counter inflation and unemployment. For the younger generations, which had not yet reached family-forming age in the phase of the economic shock, it still appears to be difficult to act in line with new value systems since their everyday experience still leads them to orientate their conduct in line with the criteria of economic rationality. It is possible to derive from this the lack of increase in the birth rate and to hypothesise that the birth rate will not increase for quite some time.

On the whole, concerning family formation the post-Socialist countries are typified by a combination of poverty shocks and an anomie of standards caused by the parallel course of the economic structural changes and the changes in social institutions. Both situations, amplifying one another, lead to economic rationality being expanded to cover the field of family formation. This initially explains the clear fall in births in all post-Socialist countries in the transformation phase. The lack of social improvement with the economic upswing then leads to the hypothesis that economic rationality continues for longer, and hence that there will be a longer phase of lower birth and marriage rates.

## 1.8 Conclusions

One of the important questions in this context is: Were the pace and magnitude of the fertility decline influenced by the intensity and the duration of the economic downturn? This question cannot be fully answered on the basis of the available data. The link between macroeconomic trends and generative decisions is not so direct that analyses comparing, for instance, the trend in gross national product with the decline in fertility could directly reveal the degree to which economic shocks may cause such a decline. "Needless to say, bivariate analysis is a primitive tool and GDP is only a crude indicator of the state of the economy and the living standard of the population" (Economic Survey of Europe, 1999: 189). The decline in fertility is a reaction to the complex social changes taking place in the post-Socialist countries, and is not solely set off by the economic shocks experienced. The collapse of Socialism, the political crises and changes in government, the enforced reorientation to a changing society, social restructuring, the devaluation of traditional vocational qualifications and training, the need to accumulate new knowledge and the expansion of western ways of thinking and acting, have combined to lead to a change in family formation, as has the fall in production caused by the change in the industrial structure, which has led to a considerable change in the lives of the population. It nevertheless appears to be legitimate to investigate the connection between fertility and changes in the economic macro-indicators since economic change forms the basis of the transformation process.

Fig. 6 shows the connection between the fall in the Total Fertility Rate and the change in gross national product between 1989 and 1999. Gross national product of 1989 was set at 100 %. Observing this connection shows that highly specific developments took place in the individual countries. However, it is also possible to identify generally valid patterns. The following connections can be seen.

The trend is for the fall in gross national product to result in a fall in fertility. These falls have however not been uniform. In most countries, the fall in gross national product was not linked to an immediate fall in fertility (Fig. 1.6). Initially, gross national product had fallen relatively clearly for two or three years after 1989. In the period when gross national product was falling rapidly, fertility remained unchanged or fell only slightly. As gross national product stabilised, fertility began to fall. "The one-year lag is introduced in order to relate economic conditions at a given time to the reproductive decisions of couples, a decision that effects the number of births about a year later" (Economic Survey of Europe, 1999: 189). Fertility followed the fall in gross national product not only with the natural time lag, but, with the exception of the GDR, it took between one and two years longer for that social and economic change to become reflected in changed decisions as to conduct. In addition to the forerunner transformation countries of Hungary, the Czech Republic, Poland, Slovenia and the Slovak Republic, this group includes countries such as Lithuania and Latvia, as well as Croatia, Moldova, Armenia, "the former Yugoslav Republic of Macedonia", the Federal Republic of Yugoslavia and Azerbaijan.

In a second, smaller group of countries, the fall in gross national product was followed immediately by a fall in fertility. This was the case in Estonia, Bulgaria, the Russian Federation, Ukraine, Belarus and Romania.

The increase in gross national product in the economically successful countries was not accompanied by an increase in fertility. It was not until 1999 that weak upward trends were observed in a small number of countries, which did not start until after gross national product had been clearly rising for several years.

The scale of the fall in gross national product does not permit conclusions to be drawn concerning the scale of the fall in fertility. In the successful transformation countries (particularly noticeable in Hungary, the Czech Republic, Poland and Slovenia) restricted falls in gross national product led to equally clear falls in fertility to those occurring in countries where gross national product fell rapidly (e.g. the Baltic countries). One can also perceive that the fall in fertility is much lower in those countries where the level was already low in 1989 than in those countries with a higher level of fertility.

It is evident that the falling trend in gross national product reflected a relationship with the economic shocks in their complexity, which also led to a fall in fertility. One may presume that the economic shocks kick-started the fall in fertility. Here, however, there were very different reactions revealing that there is no linear link between the changes in gross national product and in fertility. In particular one may not deduce the scale of the decline in fertility from that of the fall in gross national product. Additionally, the link seems to be only negative in nature. The fall in gross national product shows a situation of economic crisis which, via a variety of factors, as a rule causes a delayed fall in fertility. Conversely, economic growth does not automatically lead to an increase in fertility. For this to happen, a corresponding change is needed in conduct resulting from changes in social conditions, and these social conditions have not yet arisen in the post-Socialist countries.

**Fig. 1.6 – Total Fertility Rate and Gross Domestic Product in the post-Socialist countries, 1989-1999**

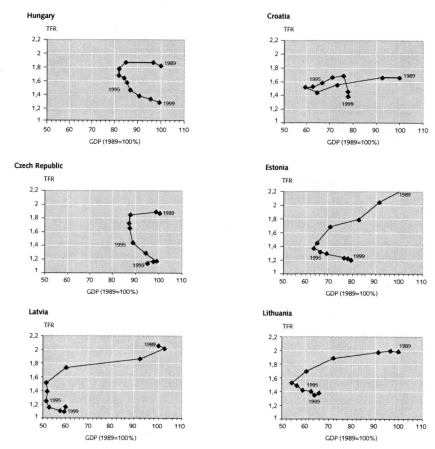

**Poland**

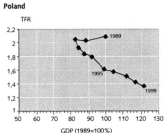

GDP (1989=100%)

**Slovak Republic**

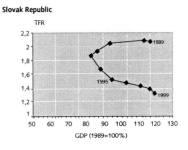

GDP (1989=100%)

**Slovenia**

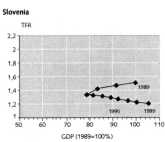

GDP (1989=100%)

**Bulgaria**

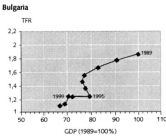

GDP (1989=100%)

**Russian Federation**

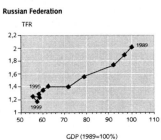

GDP (1989=100%)

**Romania**

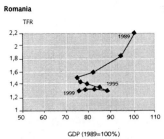

GDP (1989=100%)

**Ukraine**

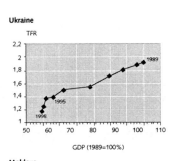

GDP (1989=100%)

**Macedonia**

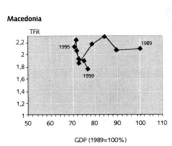

GDP (1989=100%)

**Moldova**

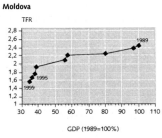

GDP (1989=100%)

**Yugoslavia**

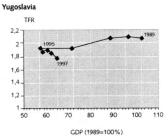

GDP (1989=100%)

65

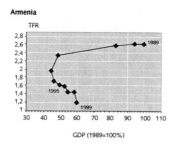

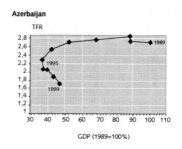

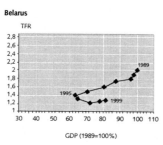

If one takes a look at the link between the change in economic indicators such as the inflation rate or unemployment, which in contrast to global economic trends are directly felt by the population, the impression that individual factors appear to be unsuited to explaining the decline in fertility rate becomes stronger. This is to be made clear by an example showing the link between unemployment and fertility trends for several countries. The data show two different patterns for the link. On the one hand, unemployment increases quickly at the beginning of the nineties, and the decline in fertility starts with a delay of one or two years. After this, the unemployment rate remains unchanged, but the level of fertility falls further. This situation was observed for instance in Hungary and in the Czech Republic (Fig. 1.7). In the Czech Republic, fertility initially fell even when unemployment was relatively low. Unemployment in the Czech Republic did not clearly increase until the second half of the nineties, and this increase was not accompanied by a fall in fertility. On the other hand, in some countries, represented here by the Russian Federation and Ukraine (Fig. 1.7), there was no major unemployment. Nevertheless, fertility fell to a very low level.

There appears to be virtually no direct link between the increase in unemployment and the decline in fertility. If at all, it applies to the advanced transformation countries in the following sense: after the collapse of the Socialist regimes, of necessity there was a political and economic structural caesura. Unemployment is one of the factors which indicated to the population that the economic changes were beginning. Together with hitherto unknown social manifestations such as hyperinflation or existential uncertainty, it caused behavioural shocks based on value anomie.

On the whole, one may presume that the post-Socialist countries are characterised by a combination of shocks and standards anomie concerning family formation, caused by the parallel course taken by the changes in economic structure and the change in social institutions. The radical social change leads to a devaluation of previous values and to economic rationality expanding to affect family formation. Children come to be regarded as a cost, as factors in social insecurity and inequality, as obstacles to the labour market and as restrictions to mobility.

Creating a link between economic change and the decline in fertility alone has shown itself to be insufficient to explain the decline in fertility. Linear connections between changes in the economic indicators and the decline in fertility have not been found. No influence has been found on the scale of the decline in fertility, and it has been shown that an economic upturn does not lead directly to increased fertility. Indicators showing complex economic circumstances such as gross national product show a closer link to the decline in fertility than do more specific indicators such as unemployment or the proportion of the poor population. One may therefore presume that the economic shocks were only one of many factors leading to the decline in radical social change causing value anomie, giving rise to economic rationality and hence to the decline in fertility.

The lack of social improvement with the economic upturn leads one to presume that economic rationality continues for quite some time, and that this leads to a longer phase of lower fertility and marriage rates, the precise influence of which cannot however be proven.

**Fig. 1.7 – Unemployment rate and Total Fertility Rate 1990-1999 in Hungary, the Czech Republic, the Russian Federation and Ukraine**

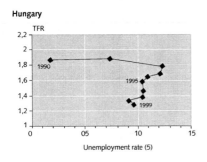

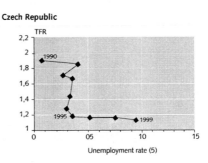

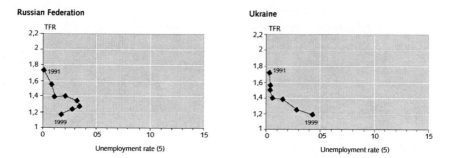

Sources: Council of Europe, Recent Demographic Developments in Europe 2000; Economic Commission for Europe, Economic Survey s of Europe 2001

# Chapter 2

## Changes in demographic trends

*Dimiter Philipov*
*Jürgen Dorbritz for sections 2.3 and 2.7*

This chapter gives a *quantitative* description of the demographic trends, such as marriage and cohabitation, fertility, family formation, divorces and dissolution, and mortality. The third chapter suggests a discussion of possible explanations of these trends. Family planning and abortion are related to family change and therefore will also be considered here. The following terminology applies throughout the chapter. Family formation encompasses events such as first entry into cohabitation, first marriage, and birth of the first child. In a broader context it includes remarriages and births of higher order. Cohabitation is a non-marital (extra-marital) union, and a union can be either a marriage or a cohabitation. Dissolution refers to the disruption of a cohabitation.

This chapter includes six sub-chapters. The first five discuss demographic events that are related to some extent and generally refer to family formation and dissolution. The following introductory notes refer to these sub-chapters. The sixth sub-chapter describes mortality trends that differ from the trends related to the family. The introductory notes to this sub-chapter are placed in its beginning.

The discussion in the first five sub-chapters comprises two main time periods. The first one starts in 1980 and ends with the onset of the transition. The second period starts with the transition and ends in the year of last available data, in most cases 1999. The transition in the non-Soviet ex-socialist countries started in 1990, after the collapse of the socialist regimes at the end of 1989, while in the ex-Soviet countries it started in 1992, after the collapse of the USSR at the end of 1991. The description of the pre-transition trends serves as a relevant point for the study of the transition drifts.

The text describes the demographic trends from the point of view of their levels, direction and pace of change, and variations in the age compositions. The demographic data on changes in nuptiality and fertility refer to women only. Such data for males are scanty. Nearly all data in the first four sub-sections were taken from the latest available Demographic Yearbook issued by the Council of Europe (Council of Europe, 2001). Exceptions are explicitly stated.

Levels of nuptiality, fertility, and divorces can be measured by diverse demographic rates, such as the crude rates, the general rates, and the total rates. Here use is made of the total rates: the total first-marriage rate (TFMR), the total fertility rate (TFR), and the total divorce rate (TDR). The TFR by birth order is denoted as TFR(i) for the i-th birth; for example TFR(1) is the total fertility rate for first births. In addition to levels we study age distributions by using mean ages and standard deviations of the corresponding age schedule. The values for these level and age indicators are not independent. For example, a postponement of first marriages to later years in life increases the mean age at first marriage (MAFM), and it is known in demography that during a period of postponement the TFMR will decrease. Inversely, advancement of first marriages that results in a decline in the MAFM, will cause the TFMR to increase.

The TFMR, TFR, and TFR(1) have interpretations that are often used in practice. The TFMR multiplied by 1000 is interpreted as the number of women out of 1000 who will ever marry by age 50 if they were subject to the period age-specific first-marriage rates observed during the year under consideration. Analogously the TFR(1) multiplied by 1000 gives the number of women out of 1000, who will eventually have a first child towards the end of the reproductive span, say age 50, and the TFR denotes the average number of children per woman. The interpretations may be misleading during periods of abrupt changes in the demographic trends under consideration. For example, the TFMR observed during a particular year may be higher than one. According to the interpretation this would mean that 1000 women would have more than 1000 first marriages. The absurd result is due to changes in the timing in marriages that affect the value of the period rate, as mentioned above. The TFMR was often higher than 1 for some central and eastern European countries (figure 2.2.1). Hence the interpretation can be wrong and will be used only where there were no significant postponement or advancement of events. The same applies to the TFR(1) and the TFR whose interpretation as the average number of children per woman is well known beyond the circle of demographic scientists. Section 2.4.3 gives more details on this topic.

The central and eastern European countries have a diverse historical economic and social life. Before the establishment of the socialist regime, most of them were economically less developed than the western countries, with the exception of a few, namely those from central Europe. The historically formed demographic patterns were also diverse. During the prevalence of the socialist regimes the demographic tendencies referring to family formation were convergent, but diverged from trends that developed in the other European countries. The start of the transition contributed to an abrupt change in nuptiality and fertility, and this change spread all over the region. The direction of change was, and is, towards patterns observed earlier in the western countries. For this reason the chapter begins with a brief description of recent demographic trends observed in the West. The discussion proceeds with descriptive analyses of marriages, fertility, divorces, and timing of marriages and births. The fifth section addresses issues related to family planning.

These topics have been widely reflected in the demographic literature, but the studies are usually country-specific. Few studies were deliberately designed for international comparisons, for example Kučera et al. (2000), as well as the FFS country reports[1]. The Reproductive and Health Surveys (RHS) were carried out in Romania, the Czech Republic, Georgia, Moldova, Ukraine, and the Russian Federation. Few studies focus on the region as a whole, and most of them appeared in the beginning of the 90s (Monnier and Rychtaříková, 1991). Recent studies were suggested for example by United Nations (1999, 2000) and Philipov (2001).

For the purpose of the graphical presentation in figures and sometimes in the text the countries are grouped as follows:

• Countries from central Europe (ex-GDR, Czech and Slovak Republics, Hungary).

• Eastern Balkan countries: Bulgaria and Romania.

• Baltic countries: Estonia, Latvia, Lithuania, plus Poland. Poland is included in this group because of its close resemblance with Lithuania where demographic trends after the transition are considered.

• Countries from the Commonwealth of Independent States (CIS). They are: Belarus, Moldova, the Russian Federation, Ukraine. The Trans-Caucasian countries could also be included in this group where the data are available: Armenia, Azerbaijan, Georgia.

• Western Balkan countries: Bosnia and Herzegovina, Croatia, "The former Yugoslav Republic of Macedonia", Slovenia, Federal Republic of Yugoslavia.

Few countries from the last two groups provide convenient data for graphical presentation. Hence most of these countries are not included in the figures.

Albania is not included in any group. The demographic situation in this country cannot be compared to that in any other country in Europe; moreover the data are insufficient for graphical presentation. This grouping of the countries is not used in the tables.

---

[1] The FFS was organised by the Population Activities Unit at the Economic Commission for Europe, UN, Geneva. The survey was carried out in 22 countries, including Bulgaria, the Czech Republic, Hungary, Latvia, Lithuania, Poland, and Slovenia. The country reports were standardised by contents. Citation: "Fertility and Family Surveys in Countries of the ECE Region. Standard Country Report. (name of country)."

## 2.1 Demographic changes in western European countries

The European countries in the West experienced substantial demographic transformations after the Second World War. The 60s divide the period since the War up to present times in two stages. A celebrated pattern during the first stage was the "baby boom" which appeared in the end of the 50s and peaked during the first half of the 60s. During this stage fertility was considerably above replacement, and the TFR was often higher than 2.5. Marriages were nearly universal: according to the prevailing rates more than 90 percent of all people would have ever entered into a marriage. Mean ages of marriages and births were lower than in the past.

The end of the 60s and the beginning of the 70s marked the rise and establishment of a new marital behaviour. Marriage rates began to decline, first in Sweden followed shortly by the other Nordic countries, Norway and Finland. During the 70s there followed countries from western Europe and during the 80s countries from southern Europe. Thus the changes set firmly in all countries situated in this half of the continent. Mean ages of first marriage began to rise rapidly as a result of postponement behaviour. Frequency of marriages decreased significantly. These changes in level and timing of marriage were established as long-lasting trends. During the 90s the trends continued, being firmly set all over the West. They were paralleled in most of the countries by a rise in non-marital cohabitation. It spread first in the Nordic countries, and later in western and central European countries, but remained rare in southern Europe. Cohabitation first appeared among young adults and usually preceded marriage. Gradually it developed into a new family form that is not necessarily a predecessor of marriage, characterised also by extra-marital but intra-cohabitation births.

The decrease in marriages during the 80s was accompanied by a significant increase in the total divorce rate in all countries except those from southern Europe (sub-chapter 2.3 gives more details). Indeed, during the 90s the number of divorces decreased but this trend was due to the decreased number of marriages. There is little information about the dissolution of cohabitation that is not observed by vital statistics. Scientific research available for many western European countries indicates that non-marital unions are less stable than marital ones, in that their dissolution is higher than the divorce rate.

The general patterns observed for marriages were also observed for fertility. The TFR declined in all European countries and the mean ages of childbearing by birth order rose. The timing of these events differs among different parts of the continent. The drop in fertility started first in Sweden and Finland around the middle of the 60s, speeded up in a few years and quickly dropped below replacement level. Western European countries followed the same pattern in a few years. Towards the end of the 70s the TFR dropped to low levels such as 1.6-1.8. During the next two decades it has been at approximately this level. An increase that appeared since the start of the 90s still keeps fertility below replacement. The countries of southern Europe experienced a considerable delay in this pattern. Fertility began to drop there later but at a speeded pace. The TFR dropped to extremely low levels such as 1.3-1.4 at the beginning of the 90s, and these low levels were attained during the 90s.

The mean age of childbearing experienced a steady increase along with the start of the fertility decline. The mean age at the birth of the first child increased by several years from the middle of the 60s up to the end of the 90s, and the rise was observed throughout the period. This augmentation has an impact on the value of the period TFR. Its delineation and adjusted for tempo effects on TFR are considered in section 2.4.3.

The drop in fertility did not considerably change the distribution of births by order. That is, the share of births of a given order did not change considerably through time. Therefore the proportion of women who have experienced a first birth decreased. This nearly 20-year long trend allows for a cohort interpretation, namely that the proportion of childless women tends to increase.

Thus since the middle of the 60s there appeared new demographic trends characterised by later and less frequent marriages and childbearing, rise in cohabitation and extra-marital births, increased union disruption. These unprecedented changes have been the topic of extensive research and explanations. Sometimes they are referred to as the *"second demographic transition"* (Lesthaeghe and Van de Kaa, 1986; Van de Kaa, 1987) – a term that has become popular among demographers in the central and eastern European countries (see for example Kotowska, 1999). The basic explanations of the "second demographic transition" are founded on ideational changes that have spread through the European populations in recent decades. This topic is discussed in the next chapter.

## 2.2 Nuptiality in central and eastern Europe

The following description of nuptiality focuses mainly on first marriages as a fundamental event in the formation of a new family. Some information is provided for extra-marital cohabitation and remarriages. The discussion of the latter is short because of the scarce data. The discussion first considers the period before the start of the transition and then proceeds to the transition period. Three western countries are considered as a reference: Austria, Finland, and Italy, from western central Europe, northern Europe, and southern Europe correspondingly.

### 2.2.1 First marriages before the transition

The discussion of these trends is necessary in order to outline the general demographic situation that immediately preceded the trends during the transition period.

The data indicate that during the pre-transition period trends in both level and timing of nuptiality were generally stable over a long period, covering some two to three decades. Some moderate changes were due primarily to the effect of the pronatal policies where they were introduced in that they provoked a slightly earlier entry into first marriage (chapter 3.3.2 gives more details on population policies). Hence it is sufficient for the discussion here to consider the period from 1980 up to the end of the decade.

*TFMR*

The levels of first marriages as measured by the TFMR are presented on the left panels of figure 2.2.1 for countries where data were available. The figure shows that the TFMR was particularly high in the C.I.S. and Baltic countries, where one can note observed values higher than 1. It was above or around 0.9 in Poland, the Czech and Slovak Republics, Bulgaria, Romania, and Hungary. The latter two countries are the only ones except the western Balkans where the TFMR had a clearly exhibited tendency of a decrease during the 80s. In the GDR, Croatia and Yugoslavia the TFMR was around 0.8, and it was considerably higher in "the former Yugoslav Republic of Macedonia". The lowest values were observed in Slovenia.

**Figure 2.2.1 – Total first marriage rates (left panel) and mean ages at first marriage (right panel)**

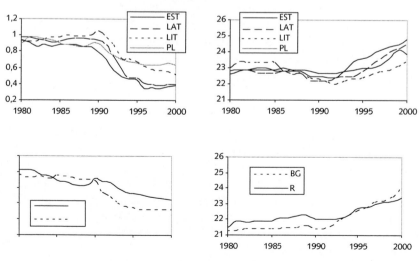

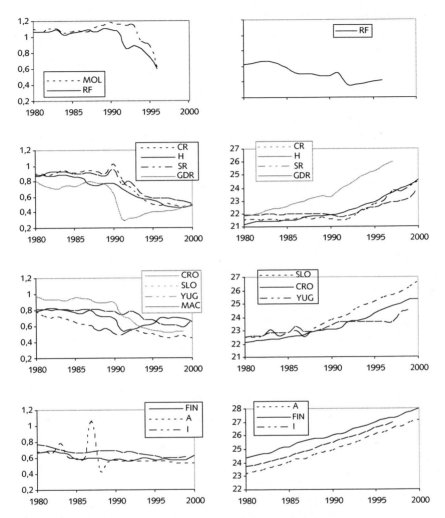

*Note: The mean ages for Moldova and "The former Yugoslav Republic of Macedonia" were not available.*

Table 2.2.1 includes additional countries, where the data were insufficient for graphical representation in figure 2.2.1. It also includes four countries from western Europe placed in the lower part of the table (Austria, Finland, FRG. and Italy). In this sub-chapter we consider only the values referring to the years 1980 and 1990; the adjusted TFMR are discussed in sub-chapter 2.4.3.

In addition to the information displayed by figure 2.2.1 the table shows that Bosnia and Herzegovina had the lowest TFMR in 1980, comparable with that observed in the western European countries. Towards the end of the decade the western Balkan countries, except for "the former Yugoslav Republic of

Macedonia", had a TFMR that was close to the levels observed in the West. (The table also indicates that the 80s have been a decade of a fall in the TFMR in western European countries.)

The changes in the TFMR were the result of diverse reasons. In the CIS and the Baltic countries as well as in Romania they were due mainly to the maintenance of the adopted pronatal policies that caused advancement of first marriages and hence TFMR larger than 1. In Bulgaria the policies had little effect on nuptiality because universal entry into marriage was traditional and was preserved during the 80s. In Hungary, the GDR and in the western Balkan countries the decrease in the TFMR was a result of ideational changes that have lead to the postponement and later refusal of entry into marriage. The latter topic is discussed in the next chapter.

Consider the three western European reference countries. While in Finland and Italy the changes during the 80s were smooth this was not the case in Austria. The adoption of specific family laws caused a sudden increase in 1986 followed by a compensatory decrease. Therefore policy-induced changes were characteristic for some western countries too. Otherwise the level of the TFMR was quite analogous in the three countries. The MAFM increased smoothly and the pattern of increase was one and the same, thus producing parallel trends.

*Age at first marriage*

The right panels on figure 2.2.1 present the mean ages of entry into first marriage for women (MAFM). They remained around constant during the 80s in Poland, Bulgaria, the Czech and Slovak Republics. The MAFM marked a temperate decrease in the Baltic countries and the Russian Federation, particularly during the second half of the decade thus reflecting changed preferences towards earlier entry into marriage as a result of the pronatal policy. This advancement has caused a tempo-driven[2] increase in the TFMR making it higher than unity: a clear example of the invalidity of the interpretation of the TFMR, when multiplied by 1000, as the number of first marriages per thousand women. Inversely to the trend observed in the then USSR countries, the MAFM exhibited a moderate increase in Hungary and Romania, a significant increase in Slovenia, Croatia, the Federal Republic of Yugoslavia and particularly high increase in the GDR.

Table 2.2.1 reveals that in 1980 the MAFM in Austria, 23.2, was higher than that in all central and eastern European countries. This value is low for a western country. Hence the MAFM clearly delineated the continent into two parts: central and eastern European countries with low values and the West with higher values. A value of around 23 was a convenient division mark.

---

[2] Tempo effects are discussed in section 2.4.3.

| | TFMR | | | MAFM | | | TFMR adj [3] |
|---|---|---|---|---|---|---|---|
| | 1980 | 1990 | 2000 | 1980 | 1990 | 2000 | 1998 |
| Albania [1] | 0.77 | 0.99 | - | 22.2 | 23.2 | 23.5 | - |
| Armenia | - | 0.93 | 0.34 | - | 22.4 | 23.1 | 0.45 |
| Azerbaijan | 0.98 | 1.05 | 0.54 | - | 24.2 | 23.7 | 0.65 |
| Belarus | - | - | 0.65 | 22.9 | 22.0 | 22.6 | - |
| Bosnia and H. [1] | 0.69 | 0.67 | 0.75 | 22 | 23.3 | 24.6 | 0.75 |
| Bulgaria | 0.97 | 0.90 | 0.52 | 21.3 | 21.4 | 24.1 | 0.76 |
| Croatia | 0.79 | 0.70 | 0.64 | 22.1 | 23.1 | 25.3 | 0.80 |
| Czech R. | 0.90 | 1.02 | 0.50 | 21.5 | 21.6 | 24.5 | 0.76 |
| Estonia | 0.94 | 0.79 | 0.39 | 22.6 | 22.5 | 24.8 | 0.49 |
| Georgia | 0.99 | 0.80 | 0.41 | -[2] | 23.5 | 24.6 | 0.64 |
| Hungary | 0.89 | 0.77 | 0.49 | 21.2 | 21.9 | 24.6 | 0.71 |
| Macedonia | 0.91 | 0.86 | 0.83 | 22.2 | 22.6 | 23.6 | 0.96 |
| GDR [1] | 0.81 | 0.64 | 0.47 | 21.8 | 23.3 | 26.0 | 0.61 |
| Latvia | 0.97 | 0.92 | 0.40 | 22.8 | 22.2 | 24.5 | 0.60 |
| Lithuania | 0.94 | 1.06 | 0.51 | 23.0 | 22.3 | 23.5 | 0.77 |
| Moldova [1] | 1.11 | 1.19 | 0.62 | -[2] | 22.3 | 21.0 | - |
| Poland | 0.90 | 0.91 | 0.63 | 22.8 | 22.7 | 23.9 | 0.85 |
| Romania | 1.02 | 0.92 | 0.64 | 21.5 | 22.0 | 23.4 | 0.78 |
| Russian F. [1] | 0.96 | 1.00 | 0.60 | 22.4 | 21.9 | 22.1 | - |
| Slovak R. | 0.87 | 0.96 | 0.52 | 21.9 | 21.9 | 24.0 | 0.79 |
| Slovenia | 0.79 | 0.51 | 0.45 | 22.5 | 23.7 | 26.7 | 0.71 |
| F.R.Yugoslavia | 0.82 | 0.78 | 0.68 | 22.5 | 23.4 | 24.6 | 0.69 |
| Austria | 0.68 | 0.58 | 0.54 | 23.2 | 24.9 | 27.2 | 0.69 |
| Finland | 0.67 | 0.58 | 0.62 | 24.3 | 26.0 | 28.0 | 0.72 |
| FRG [1] | 0.66 | 0.64 | 0.64 | 23.3 | 25.7 | 26.8 | 0.47 |
| Italy [1] | 0.78 | 0.69 | 0.62 | 24.6 | 26.6 | 27.0 | 0.54 |

[1] The last available year for Albania is 1999; for Bosnia and Herzegovina 1998; for the ex-GDR, FRG and Italy 1997; for Moldova and the Russian Federation 1996.
[2] The 1980 values for the are unlikely high.
[3] The given adjusted TFMR is an average of the estimated values for 1997, 1998, and 1999.
Source: Council of Europe (2001); adjusted TFMR estimated by the author.

While the MAFM synthesises the age distribution of first marriages, it does not reveal changes specified by age. The latter are exemplified with the age-specific first-marriage rates for Hungary, as observed in 1986, 1990 and 1996 (figure 2.2.2). The figure gives both the observed values in panel (a) and their standardised values in panel (b). The latter are estimated such that the area under the schedule is equal to 1. Here the schedules for 1986 and 1990 are of interest; the one for 1996 is considered in the next sub-chapter.

The exhibited age schedules are typical for the region. The plot shows that the schedule observed in 1986 is slightly higher than the one observed in 1990, thus revealing a more or less proportionate decrease of the rates. In the other countries the schedule either practically did not change, or somewhat increased or decreased, like in Hungary. A move towards left or right was very small where existent.

**Figure 2.2.2 – Age-specific first-marriage rates in Hungary 1986, 1990, 1996: (a) observed values and (b) standardised values**

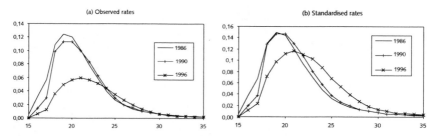

Another characteristic of the Hungarian schedule is its narrowness, in that a large part of the events are clustered in a narrow age interval. This characteristic is typical for other countries from the region too. It can be measured by the standard deviation around the mean age. The latter should be estimated using single-year age groups. In the case of Hungary it is 3.8 in 1980 and 3.7 in 1990. Using 5-year age groups could provide only a crude estimate. In Hungary it is equal to 4.2 and 4.4 for 1980 and 1990, while in Austria it was 4.9 and 5.0 correspondingly. The insufficient data do not allow a generalisation of this pattern over all countries.

Thus the trends in first marriages before the start of the transition can be briefly described as:

• *nearly universal entry into marriage;*
• *entry into marriage early in life.*

These trends are common for all countries in the region, with the exception of some countries from the western Balkans where there were certain signs of a change of the first marriage indicators towards values observed in the

West. In addition to the countries from the western Balkans, they were noticeable also in Hungary, where a slight decrease in the TFMR could be noted before the start of the transition.

Table 2.2.1 gives data for the two parts of Germany: ex-GDR and the western provinces of FRG The TFMR in the GDR in 1980 was like the one observed in the central European countries and considerably higher than the one for the FRG, while in 1990 the two parts of Germany had similar levels of first marriages (TFMR=0.64). The MAFM in the GDR was considerably lower than that in the FRG: the GDR 1990 value was equal to the 1980 FRG value. In general, the demographic indicators for first marriages were changing much faster in the GDR than in any other central and eastern European country, but they were still more characteristic for an eastern European rather than a western European country for that period.

### 2.2.2 First marriages after the start of the transition

The picture outlined in the above sub-chapter changed entirely only in a few years after the start of the transition.

### TFMR

We consider first the start of the changes in the TFMR during the 90s, i.e. the first couple of years of the transition period. Figure 2.2.1 shows that the TFMR noted a slight increase during the first 1-2 years of the transition, particularly notable in the Czech and Slovak Republics. The western Balkan countries are an exception: the start of the transition brought about an initial drop in the TFMR. A drastic initial decrease was recorded in the ex-GDR, where the TFMR went down from 0.64 in 1990 to 0.31 in 1991. Hence, with the exception of the GDR and the western Balkans, the populations of the central and eastern European countries reacted to the start of the transition with a modest increase in first marriages.

This initial change was shortly followed by an abrupt decrease in the TFMR, with western Balkan countries again being an exception (discussed below). It was steeper during the first half of the 90s, that is, immediately after the initial relative increase mentioned above. During the second half of the decade its decrease smoothened. Towards the end of the 90s it dropped down to unprecedented levels, reaching in 2000 low values such as 0.39 in Estonia, 0.40 in Latvia and 0.49 in Hungary (table 2.2.1). A drastic decrease was also registered in Armenia and Georgia as well as in Azerbaijan, as table 2.2.1 indicates in addition to figure 2.2.1. The data do not indicate an upturn towards an increase in the TFMR as one might have expected after such a drastic fall. Indeed, for some countries the TFMR values observed in 2000 were somewhat higher than those observed in 1999, but similar reversals have been observed in previous years too.

It is important to note that the fall in the TFMR began from high levels that corresponded to traditional marital behaviour. The 90s therefore witnessed a break in behaviour that can only be the result of a break in social norms: an important topic discussed in more detail in the next chapter.

Now we go back to the exceptional cases: the western Balkan countries and the ex-GDR. During the 90s Slovenia did not experience a sudden change in the TFMR at all; the decrease observed during the 80s was stronger than the moderate one observed during the 90s. In Croatia there was a moderate increase, while "the former Yugoslav Republic of Macedonia" is the only one where changes were similar to those observed in the other central and eastern European countries. In the ex-GDR the initial sudden fall was followed by a modest increase up to the value of 0.47 in 1999. It remained the country (strictly, a region of a country) with the lowest TFMR during the 90s.

The TFMR in the western European countries have reached similar low levels over a longer period and therefore the drop was considerably smoother than in the East. Like in Slovenia, and unlike in the other central and eastern European countries, there was no sudden drop in the TFMR in the West. Moreover, although the three countries refer to three different regions of Europe, the trends of change in their TFMR are difficult to distinguish during the second half of the 90s, i.e. these trends have become uniform.

It can be generalised that the universality of marriage was lost all over the eastern part of Europe. Albania is the only European country where this inference could not hold; the lack of data for this population does not allow for a firm conclusion. Note should be taken that this generalisation depends on the extent to which the TFMR measures correctly the level of marriages. A distortion of the TFMR is discussed in chapter 2.4.3 along with the related adjustment included in table 2.2.1.

*Age at first marriage*

The trends in the MAFM were usually opposite to those in the TFMR: during the first 1-2 years it decreased a little and later there followed a significant rise. Table 2.2.1 shows that during the 90s it has risen by as much as 2-3 years. The highest rises between 1990 and 2000 were observed in Slovenia (3 years) and the Czech Republic (2.9 years), followed by the GDR, Hungary and Bulgaria with 2.7 years. The rise was very small in most of the C.I.S. countries, although the TFMR marked a huge drop. In the western Balkans the rise was positive but moderate, with the exception of Slovenia and Croatia.

The three western countries exhibit a rise in the MAFM too. It is pronounced in Austria, where its level in 1990 was very low as compared to western Europe. The steep increase in the MAFM during the 90s did not ruin the demarcation between East and West in Europe, where its values are considered. First marriages continue to be younger in the East and the difference was more pronounced in 2000 than it was in 1980. In fact the values observed in the West in 1980 were roughly similar to those observed in the East in 2000. The two parts of Europe differed by about two decades.

The steep rise in the MAFM did change the traditional behaviour of an early entry into first marriage. A new behaviour is on the rise; entry into marriage is being postponed into later years. This process continues and additional research is necessary to indicate the length of postponement in time and hence the level of MAFM where postponement could halt. If one makes a simple comparison with western Europe, this period will hardly be shorter than 2 decades.

Thus the 90s established new trends of first marriages, observed earlier in the western European countries. The traditional patterns of early and universal entry into marriage were broken. Traditional social norms were broken. The trends during the 90s are not as homogeneous among the different countries as the trends before the transition. Figure 2.2.1 indicates that several groups of countries can be delineated. Two countries around the Baltic Sea delineate vividly from all others: Estonia and Latvia. They have experienced the swiftest drop in the TFMR and rise in the MAFM. The same change was observed in the ex-GDR. Poland and Lithuania contrast with smoother changes in the two indicators. Poland and Lithuania have a number of common demographic features. These two countries have experienced common trends with some other central European countries, namely Hungary, Bulgaria, Romania, and the Slovak Republic. The CIS countries form another group of countries, characterised by a swift drop in the TFMR but a modest rise in the MAFM. Finally, the western Balkans are atypical with its earlier start of the changes that were not as abrupt as in the other central and eastern European countries.

One can notice towards 2000 similarities among countries that before the start of the transition belonged to larger countries: the USSR, Yugoslavia, Czechoslovakia.

*Cohort changes*

Cohort indicators are less affected by period changes and therefore are expected to reveal softer changes where cohorts are considered. Figure 2.2.3 gives two cohort indicators that were available for seven countries, estimated by age 50 of the cohort. The proportion of women ever married by age 50 was above 90% for all cohorts in Bulgaria and Romania, while in the Czech and possibly in the Slovak Republics only the cohorts born in 1966 and 1967 were below that level. In Hungary the last four cohorts dropped below 90%. In Poland and in the GDR this was observed for cohorts born before 1960. A significant rise in this proportion was observed in the Czech and Slovak

81

Republics for the cohorts born in 1964 and 1965. It can probably be connected to the pronounced rise in the period TFMR observed in the start of the transition, when they were 24-25 years old.

The proportion ever married exhibits a clear decline by cohorts in the GDR and Hungary. Indications of a decline are clear for the other countries too. Therefore this cohort indicator supports the findings that referred to the period TFMR.

The mean age of entry into first marriage is considerably below 23 for all the countries. It is considerably lower than that observed at the period level. A clear tendency of increase is notable in the GDR, Hungary, Romania and to some extent in Bulgaria. For the remaining three countries the tendency of change in the cohort MAFM is diverse. Real cohorts behave differently than the synthetic ones.

The cohort data conveniently support the finding that in the central and eastern European countries marriages were universal and early. While these inferences are typical for the eastern European marriage pattern (described in section 3.2.1), they cannot necessarily be associated everywhere with its historical origin, only where the most recent 1-2 decades are considered. One would expect that changes similar to those observed in the West would start to develop, but they were delayed until the fall of the socialist regime. Hence the latter had a certain impact on the domination of the pattern. It was during the 80s that this recent pattern began changing towards approaching the western characteristics, notably in Hungary, ex-GDR and particularly in Slovenia and Croatia.

**Figure 2.2.3 – Proportion ever married women in cohorts born between 1947 and 1967 (thick line – left axis) and mean age at entry into first marriage of the same cohorts (dotted line – right axis)**

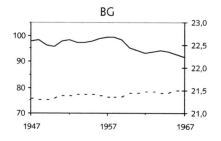
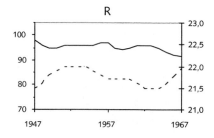

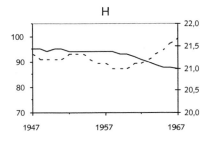

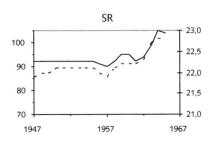

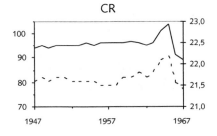

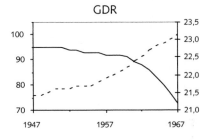

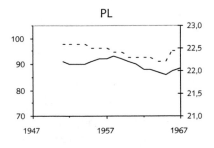

## 2.2.3 Extra-marital unions

The data on extra-marital unions (cohabitation) in the central and eastern European countries are scarce. Some information is available from the WVS (Inglehart *et al.* 2000), carried out in this region in 1990-1992 (wave 2) and in 1995-1997 (wave 3). A question on marital status at the time of the survey includes an option for an answer "living together like married". The percentage of respondents aged 20-29 who gave this answer were estimated for groups of countries where the number of positive answers was very small. The results are:

- in Estonia, 13% and 26% for waves 2 and 3 correspondingly;

- in Latvia, 8% and 10%;

- in Poland grouped with Lithuania, as well as in Bulgaria separately, 1% and 4%;

- in Slovenia, 13% and 17%;
- in the Czech Republic, 8% in wave 2;
- in Hungary, 5% in wave 2;
- in the group comprising Ukraine, the Russian Federation, and Moldova, 2.5% in wave 3;

Very low numbers were observed for one of the waves in the Slovak Republic, Romania, "The former Yugoslav Republic of Macedonia".

In Austria, 12% of the respondents answered that they resided in a non-marital union; in the Netherlands this was 18%, and in Italy only 2%.

In all the countries the sample size was very small and the results are therefore with a high variation. Yet it becomes clear that in general the level of extra-marital cohabitation in central and eastern Europe is low, with the exception of Estonia, Latvia, and Slovenia. However, there is a slight tendency of an increase as from the beginning of the 90s towards the middle of the decade.

The same inference can be made with another data source, namely the Fertility and Family Surveys (FFS). The FFS data allow for the estimation of the cumulative percentage of those who have ever been in extra-marital unions by exact age 20, classified by age at interview. Table 2.2.2 presents the results for the females for seven central and eastern European countries where the data were available, as well as for Austria, Finland, and Italy.

The data are difficult to compare because the interviews were done at different years during the 90s. Still they allow for making some important inferences. Given the low MAFM it can be expected that at age 25 a large proportion, if not nearly all women, should have already experienced either a first marriage or a first cohabitation.

In Estonia the cohabitation by age at interview is strikingly close to that observed in Finland. Its level is much higher compared with any other central and eastern European country. An inverse analogy can be made between Poland and Italy where cohabitation is rare. The percentage of first cohabitation is high in Slovenia, but it is lower than neighbouring Austria. Cohabitation is high in Latvia too, while in Lithuania it is far either from that observed in Poland, or from that observed in the other two Baltic countries.

There is a noticeable tendency of an increase in this level among younger respondents. This observation is valid for all countries included in the table. It may be concluded therefore that cohabitation is gaining ground at least in some central and eastern European countries, and it has significantly advanced in the Baltic countries and Slovenia.

**Table 2.2.2 – Cumulative percentage of females who by exact age 25 have ever entered first partnerships that were non-marital unions**

| Country | Year of interview | Age at interview | | |
|---------|-------------------|------|------|------|
| | | 25-29 | 30-34 | 35-39 |
| Czech Rep. | 1997 | 29.3 | 25.5 | 20.5 |
| Estonia | 1994 | 64.0 | 60.8 | 48.9 |
| Hungary | 1992/93 | 18.1 | 14.8 | 8.9 |
| Latvia | 1995 | 40.0 | 28.6 | 25.4 |
| Lithuania | 1994-1995 | 15.3 | 9.5 | 12.2 |
| Poland | 1991 | 4.1 | 3.6 | 2.8 |
| Slovenia | 1994-1995 | 42.5 | 36.0 | 23.1 |
| Austria | 1995-96 | 57.5 | 54.6 | 44.6 |
| Finland | 1989-90 | 68.4 | 60.8 | 42.9 |
| Italy | 1995-1996 | 4.8 | 5.0 | 3.4 |

Source: Tables 8c from the series "Fertility and Family Surveys in countries of the ECE region" for the corresponding countries.

Entry into cohabitation before, or instead of, first marriage is a new behaviour that spread rapidly during the 90s. It complements the other behavioural changes described above and join them into a general picture typical for the second demographic transition.

### 2.2.4 Remarriages

The data on remarriages are scanty and are insufficient for the estimation of proper indicators such as a total remarriage rate. Here use is made of a crude indicator, namely the share of remarriages to all marriages. This share depends on the level of first marriages. Since the latter were studied above it is possible to trace levels of remarriages relative to those of first marriages, as far as allowed by a crude indicator, not adjusted for the age distribution of the events and of the population. Regretfully even this indicator was available only for separate years and countries.

During the 90s the share of remarriages was around 10% in the Slovak Republic, Bulgaria, and Poland, and 10-14% in Romania. Higher levels were observed in Lithuania (16-19%), Hungary (20%), and the Czech Republic (24%). During the 80s and the 90s the share of remarriages was nearly constant around the values cited above in the Slovak Republic, Hungary, Poland and Bulgaria. In Lithuania, a sudden drop from 19.5% in 1991 down to 16.6% in 1993 was followed by a slow rise; the 1991 level was reached again in 1999. In Romania, a gradual increase started in 1991 from the level of 10.4% up to 13.9% in 1998.

The constant levels indicate that changes in remarriages could be similar to those in first marriages. Lithuania and Romania are two different exceptions. In Lithuania the decrease in the share of remarriages indicates a steeper decline as compared to that in first marriages, while in Romania remarriages decreased less than first marriages. In general, the abrupt decrease in first marriages during the 90s was characteristic for nuptiality as a whole. Remarriages consist nearly of second marriages only. Higher-order marriages are very rare, if not exceptional. The data do not reveal a significant break from this pattern during the 90s.

## 2.3 Divorces

### 2.3.1 The general trend in Europe since 1970

The primary trend in the divorce rate in Europe has been upward since the seventies, measured against total divorce rates. In most countries that have provided divorce data to the Council of Europe, particularly in northern and central Europe, the total divorce rates have more than doubled since the seventies. If one takes a closer look, however, the trends have run highly divergently. Nevertheless, a few typical groups of countries can be found which do indeed form regional patterns. With some exceptions, it is possible to find a North-South divide in the divorce rate in Europe. Seen as a trend, the divorce rate quickly reached a high level in northern Europe first, confirming the North's role as the forerunner in demographic change. In western Europe, the increase in the divorce rate was constant, but was slower than in northern Europe. It is a characteristic of southern Europe that the divorce rate has remained low. The reforming states of eastern and central Europe do not form a uniform cluster, and can be alternately allocated to one or other group of countries. In general terms, it is possible to distinguish between three groups:

Firstly, countries in which a rapid increase in the divorce rate had already begun in the seventies. This group of countries consists largely of the northern European states: Denmark, UK, Sweden, and to a lesser extent Finland and Norway. The upward trend already started to slow in the eighties in these countries, and then stagnation set in. This group also registered the highest divorce rate in Europe in the nineties. The total divorce rates vary between 0.4 and 0.5. On the one hand Finland and Norway constitute exceptions to the trend, as does Sweden. In Finland and Norway, the clear rise in the divorce rate took place relatively late, namely in the second half of the eighties. In Sweden, the very high divorce rate had already been reached in the mid-seventies. Since then, the values of the total divorce rates have remained constantly high.

Secondly, countries with a trend towards divorce which has been rising since the seventies. This group consists largely of western European countries, namely Austria, Belgium, France, West Germany, Luxembourg, Switzerland, Iceland and the Netherlands. A divorce rate of at least 30 % was reached in the nineties. The typical profile for this trend is that the upwards movement slowed around 1990, but intensified once more in the second half of the nineties. This led to the total divorce rate also exceeding the 40 % threshold in some countries, for example Switzerland, Austria and West Germany.

Thirdly, there is a group of countries in which the total divorce rate has been consistently low since the seventies. This group includes the southern European countries: Greece, Italy, Cyprus, and also a large number of the former Socialist countries. In this group of states, divorce rate figures were only occasionally recorded at higher than 20 % over the entire observation time of the period measurement.

### 2.3.2 The situation in the eastern and central European reform states taking particular account of the situation in the nineties

Figures 2.3.1 to 2.3.4 provide an overview of the course typically taken by the divorce rate since 1960[3]. The former Socialist countries can also be subdivided into three groups by analogy to their position within Europe.

#### Group 1
#### The Baltic Republics: Estonia, Latvia and Lithuania

The divorce level has been extraordinarily high since the first calculation of total divorce rates, and is comparable with the situation in northern Europe (fig. 2.3.1). It varied in the seventies and eighties by 50 % in Latvia and Estonia. In Lithuania, the divorce rate was a little lower in the seventies and eighties. The values vary within a range of 30 to 40 %. Because of this situation, the Baltic countries held a special position among the central and eastern European reform states in the seventies and eighties.

Considerable variations are characteristic of the nineties. Thus, the total divorce rate reached a value of 0.65 in Estonia in 1995 (1996: 0.51). A similar situation was observed in 1992 in Latvia, where an increase to 0.6 was registered (1993: 0.44). In Lithuania, variations were also observed, but at a lower level. These variations in the total divorce rate make it more difficult to assess the situation in this group of countries. Irrespective of this, the divorce rate has generally remained high.

---

[3] There is no total divorce rate for: Albania, Georgia, Moldova, the Russian Federation, the Slovak Republic, "The former Yugoslav Republic of Macedonia", Armenia, Azerbaijan or Belarus.

**Figure 2.3.1 – Total divorce rates in Estonia, Latvia and Lithuania, 1960-2000**

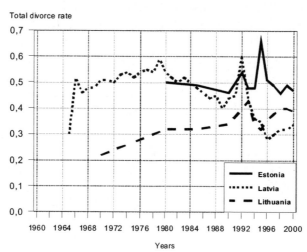

Source: Recent demographic developments in Europe, 2001

These variations were caused by a wide variety of factors. In Estonia, divorces were made easier in the mid-nineties as a result of a new family law, which explains the peak in the divorce rate in 1995. If both partners take a joint, agreed position, fast divorces are possible by virtue of a much simplified divorce procedure. The drop which followed in 1996 and 1997 indicates preference being given to 'standard' divorces, as against the expedited divorce procedure.

In contrast, divorce law in Latvia and Lithuania remained unchanged in the nineties. The variations in these two countries are based on particularities in the way in which existing marriages and divorces are counted. In Latvia, the increase at the beginning of the nineties can be explained by a fall in the number of registered marriages. No explanation can be offered for the subsequent drop. In Lithuania, the changes are mathematical in nature. It is possible to divorce in two ways. If there are no children in the marriage under the age of 18, marriages are dissolved at the Civil Registration Office. In all other cases, divorces are arranged in court proceedings by the Civil Justice Authority. These divorces gain the force of law if at least one of the divorced partners has the divorce counted at the Civil Registration Office. Fluctuations can hence be largely attributed to the time lag between actual divorces and their registration, which is counted in the statistics.

No clear change in conduct appears to have taken place in any of these three countries in the nineties, in other words there was no change in the tendency towards divorce. However, the major changes resulting from the causes described make it virtually impossible to reach a final assessment.

*Group 2*
*The Czech Republic, the Slovak Republic, eastern Germany and Hungary*

This group tended to follow the trend in western Europe, at least until the end of the eighties, but at a higher level. Total divorce rates had already reached a relatively high level at the beginning of the seventies, and then rose further, reaching 30 to 40 % by the second half of the eighties (fig. 2.3.2). Thereafter, the homogeneity of this group of countries was lost.

For eastern Germany, at the beginning of the nineties, as a result of the so-called 'demographic shocks', a dramatic fall in the divorce rate began, reaching its lowest point in 1991 (6.4). This special situation can be explained as a result of two factors acting together. On the one hand, delays occurred in the divorce applications received. German Reunification created an entirely new economic, social and legal order for eastern Germany. This also meant a change in the divorce law (the introduction of the separation year) and changes in the labour and family courts, leading to what may be termed a divorce gridlock. On the other hand, because of the fact that equally clear reductions were observed in the numbers of births and marriages, demographers claim that the rapid social changes led people to keep their individual lives stable, in other words they chose to remain in marriages which had in fact irreconcilably broken down. Starting in 1993, rapid growth was observed once more. This can be explained by the gradual reduction in the 'divorce gridlock' and the implementation of divorces postponed around 1990. In Hungary and the Czech Republic, the upward trend in the divorce rate was interrupted (Czech Republic) and there was even a slight drop (Hungary). The divorce rate started increasing once more in both countries in the second half of the nineties.

Whilst the divorce law remained unchanged in Hungary and the Slovak Republic in the nineties, western German divorce law became valid in the former GDR following its accession to the Federal Republic of Germany. The divorce law was amended on 1 August 1998 in the Czech Republic. With these statutory amendments, divorce law became more conservative once again, after previous liberalisations. The new divorce law allows the court to dissolve a marriage after an irretrievable breakdown of relations if the marriage has lasted at least one year, the husband and wife have lived separately for at least six months and the petition of divorce has the agreement of the other partner. If one of the partners does not agree to the divorce and did not have the major responsibility for the break-up of the marriage, divorce is only possible after at least three years of separation. The new law also sets a requirement of a written agreement as to the separation of shared property, rights and responsibilities in cohabitation, an agreement on the upbringing of dependent children and, where relevant, the payment of maintenance. No impact on the divorce rate has yet been observed using the data available.

One must however presume that, because of the introduction of separation periods prior to divorce, initially the divorce figures will fall.

**Figure 2.3.2 – Total divorce rates in the Czech Republic, eastern Germany, Hungary and the Slovak Republic, 1960-2000**

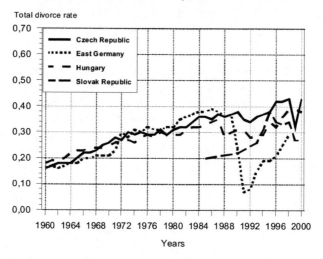

Source: Recent demographic developments in Europe, 2001

In Hungary, after the divorce law had been amended in 1987, no further amendments were carried out in the nineties. The new divorce law prescribed a preliminary agreement between the spouses concerning the separation of common property, the situation of the child(ren) and payment. A six-month separation period prior to divorce is prescribed. The amendment of the divorce law led to a slight drop in the divorce rate in 1988. No long-term stabilisation effect has yet occurred, however.

*Group 3*

*Bulgaria, Croatia, Poland, Romania, Slovenia, "The former Yugoslav Republic of Macedonia", Bosnia-Herzegovina and the Federal Republic of Yugoslavia*

The third group of countries includes the majority of former Socialist countries for which data are available. The divorce rate has remained at a stable, low level since the 1960s (figs. 2.3.3 and 2.3.4).

**Figure 2.3.3 – Total divorce rates in Bulgaria, Croatia, Poland and Romania, 1960-2000**

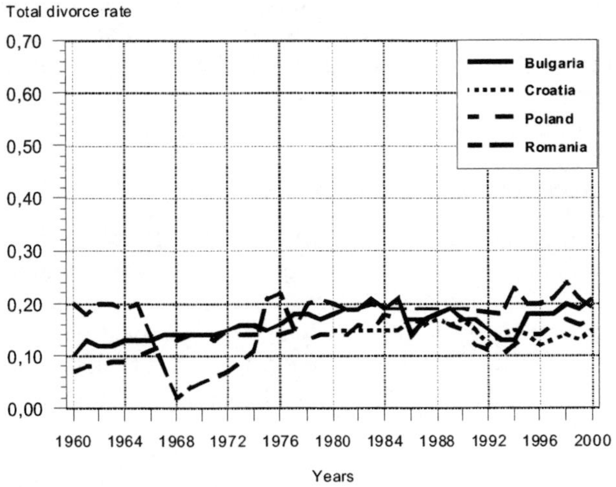

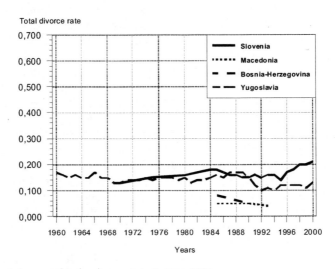

Source: Recent demographic developments in Europe, 2001

**Figure 2.3.4 – Total divorce rates in Slovenia, "The former Yugoslav Republic of Macedonia", Bosnia-Herzegovina, the Federal Republic of Yugoslavia, 1960-2000**

Source: Recent demographic developments in Europe, 2001

The value of 20 % was only exceeded in a small number of exceptional years. Variations such as that which occurred in Romania in the second half of the sixties are extraordinarily rare. Nor did the situation change much in the nineties. In a small number of countries (Bulgaria, Romania and Slovenia) an upward trend is indicated after 1993/94 which at present cannot be finally judged. In these countries a divorce rate is found which is similar to that in the southern European countries.

### 2.3.3 Divorces according to duration of marriage

Statistics on divorces according to duration of marriage are available for only a small number of countries in transition. The courses comparing 1990 and 1999 are portrayed in Fig. 2.3.5. The trend in all the countries observed was towards a longer duration of marriages ending in divorce. The divorce peak observed in 1990 in the first years of marriage was no longer so pronounced in 1999. Divorces after the fifth year of marriage, on the other hand, have increased. This situation can be clearly observed in particular in Croatia, eastern Germany and the Slovak Republic. The trend is still relatively easy to recognise in Hungary and the Russian Federation, whilst it is only hinted at in Romania. The consequence of this change is that, for instance in the Slovak Republic, the average duration of dissolved marriages increased between 1990 and 1999 from 10.7 to 12.3 years (Population Development in the Slovak Republic, 1999:25). In eastern Germany, the duration of marriage increased from 9.6 to 14.0 years in the same period.

One may presume several causes to have led to these increases. One is that because of the fall in marriage frequency which took place in the nineties the proportions of marriages with a short duration fell so that the structure of dissolved marriages changed as to their duration. This influencing factor is presumed to apply in the Slovak Republic. For eastern Germany, however, another factor is added. The introduction of western German divorce law, with the separation year prior to divorce that was prescribed from 1991 onwards, also contributed to the distinct increase. A third hypothesis, according to which conflicts between partners are initially glossed over in times of social crisis, and hence willingness to dissolve marriages is reduced, cannot be precisely examined with the data available. Such an influence is presumed for Georgia: "Some years ago, when the divorce rate began to fall in Georgia, family researchers supposed this to be a result of the difficult economic situation in Georgia, where the living standards of the majority of the population are low, and money is not available for the legal proceedings involved in obtaining a divorce. The difficult economic situation faced by families makes family problems which in other cases might lead to a divorce appear to be luxuries." (Population Information of Georgia, POPIN: 15). If this presumption is correct, one should anticipate the years to come to entail a renewed increase in the divorce rate in those countries in which worries about the future lead to people opting against or postponing divorce.

## Figure 2.3.5 – Divorces by duration of marriage, selected countries in transition, 1990 and 1999

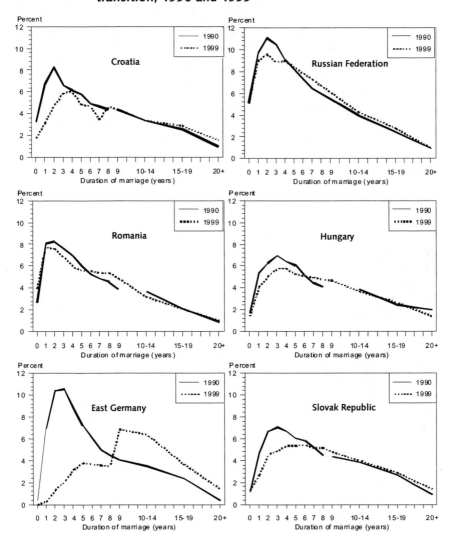

### 2.3.4 Divorces: summary and conclusions

The divorce rates of the countries in transformation in eastern and central Europe offer a highly divergent picture. This applies both to the trends in the Socialist period until the end of the eighties, and to the transformation phase in the nineties. Diverging trends had emerged in the former Socialist countries in the seventies and eighties. This situation is no different to those in the other countries of Europe, which also demonstrate considerable divergence.

In a larger number of the countries of central and eastern Europe, the divorce rate remained very low (Bulgaria, Croatia, Poland, Romania, Slovenia, "The former Yugoslav Republic of Macedonia", Bosnia-Herzegovina and the Federal Republic of Yugoslavia). In the other countries included in the analysis, it increased to a high level (Czech Republic, eastern Germany, Hungary and Slovak Republic) or indeed to very high level (Estonia, Latvia and Lithuania). The total divorce rates range from 0.05 to 0.5 at the end of the nineties.

The impact of economic, social and legal change on the divorce rate can be observed only in a small number of countries. In general it is true that, where the divorce rate has remained low, virtually no changes occurred in the nineties. In the groups of countries with a higher divorce rate, relatively large variations have taken place, caused by differing factors. The most obvious changes occurred in the former GDR. The radical nature of social change on accession to the Federal Republic of Germany, in other words the introduction of a completely new economic, social and legal order, led to a drastic drop in the divorce rate. In the second half of the nineties, however, a rising trend set in once again, so that one should not presume that social change has led to a long-term change in conduct concerning divorce. Strong variations also occurred in the Baltic Republics. This was caused by technical details in methods of counting existing and dissolved marriages (Latvia and Lithuania) and by a relaxation of the rules for divorce in Estonia. In none of the former Socialist countries did economic and social change lead to fundamental changes in conduct towards divorce. Where changes did occur, they are due to timing effects. No link between the economic structural caesura, represented by the changes in gross national product and divorce rate, could be demonstrated in any of the countries. No evidence was found to support the poverty theory (divorce not being affordable) or the theory according to which fewer divorces take place in times of crisis since there are more important things to do than engage in marital conflicts.

The amendments to divorce law were equally non-standard. Divorce law remained unchanged in most countries. Where new regulations have been set in place, they also differed in their nature. Thus, on the one hand, the liberal divorce law was revoked in the Czech Republic, making divorce more difficult. On the other hand, in Estonia there was a partial relaxation of regulations on divorce if the dissolved marriage did not involve children aged under 18.

## 2.4 Fertility

The discussion on fertility proceeds in a similar manner to that of nuptiality. We consider first the level of fertility measured by the TFR and then the mean age of childbearing.

### 2.4.1 Trends observed before the transition

*TFR*

The left panels on figure 2.4.1 illustrate the trends in the TFR. Table 2.4.1 exhibits data for additional countries. The lowest two panels on the figure as well as the last three rows inform about the three western reference countries. The following observations can be made by groups of countries.

The TFR was on the rise in the CIS and the Baltic countries, as a result of the pronatal policy introduced in the ex-USSR in the beginning of the 80s. Towards the end of the decade it was around replacement level, app. 2.1. Moldova was an exception among these countries, in that the level of fertility as measured by the TFR was considerably higher.

The TFR was slightly below replacement level in Bulgaria, the Czech Republic, and Hungary. In Poland and in the Slovak Republic, fertility was higher and there was a trend towards its decrease. The same was observed in the Federal Republic of Yugoslavia and "The former Yugoslav Republic of Macedonia". The lowest fertility level in the region was observed in the GDR, Slovenia and Croatia, where the TFR was lower than 1.8 before the middle of the 80s.

**Figure 2.4.1 – TFR (left panel) and mean age at birth of first child (right panel)**

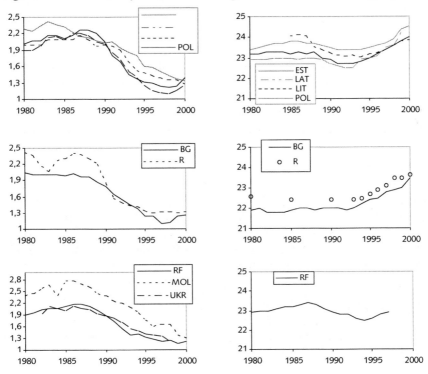

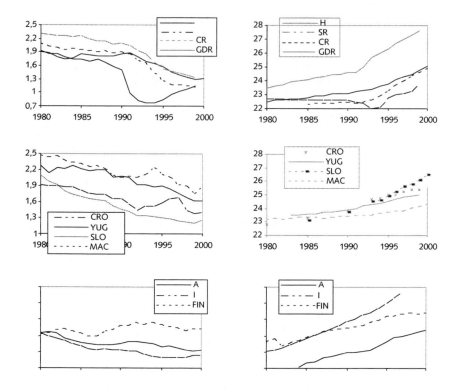

Aside of these country differences some generalisations can be made. First, the TFR was between 1.9 and 2.3 in most of the countries, i.e. it was not far from the replacement level. "The former Yugoslav Republic of Macedonia", Albania, Azerbaijan and Armenia were the only countries where the TFR was higher than 2.3 and hence higher than replacement in 1980, if disregarding policy effects in Romania and the ex-USSR countries.

Second, the level of fertility decreased a little during the 80s, except for the ex-USSR countries and Romania where it peaked around the middle of the decade. Were no pronatal policies adopted, this decrease could have been faster in Bulgaria, the Czech and Slovak Republics, GDR and Hungary. Diverse reasons have been discussed for this decrease, such as the shortage of housing, increased female labour-force participation, ideational changes: a topic discussed in the next chapter.

The level of the fertility in the central and eastern European countries was high as compared to that in the western countries. The TFR in the three reference countries was around 1.6 in 1980, and it fell even lower towards 1990 in Austria and Italy. The decrease in Finland was halted during the second half of the 80s with the adoption of relevant social policies.

**Table 2.4.1 – Total fertility rates (TFR) and mean age at first birth (MAFB)**

| | TFR | | | MAFB | | |
|---|---|---|---|---|---|---|
| | 1980 | 1990 | 2000 | **1980** | **1990** | **2000** |
| Albania | 3.62 | 3.00 | 2.10[1] | - | - | - |
| Azerbaijan | 3.23 | 2.74 | 1.71 | - | - | 24.7 |
| Armenia | 2.33 | 2.63 | 1.11 | 22.1 | 22.8 | 23.0 |
| Belarus | 2.04 | 1.90 | 1.31 | - | 22.6 | 23.4 |
| Bosnia and H. | 1.93 | 1.71 | 1.21[2] | 23.3 | 23.6 | - |
| Bulgaria | 2.05 | 1.82 | 1.26 | 21.9 | 22.0 | 23.5 |
| Croatia | 1.92 | 1.67 | 1.36 | 23.4 | 24.1 | 25.4[1] |
| Czech R. | 2.10 | 1.90 | 1.14 | 22.4 | 22.5 | 24.9 |
| Estonia | 2.02 | 2.04 | 1.39 | 23.2 | 22.9 | 24.0 |
| Georgia | 2.26 | 2.19 | 1.35 | - | - | 24.2 |
| Macedonia | 2.47 | 2.06 | 1.88 | 23.2 | 23.4 | 24.3 |
| GDR [1] | 1.94 | 1.50 | 1.15[1] | 23.5 | 24.6 | 27.6[1] |
| Hungary | 1.91 | 1.87 | 1.32 | 22.4 | 23.1 | 25.1 |
| Latvia | 1.90 | 2.01 | 1.24 | 22.9 | 23.0 | 24.4 |
| Lithuania | 1.99 | 2.02 | 1.27 | 23.8 | 23.2 | 23.8 |
| Moldova | 2.41 | 2.39 | 1.30 | - | - | - |
| Poland | 2.26 | 2.05 | 1.34 | 23.4 | 23.3 | 24.5 |
| Romania | 2.43 | 1.84 | 1.31 | 22.4 | 22.6 | 23.6 |
| Russian F. | 1.86 | 1.90 | 1.21 | 23.0 | 22.6 | 23.0[3] |
| Slovak R. | 2.31 | 2.09 | 1.29 | 22.7 | 22.6 | 24.2 |
| Slovenia | 2.10 | 1.46 | 1.26 | 22.9 | 23.1 | 26.5 |
| Ukraine | 1.95 | 1.89 | 1.10[1] | - | - | - |
| F.R.Yugoslavia | 2.29 | 2.10 | 1.67 | 23.2 | 23.9 | - |
| Austria | 1.65 | 1.45 | 1.34 | 23.3 | 23.9 | 25.0[1] |
| Finland | 1.63 | 1.78 | 1.73 | 25.6 | 26.5 | 27.4 |
| Italy | 1.64 | 1.33 | 1.23 | 25.0 | 26.9 | 28.7[3] |
| FRG | 1.45 | 1.45 | 1,41[1] | 25.5 | 27.0 | 28.0[1] |

[1] in 1999; [2] in 1998; [3] in 1997
Source: Council of Europe (2001)

## Order-specific fertility

A value of TFR close to 2 prompts the prevalence of a two-child family model in most of the countries in the region. This inference is supported by the data on births by order of children (not given here; see tables 5 for each country in the country-specific part in Council of Europe, 2001). The number of first births was only slightly higher than that of second-order births during the 80s, and both numbers were much higher than that of the higher-order births. The same inference is re-enforced by the high values of the first- and second-order TFR (table 2.4.2).

**Table 2.4.2 – Order-specific TFR, mean age, and standard deviation for first and second births, selected countries, 1988 (Croatia, Poland, Romania and the Russian Federation 1989)**

|  | First births | | Second births | |
| --- | --- | --- | --- | --- |
|  | TFR(1) | mean age | TFR(2) | mean age |
| Bulgaria | 0.91 | 21.9 | 0.80 | 25.1 |
| Croatia | 0.73 | 23.6 | 0.61 | 26.4 |
| Czech Rep. | 0.91 | 22.4 | 0.73 | 25.6 |
| GDR | 0.79 | 22.1 | 0.62 | 25.7 |
| Hungary | 0.82 | 23.1 | 0.66 | 26.2 |
| Lithuania | 0.98 | 23.6 | 0.73 | 27.4 |
| Poland | 0.84 | 23.3 | 0.70 | 26.4 |
| Romania | 0.81 | 22.1 | 0.65 | 25.0 |
| Russian F. | 1.00 | 22.8 | 0.70 | 27.0 |
| Austria | 0.67 | 24.6 | 0.47 | 27.4 |
| Italy | 0.65 | 26.5 | 0.50 | 29.4 |

The TFR(1) is high in all the central and eastern European countries included in the table, except in Croatia. It indicates that a very high proportion of the women would ever have at least one child. Possibly only the infertile women are not in this group. This high level of first births corresponds to a traditional pattern that is not observed in the West.

These important observations hold for a longer period before the start of the transition. The trends depicted on figure 2.4.2 provide a support. The figure shows that the TFR(1) has been high during the 80s (upper left panel).

**Figure 2.4.2 – First-order TFR**

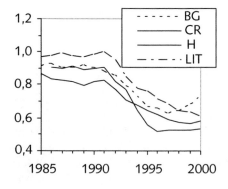 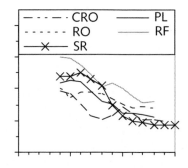

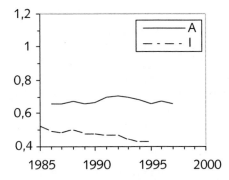

The figure also shows that the TFR(1) had a clear tendency for a decrease in Hungary during the 80s. A similar decline was observed in the GDR. In both countries it dropped down below 0.8 in 1989: a decrease that indicates a loss of universality in the birth of a first child. There were no signs of such significant behavioural change in the other countries. No data were available for Slovenia and it could be expected that in this country first-order fertility could have significantly decreased during the 80s. Such a decrease would agree with the other changes discussed up to now.

The first-order TFR observed during the 80s in the central and eastern European countries were considerably higher than those observed in Austria and Italy. This illustrates the difference between the West and the East mentioned above.

The second-order TFR is also considerably higher in the East than in the West. The two-child model was widely spread over the East and it was characteristics for this period of time.

*Age of fertility*

The mean age at birth of the first child (MAFB) was low, similarly to the mean age at first marriage. This is expected because it was common for a newly formed family to have the child soon after the marriage. Table 2.4.2 gives data for several countries. The highest MAFB was 23.6 years. In the previous sections in this chapter the value of 23.5 was suggested as a demarcation between East and West where first marriage is considered. Hence a value a little higher could serve as a demarcation line where timing of first births is considered. Family formation in eastern Europe during the 80s took place considerably earlier in life than it did in the West.

Similar inferences can be made where the mean age at second birth is considered (table 2.4.2). Spacing of children, at least between the first and the second child, seems to have been similar to that in the West. Given the prevalence of the two-child family model, it can be deduced that the family size was completed earlier in the East as compared to the West.

The age distribution of fertility is subject to change as a result in changes in the structure of births by order. A decrease in fertility usually takes place by decreasing the number of children per woman, i.e. births of higher order decrease more rapidly than those of lower order. This may cause a decrease in the mean age at childbearing, although the mean ages by order of birth could remain constant or even increase. Inversely, an increase in fertility may cause the mean age to rise. That is why the order-specific mean age of childbearing reveal better the trends in age changes. The age distribution of first births is discussed below.

**Figure 2.4.3 – First-order age-specific fertility rates for the Czech Republic, Hungary, and GDR (left panel) and Austria, Italy and the Netherlands (right panel) 1988**

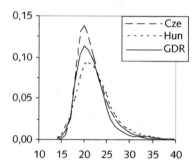
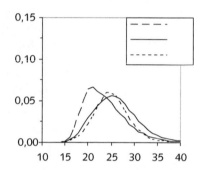

Figure 2.4.3 represents the first-order age-specific fertility rates observed in 1988 in several European countries. The contrast between the two groups of countries is evident. The age schedules observed in the three ex-socialist countries are considerably higher, more narrow, and placed to the left. The difference in the height reflects the higher level of first births as discussed above. The difference in the width of the curve is a result of the clustering of the births into a narrow age interval, and the placement to the left indicates a considerably lower mean age at the birth of the first child (table 2.4.2). The Czech curve is typical for most of the countries in the region. It is also typical for a period of 10-20 years preceding 1998. The changes in the TFR(1) in the GDR and Hungary mentioned above caused a decrease in these two curves; in addition there is a shift to the right and a slight widening. Still their shape is much closer to that of the Czech curve than to those of Austria, Italy, or the Netherlands. Hence the trends that occurred during the 80s were modest and still not typical for those observed in the West.

The order-specific age schedules of fertility did not experience considerable changes during the 80s, except for the effect of the population policies. The latter caused some youngering of fertility, i.e. a decrease in the mean age. A temperate increase was observed in Slovenia, the GDR and Hungary.

The width of the age schedule is measured by the standard deviation. The Austrian curve exhibited on figure 2.4.3 has a standard deviation of 4.5 and the Italian 4.7, while for the Hungarian curve it is 4.1, for the Czech Republic 3.6, and for GDR it is 3.3. The data show that the standard deviation in Hungary remained constant around that level during the 80s. The same is true for the other central and eastern European countries in the region: this measure was generally low and constant, as compared to higher and increasing values in the western European countries. The female population in the central and eastern European countries was more uniform with respect to timing of the first birth than it was in the West.

*Extra-marital births*

Before the start of the transition, the ex-socialist countries were more divergent in the patterns of extra-marital births than in any other fertility-related event. In 1970 the number of extra-marital births per 100 live births was above 10 in Estonia (14.1), GDR (13.3), Latvia (11.4), Russia (10.6), Yugoslavia (11.7); in Bulgaria it was 9.4, while in the other countries from the region it was lower. These levels were typical for a long period and remained stable up to the beginning of the 80s. The decade of the 80s marked a moderate increase in most of the countries, and particularly in Estonia, GDR, and Slovenia. The absolute number of extra-marital births rose too. In Estonia for example, it increased by 50% in 1990 as compared to 1980.

The information allows for the following generalisation of fertility patterns that were preponderate in the central and eastern European countries before the start of the transition:

- Nearly universal birth of a first child;
- Early birth of the first child;
- Prevalence of a two-child family model;
- Completion of family size at an early age in life.
- Dominance of marital fertility with the exception of few countries.

### 2.4.2 Trends observed after the start of the transition

*TFR*

Analogously to first marriages, the drop in fertility was abrupt and substantial (figure 2.4.1). Its timing differs from that of first marriages in that the decrease began at least one-two years earlier in most of the countries. There was no temporary rise during the first 1-2 years of the transition, as the one observed for marriages. In fact the drop in the TFR began before the start of the transition, and the latter has speeded it up. The figure shows that in nearly all countries its fall began during the second half of the 80s.

The drop in the TFR is substantial and indicates record low levels of fertility in all the countries. Everywhere it went from a little below replacement level down to below 1.4. The lowest value was observed in the ex-GDR, being a part of united Germany. The value of 1.09 registered in Bulgaria in 1997 and in Latvia in 1998 is the world record low level of the TFR registered for a whole country, except perhaps for years of war and famine. Several other countries had a TFR very close to this value. An even lower level was registered in the ex-GDR in 1993-1994, namely 0.77, when its territory was part of united Germany. The tremendous fall in this ex-country was temporary. The TFR began to rise towards the levels observed in the other ex-socialist countries, though remaining throughout the 90s the lowest one.

Where groups of countries are considered it needs to be noted that Poland and Lithuania are again closer as compared to the other two Baltic countries. The TFR in the Slovak Republic towards the end of the decade was closer to that observed in Hungary than in the Czech Republic. The fall of fertility in the Federal Republic of Yugoslavia and "the former Yugoslav Republic of Macedonia" is not as steep as in Croatia and Slovenia. In Moldova the fall is drastic, while it can hardly be distinguished where the Russian Federation and Ukraine are considered. Table 2.4.1 shows that in 2000 the TFR dropped significantly in all other countries not included in figure 2.4.1. Even traditionally high-fertility countries such as Albania and Azerbaijan can no longer be associated with high fertility. The drastic fall in fertility was universal all over the eastern part of Europe with no exceptions.

During the last few years of the period considered here there are indications of levelling off in the fall of the TFR in all countries except Moldova. A moderate increase could even be noticed in 2000 in Estonia and Latvia. Probably the decrease in the TFR has reached its lowest level in the end of the 90s. No firm statements can be made about its value in the beginning of the first decade of this century.

The abrupt fall of the TFR in the central and eastern European countries is unique, where the speed of decrease is considered. It has not been observed in other parts of the world. In other low-fertility countries a drop towards similarly low levels was experienced over longer periods of time. In the southern European countries it was quicker than elsewhere in western Europe, but not as quick as in the central and eastern European countries. Lowest levels were achieved in 1998, in Italy 1.15, in Spain 1.16, and in Greece 1.29.

### Age of fertility

The mean age at first birth marked an abrupt increase shortly after the start of the transition. It rapidly rose to levels 1.5 to 2 years higher than those observed in 1990. The increase was steepest in the ex-Yugoslav countries,

Hungary, and the Czech and Slovak Republics (figure 2.4.1). Notably the Russian Federation and the Baltic countries marked a decrease in this mean age during the first half of the decade, observed also in Poland.

What is remarkable in this change is its speed, rather than the high level achieved.

Table 2.4.1 shows that in the three western countries the mean age of birth of first child has increased considerably too.

Figure 2.4.4 exemplifies, in the case of Hungary, the way the period age-specific fertility schedule changed. While those observed in 1986 and 1990 are very close, the schedule observed in 1996 is significantly different. It is considerably lower (thus reflecting the drop in the TFR) and is moved to the right (reflecting the increase in the mean age at childbearing). The 1996 schedule has also become wider, even though a decrease in the number of births contributes to its shrinking.

**Figure 2.4.4 - Age-specific fertility rates, Hungary 1986, 1990 and 1996**

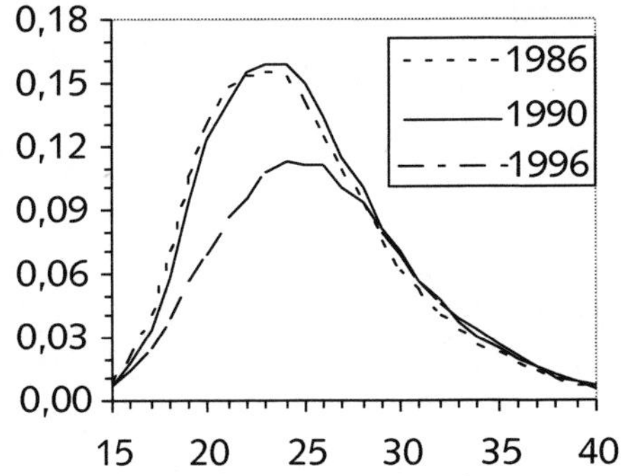

The swift rise in the mean age at birth of the first child and of childbearing in general indicates a preference of shifting births towards higher ages. Like in the case of first marriages this is a new behaviour that has stretched over the central and eastern European countries.

*Fertility by birth order*

Figure 2.4.2 shows the TFR(1) during the 90s in some countries. The patterns in the figure are like those discussed for the overall fertility. Where the central and eastern European countries are considered, the TFR(1) dropped considerably and levelled off during the last few years. There are no significant changes in the level of first births in the two western European countries.

Higher order fertility decreased too (data not shown). The decrease is not as steep though. In some countries the TFR for order 3 and higher decreased only a little. This indicates most probably the existence of a sub-population whose fertility has not changed significantly during the transition period. The data do not allow distinguishing this group. It could be characterised for example by ethnicity, or religiosity. The share of these higher-order births of all births is very small and practically does not have an impact on the overall fertility level.

## Extra-marital births

The number of extra-marital births relative to all births increased drastically during the 90s (table 2.4.3). In most of the countries it went up more than twice as compared to the level of 1990. Moderate changes were observed only in Croatia, "The former Yugoslav Republic of Macedonia", and Bosnia-Herzegovina. It is notable that a drastic increase was observed even in catholic Poland. The rise in extra-marital births relative to all births was high in other European countries too, as table 2.4.3 shows. Hence this was a trend common for most of Europe.

**Table 2.4.3 – Extra-marital births per 100 births**

|  | 1990 | 1995 | 2000 |
|---|---|---|---|
| Bulgaria | 12.4 | 25.7 | 38.4 |
| Croatia | 7.0 | 7.5 | 9.0 |
| Czech R. | 8.6 | 15.6 | 21.8 |
| Estonia | 27.1 | 44.1 | 54.5 |
| GDR | 35.0 | 41.8 | 49.9[1] |
| Georgia | 18.2 | 29.2 | 40.4 |
| Hungary | 13.1 | 20.7 | 29.0 |
| Latvia | 16.9 | 29.9 | 40.3 |
| Lithuania | 7.0 | 12.8 | 22.6 |
| Moldova | 11.1 | 13.3 | 20.5 |
| Poland | 6.2 | 9.5 | 12.1 |
| Romania | ... | 19.7 | 25.5 |
| Russian F. | 14.6 | 21.1 | 28.0 |
| Slovak | 7.6 | 12.6 | 18.3 |
| Slovenia | 24.5 | 29.8 | 37.1 |
| Macedonia | 7.1 | 8.2 | 9.8 |
| Ukraine | 13.0 | 13.2 | 17.4[1] |
| Belarus | 8.5 | 13.5 | 18.6 |
| Bosnia-Herz | 7.4 | ... | 10.1[2] |
| F.R.Yugoslavia | 12.7 | 16.4 | 24.3 |
| Austria | 23.6 | 27.4 | 31.3 |
| Italy | 6.5 | 8.1 | 10.2 |
| Finland | 25.2 | 33.1 | 39.2 |
| FRG | 10.5 | 12.9 | 17.7[1] |

(1) in 1999; (2) in 1998

Absolute numbers of extra-marital births increased too, although not at the same levels. For example in Bulgaria this number was around 13,000 in 1990, and increased up to more than 25,000 in 1999, while the number of all births decreased from 102,000 down to 72,000.

These trends could have been caused by diverse reasons. One hypothesis is that people may first have a baby and then enter into a marriage. Another one is that many extra-marital births could have taken place within a non-marital union. The latter case has been observed in western European countries. It was shown above that non-marital cohabitation has increased in the central and eastern European countries, and therefore the second hypothesis seems plausible, along with the first one. This is supported by the data in table 2.4.4.

**Table 2.4.4 – Partnership status of the mother at the birth of the first child, age 20 to 24 at time of interview**

|  | married | cohabiting | not in any partnership |
|---|---|---|---|
| Czech R. | 80.7 | 9.2 | 10.1 |
| Estonia | 20.7 | 30.4 | 38.9 |
| Hungary | 82.1 | 8.0 | 9.9 |
| Latvia | 72.6 | 10.6 | 16.8 |
| Lithuania | 82.7 | 2.7 | 14.6 |
| Poland | 84.9 | 1.6 | 13.5 |
| Slovenia | 51.6 | 26.5 | 21.9 |
| Austria | 33.3 | 26.4 | 40.2 |
| Finland | 70.4 | 23.8 | 5.8 |
| Italy | 81.2 | 11.7 | 7.1 |

Source: tables 15 from the FFS SCR's

Extra-marital first births have been split between the two states: with partner and without a partner, with the exception of Poland and Lithuania. The high level of first births out of any partnership could be linked to the increased desire among women to have a child without a commitment to a partner.

Table 2.4.4 gives data for women aged 20-24 only. The original tables 15 from the FFS country reports contain data for other age groups as well. They show that the share of extra-marital births is higher among younger women and particularly among those aged below 25. The share of births in extra-marital unions has also increased. It can be concluded that the 90s gave rise to a new behaviour that is expanding among larger groups of the population.

*Completed fertility*

Figure 2.4.5 gives the completed fertility of cohorts born between 1947 and 1967, for countries where the data were available. The fertility of the older cohorts, i.e. those born before 1957-58, was close to or above replacement level in Bulgaria, Romania, Poland, the Czech and the Slovak Republic, and below replacement in the Russian Federation, Lithuania, Estonia, Hungary, Croatia, Slovenia. The fertility of the younger cohorts and particularly of those who were born after 1960 decreased by around 0.2. Such a drop in completed fertility is high in a historical perspective but can be seen as moderate when compared to the drastic period decrease in the TFR. It should be noted that the youngest cohorts have not yet completed their fertility; for example those born in 1967 were 32-33 years old towards 2000, the reference year of the data used here. Another important consideration is that the period fertility drop observed during the 90s has affected mostly cohorts who were born after 1965 and whose fertility is not yet completed. Most probably these cohorts will have a significantly lower completed fertility than the one observed on figure 2.4.5.

**Figure 2.4.5 – Completed fertility of cohorts born between 1947 and 1967**

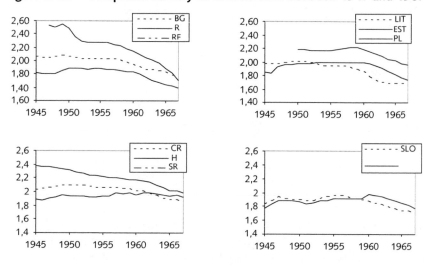

Figure 2.4.6 illustrates the way the cohort age-specific fertility rates (censored at age 35) changed for cohorts in Bulgaria. They show that the decrease in cohort fertility was not uniform by age. Teenage fertility experienced a very small change towards an increase for the youngest teenagers, while fertility for those age 20 to 30 years decreased significantly. Adult-age fertility changed little. The youngest cohort is censored at a tendency of an increase in fertility at that age; a result of postponement of births to later ages.

**Figure 2.4.6 – Age-specific fertility rates for cohorts born in 1971, 1975 and 1981, Bulgaria**

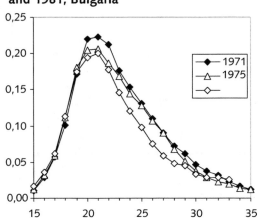

The description of the changes observed during the 90s allows for the following compact conclusions:

• The universality of the birth of the first child has become questionable if not lost; Childlessness has grown.

• Postponement of births, including first birth has lead to a break of the pattern of early childbearing.

• Completion of family size was achieved early in life due to the lower number of children achieved and in spite of the postponement of births.

• The dominance of extra-marital births was lost; single parenthood of mothers has risen considerably.

### 2.4.3 Timing of marriages and births

The rise in the mean ages of first marriages and first births indicates postponement of these events. It is known from demographic theory that postponement of events has an effect on period measures such as the TFMR, TFR, and TFR(1). The higher the postponement effect, the lower the period measure will be. Inversely, when advancement of the events is observed instead of postponement (i.e. decrease in the corresponding mean age), the period measure tends to be larger. Hence the period total rate may include a bias in its measurement of the level of the event. The part of the total rate that measures level is known *as quantum*, and the part that results from changes in the timing of events is known *as tempo*. The problem of delineating the tempo effect from the quantum has been studied extensively in demography. Bongaarts and Feeney (1998) recently suggested a simple formula for such delineation.[4] It allows for the estimation of adjusted total rates that are used in this sub-chapter.

The adjustment for tempo makes more feasible the interpretations of the TFMR as the average number of first marriages and of the TFR as the average number of children per woman. Yet the latter remain period rates and cohort-type interpretations like these should be carefully done. In particular, adjusted rates may violate the "average number" interpretation because they are not free of additional effects other than the tempo effect.

Trends in the adjusted total rate over a sequence of years allow for a better assessment of the level of the demographic event of interest. We will discuss here the post-transition period. Where the pre-transition period is considered it suffices to state that the tempo effect on the TFR and TFMR was modest and was usually the result of temporary changes in tempo caused by policy changes and particularly by the introductions of pronatal policy instruments.

*TFMR*

Figure 2.4.7 illustrates the adjusted TFMR during the period 1988-1998. They are plotted on the same time span as the one used in figure 2.2.1 in order to facilitate the visual comparisons of the adjusted to the observed TFMR. The series were smoothed. Table 2.2.1 gives the values estimated towards 1998.

### Figure 2.4.7 – Adjusted TFMR

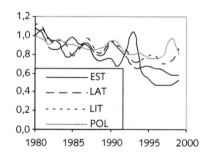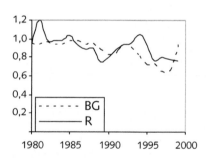

[4] In the case of the first marriages, their formula is as follows:
(1) $\qquad$ $TFMR_t(adj) = TFMR_t(obs)/(1-(a_{t+1} - a_{t-1})/2)$
where $a_t$ is the mean age at first marriage observed during the year t, $TFMR_t(obs)$ is the total first marriage rate observed in year t, and $TFMR_t(adj)$ is the adjusted for tempo effect $TFMR_t(obs)$.
In the case of fertility formula (1) is arranged as follows:
(2) $\qquad$ $TFR_t(1,adj) = TFR_t(1,obs)/(1-(m_{t+1} - m_{t-1})/2)$
where $m_t$ is the mean age at the birth of the first child observed during the year t, $TFR_t(1, obs)$ is the first-order total fertility rate observed in year t, and $TFR_t(1,adj)$ is the adjusted $TFR_t(1,obs)$. The adjustment for higher orders is done using analogous formula for each order separately. The overall adjusted for tempo effect TFR is simply the sum of the order-specific adjusted TFR.
Kohler and Ortega (2002) have shown that the Bongaarts-Feeney formula overestimates the tempo effect in cases of postponement. The tendencies it revealed are approximately valid and this is made use of here.

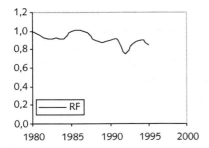

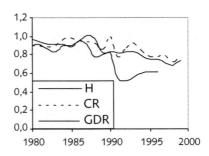

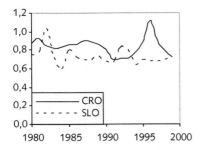

The data allow distinguishing the following stages in the changes of the quantum of first marriages.

The first stage refers to the first couple of years of the transition when the adjusted TFMR was lower than the observed one in most of the countries. After these initial years started the second stage, when the adjusted TFMR raised higher than the observed ones and their decrease was less pronounced. In some countries the difference between the adjusted and observed rates was tremendous, like in Bulgaria, the Czech and Slovak Republics, Hungary. The third stage refers to the end of the period, characterised by some convergence in the two measures of first marriages. In the case of the three western European countries, the adjusted TFMR are also lying above the observed ones, and its significant decrease is notable only in the Netherlands.

Towards the end of the studied period the adjusted for tempo effect TFMR was considerably lower than the traditional value (around and higher than 0.9) in some of the countries. Hence a significant proportion of all women, some 40% in Bulgaria in 1997 for example, will remain never married by age 50, were they subject to the age-specific first marriage rates free of tempo effect. If the assumptions underlying this inference were shaky, the numbers cited above could be inexact but the tendency they describe will remain valid, namely, that there is a clear break from the traditional behaviour of universal nuptiality and a rise in the preference to remain unmarried.

*TFR*

Figure 2.4.8 gives the observed and the adjusted TFR during the 90s. The adjusted TFR lies noticeably higher than the observed TFR. The difference between the two rates is due to a tempo effect. The latter is the result of postponement of births that has become evident through the rise in the mean age of childbearing (discussed above). Therefore a part of the fertility decline observed during the 90s is a result of birth postponements rather than to the desire not to have children. The problem remains open as to whether the postponed births will be realised. The adjustment procedure used here does not tell us anything about length of postponement and level of realised postponed births.

**Figure 2.4.8 – Observed (thin line) and adjusted (thick line) total fertility rate**

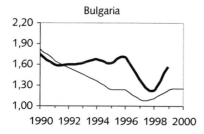
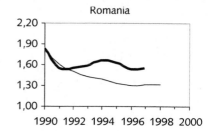
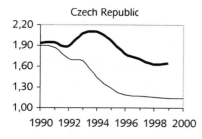
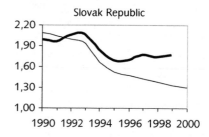
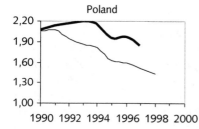
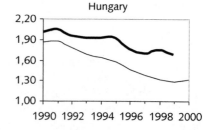

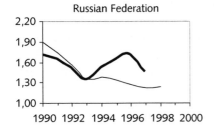

Russian Federation

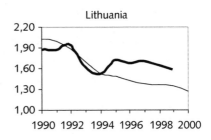

Lithuania

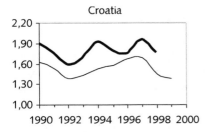

Croatia

The adjusted TFR reveals some unexpected inferences. In the Czech and Slovak Republics, Hungary, and Poland it increased until around 1994. We can suppose that if there were no postponement of births the transition would have increased fertility in these countries, rather than have decreased it. After around 1994, the adjusted TFR in these countries began decreasing. In the Russian Federation and Lithuania, the decrease in the adjusted TFR coincided with the observed one up to around 1994, and in Bulgaria this was observed up to 1991 only. Hence in these countries, inversely to the previously mentioned ones, the transition would anyway decrease fertility, were there no postponement of births. That is to say, the tempo effect was negligible. In the Russian Federation and Lithuania this initial period was followed by a temporary rise in the quantum of TFR (i.e. the adjusted TFR increased). In general, after 1994 or later the adjusted TFR decreased in all countries. Only Croatia is an exception where both the observed and the adjusted TFR show some fluctuations that could perhaps be linked to the specific political development in the country.

The adjusted TFR indicates a considerably higher level of fertility than the observed one. In Bulgaria it was around 1.6-1.7 except for 1997. Hence the record low observed TFR in this country was due by and large to a tempo effect. The tempo effect was particularly clear in the Czech Republic, where the difference between the adjusted and the observed TFR was as much as 0.6.

Results not shown here indicate that the adjusted for tempo effect TFR(1) was higher than the observed one and was crudely around the value of 0.8 in most of the countries. The traditional value of 0.9 or higher was not prevailing during the 90s. This is a clear sign of a break from the traditional behaviour of nearly universal maternity. An adjusted TFR(1) lower than 0.9 indicates that there is an increase in the number of women who will remain without any children. This behaviour, widely spread over other parts of Europe, has come to dominate in central and eastern European countries too. The stages of change in the adjusted TFMR are visible for some countries in the case of the adjusted TFR too.

### 2.4.4 General inferences

The above discussion can be conjectured as follows:

*Before the start of the transition:*
• The prevalent high levels of TFMR and TFR(1) indicate that nearly every woman will ever get married and have at least one child. Nearly every adult woman was expected to start a family life. Being single and/or childless was not a conscious choice but a fate submitted to biological reasons.

• A TFR of slightly less than 2, high TFR(1) and TFR(2), and high number of first and second births as compared to higher-order births indicate the prevalence of a two-child model. A large proportion of women were expected to have two children. Having more than two children was a rare event.

• First marriages and births of a first child were clustered into narrow age intervals. Both events took place early in life. Family formation thus competed successfully with other crucial events in the life course, such as starting a job or completion of education.

These conjectures were valid more or less for each ex-socialist country. Central and eastern Europe was not only politically, but also demographically uniform with respect to patterns of family formation.

These patterns were less explicit in some ex-Yugoslav countries and particularly in Slovenia. During the second half of the 80s the patterns began changing in the GDR, Hungary, and the Czech Republic. Inversely, Albania and the Transcaucasian countries were lagging behind in these changes and the patterns described above are less valid.

*After the start of the transition:*
The changes after 1990 indicate a clear break from past demographic behaviour. None of the inferences about the general trends observed before the start of the transition holds any more:

• There was no persistence in the universality of marriage. Being single became a common behaviour.

• The universality of maternity was lost. Being childless became a matter of choice, not fate.

- The two-child model gave way to a single-child family.

- The first marriage and birth of the first child were being postponed to later years in life. Family formation gradually gives way to other choices in the course of life, such as start of work and longer education.

- The proportion of extra-marital births as well as their absolute number marked an enormous increase. Single parenthood rose as a matter of choice.

These changes were directed towards patterns that have been observed in the west, except that its pace was much higher.

The stages in the changes of tempo and quantum effects during the 90s allow for the following complementary inferences about the marital and reproductive behaviour during the transition. The shock of the start of the transition provoked a quantum fall in marriage and fertility. Later, during the middle of the decade, the tempo effect was enforced, and towards the end of the 90s, probably after some adaptation to the new conditions of life, the tempo effect began a slight decrease in some countries, and quantum remained low.

The changes during the 90s are not uniform among the central and eastern European countries, as they were before the transition. A clear-cut grouping of the countries is difficult. However some regularities need to be mentioned.

The start of the transition had a more pronounced effect on nuptiality and fertility in the ex-USSR countries, Bulgaria, and Romania, than in the central European ex-socialist countries. In the latter group of countries the MAFM and MAFB rose faster than in the former, joined by the Baltic countries.

The ex-Yugoslav countries exhibit smoother changes that have started before the 90s. Slovenia is an extreme example. The demographic trends in this country are more characteristic of western than eastern Europe.

Drastic changes in the Transcaucasian countries bring about their inclusion to all central and eastern European countries. Changes in Albania are drastic but the demographic indicators in this country lag behind those observed in the other central and eastern European countries. It can be expected that shortly it will join the group as well.

## 2.5 Family planning, abortions and related issues

During the times of socialism, family planning was considered a part of the population and family policy. Distinctive individual-level matters, such as desired number of children and birth control were submitted to macro-social aims of the population policy. The latter stated its goal to be a moderate and positive population growth that could be achieved when families have two to three children on average. Subsequently unmarried persons and families having no children or only one child could either be subject to negative instruments of the population policy, for example the bachelor's tax used in Bulgaria and the ex-USSR, or not be subject to certain positive instruments. The centrally planned economy could easily be directed towards restricted supply of market contraceptives, and the state imposed restrictions on the implementation of clinical contraceptive methods (sterilisation). Under similar conditions it is no wonder that many ex-socialist countries experienced high abortion rates and dominant usage of classical contraceptive methods.

With the start of the transition this picture started changing too. Abortion trends started decreasing and usage of modern contraceptives (i.e. clinical and commercial, or mechanical, devices) emerged and grew. Family planning organisations developed and expanded their activities. The right of parents to have the number of children that they desired was legally formulated. Nonetheless, the transition period witnessed negative trends, such as worsening of reproductive health and rise in infertility. This section discusses these and related issues.

Data quality is a major issue in the study of such sensitive topics. It is generally considered that survey data provide less accurate information on abortions than annual statistics. For this reason the latter are preferred here. Where usage of contraceptives is considered, survey data are the major source of information and they cannot be avoided.

### 2.5.1  Ideal and expected number of children

At the start of transition the ideal number of children in a family in the central and eastern European countries was around or slightly above replacement level, i.e. 2.1 to 2.3, with the exception of the ex-USSR countries where it was considerably higher, and the ex-GDR where it was lower. The World Values Survey for example (Inglehart 2000) exemplify these observations (table 2.5.1). The course of the transition made these numbers decrease. The decrease was significant only in the Russian Federation and Bulgaria, although some decrease was noted in the other countries too.

The ideal number of children is an abstract notion. Closer to reality is the expected (ultimate) number of children. This was measured by the FFS (table 2.5.2 gives the observations for females) and is the sum of the number of children already born, plus the desired additional number of children. The expected number of children is not far from the ideal number of children, nor does it differ significantly by age groups: preferences towards family size among the females are stable with age. Other data from FFS reveal that women with lower education prefer a higher number of children.

114

**Table 2.5.1 – Ideal number of children in some central and eastern European countries, World Value Survey, 1990 and 1995-1997**

|            | 1990 | 1995-97 |
|------------|------|---------|
| Czech R.   | 2.2  | -       |
| Hungary    | 2.3  | -       |
| Poland     | 2.3  | 2.2     |
| Slovak R.  | 2.2  | -       |
| ex-GDR     | 1.9  | 1.9     |
| Slovenia   | 2.4  | 2.3     |
| Estonia    | 2.4  | 2.4     |
| Latvia     | 2.6  | 2.4**   |
| Lithuania  | 2.5  | 2.4*    |
| Bulgaria   | 2.2  | 2.0 **  |
| Macedonia. | -    | 2.3     |
| Romania    | 2.1  | -       |
| Moldova    | -    | 2.6     |
| Russian F. | 2.6  | 2.2**   |
| Ukraine    | -    | 2.1     |

* change is significant at the 0.05 level; ** at 0.01 level.
"dash" is placed where the survey was not taken.

Both the ideal and the expected number of children are considerably higher than the number of children actually born, where the latter is measured by the observed TFR (or the adjusted TFR, where the latter is available). Fertility intentions therefore remain unfulfilled. This is hardly any news for demographers. The same inference can be made for other countries (Austria and the Netherlands, as shown in table 2.5.2).

**Table 2.5.2 – Average number of children ultimately expected (number of born plus desired additional children), women**

| Country and year of survey | 20-24 | 25-29 | 30-34 | 35-39 |
|-----------------------------|-------|-------|-------|-------|
| Slovenia, 1994/95           | 2.3   | 2.3   | 2.3   | 2.3   |
| Lithuania, 1994/95          | 2.1   | 2.2   | 2.1   | 2.2   |
| Bulgaria, 1997              | 1.9   | 2.0   | 2.0   | 1.9   |
| Estonia, 1994               | 2.5   | 2.5   | 2.7   | 2.4   |
| Hungary, 1992/93            | 2.1   | 2.1   | 2.1   | 2.1   |
| Latvia, 1995                | 2.1   | 2.2   | 2.3   | 2.1   |
| Poland, 1991                | 1.7   | 2.1   | 2.3   | 2.2   |
| Austria, 1995/96            | 1.9   | 1.9   | 2.0   | 1.9   |
| Netherlands, 1993           | 2.3   | 2.2   | 2.1   | 2.0   |

Source: FFS Country Reports, table 24b.

## 2.5.2 Contraception

Usage of commercial and clinical contraceptives was severely restricted in most of the central and eastern European countries. There existed at least two reasons. One was economic: the regime could not afford the import of modern contraceptive devices. The other was based on ideological grounds: contraceptives would be a means against reaching the aims of the official pronatal policy. Personal needs for contraceptives should be submitted to the societal needs for population growth. On the other hand, restriction on contraceptives hindered the fulfilment of significant family policies aiming at relieving the conflict between women's roles as mothers and workers. During the 80s certain modern contraceptives appeared on the market in some central and eastern European countries, and to a larger extent in central European countries. In a few countries production of certain mechanical devices emerged and began growing. While before the 80s usage of modern contraceptive devices was virtually absent it marked a rise during the 80s, although at a moderate pace. The dominant methods of birth control were the traditional ones, namely abstinence and withdrawal. For example in Bulgaria in 1976, 76% of all women aged 15-44 used any contraceptive method, and only 8% used a modern method. In Poland in 1977 these percentages were 75 and 26, while in Finland they were 80 and 78 (UN 2000b, p.16).

Towards the end of the 80s and during the 90s usage of modern methods increased considerably. The FFS data in table 2.5.3 show that only Poland and Lithuania had a level of usage of modern methods lower than that in Italy. Prevalence of religious values in Italy hinders usage of modern methods and the same holds for Poland and Lithuania. Comparisons with the Netherlands show that this level is low. The same inference holds where other western countries are considered.

**Table 2.5.3 – Usage of contraceptives by fecund, not pregnant women in sexual relationship: FFS results (in percent)**

|  | 20-24 | 25-29 | 30-34 | 35-39 | 40-44 |
|---|---|---|---|---|---|
| Poland -using modern method -using traditional method -not using any method | 36 52 12 100 | 41 49 10 100 | 32 55 13 100 | 34 53 12 100 | 33 55 11 100 |
| Latvia -using modern method -using traditional method -not using any method | 77 7 15 100 | 74 12 15 100 | 74 13 13 100 | 71 19 10 100 | 62 19 19 100 |

| | 20-24 | 25-29 | 30-34 | 35-39 | 40-44 |
|---|---|---|---|---|---|
| Hungary[1] | | | | | |
| -using modern method | 74 | 82 | 78 | 75 | 67 |
| -using traditional method | 8 | 7 | 10 | 13 | 15 |
| -not using any method | 18 | 11 | 12 | 12 | 18 |
| | 100 | 100 | 100 | 100 | 100 |
| Estonia | | | | | |
| -using modern method | 55 | 56 | 61 | 58 | 49 |
| -using traditional method | 32 | 28 | 24 | 23 | 23 |
| -not using any method | 12 | 16 | 15 | 19 | 28 |
| | 100 | 100 | 100 | 100 | 100 |
| Slovenia | | | | | |
| -using modern method | 73 | 71 | 71 | 69 | 72 |
| -using traditional method | 15 | 17 | 18 | 18 | 13 |
| -not using any method | 12 | 12 | 12 | 13 | 15 |
| | 100 | 100 | 100 | 100 | 100 |
| Lithuania | | | | | |
| -using modern method | 49 | 51 | 49 | 47 | 37 |
| -using traditional method | 16 | 24 | 24 | 19 | 27 |
| -not using any method | 35 | 25 | 27 | 33 | 36 |
| | 100 | 100 | 100 | 100 | 100 |
| Netherlands [1] | | | | | |
| -using modern method | 93 | 95 | 89 | 79 | 73 |
| -using traditional method | 2 | 3 | 3 | 8 | 15 |
| -not using any method | 4 | 3 | 8 | 13 | 13 |
| | 100 | 100 | 100 | 100 | 100 |
| Italy | | | | | |
| -using modern method | 47 | 51 | 56 | 56 | 50 |
| -using traditional method | 33 | 24 | 22 | 21 | 24 |
| -not using any method | 19 | 25 | 22 | 23 | 26 |
| | 100 | 100 | 100 | 100 | 100 |

Source: estimations based on tables 19 in the corresponding FFS country reports.
[1] The last age group in Hungary is 40-41, and in the Netherlands 40-42.
Modern methods include clinical and commercial methods.
Traditional methods include periodic abstinence and withdrawal.

Where the age distribution of the usage of modern methods is considered, a lowest level is observed among women from the highest age group. Only some countries reveal a tendency of a rise in the usage of modern methods with the decrease in the age of the respondents though. Hence the spread of the methods is not explicitly age-specific. Usage of contraceptives depends on age and this makes the age-specific FFS data preferable for the purpose of a short presentation as in this report.

Table 2.5.3 shows also that the share of women in the central and eastern European countries that did not use any method remained high during the

90s, as compared with the data observed in the Netherlands, and low as compared to Italy (except for Lithuania).

Thus the start of the transition marked a radical change in the family planning. Modern contraceptive methods began to spread through the population at a fast pace and nearly independently of the women's age. The pill, the intra-uterine devices and particularly the condom are among the preferred devices. Sterilisation nearly does not exist. The family planning organisations develop large-scale activities for the spread of knowledge on modern contraceptive methods (see country chapters in David (2000).

Country-specific studies supply in-depth information: Carlson and Omori (1998) discuss Bulgaria; see also country chapters in David (1999) and in Kučera et al. (2000), as well as UN(2000b) and previous editions of this UN series.

### 2.5.3 Abortions

The topic of induced abortion as a method of birth control in the ex-socialist European countries has been a subject of numerous debates. Two major issues were examined: legal matters and levels of abortion. Legalisation of induced abortion was widely introduced around the end of the 50s. Periods of prohibitions, restrictions, and legalisation changed (see for example Frejka 1983 as well as David 1999 and the country chapters therein). This issue was closely connected to the pronatal population policy. Prohibition and restriction arose when fertility declined, and later alleviation was introduced for relieving the contradiction between the roles of a woman as a mother and worker. Poland and Romania were the two countries where abortion remain prohibited up to 1989.

Induced abortion in the ex-socialist countries reached unusually high levels. Frejka (1983) cites that as of the late 1970s, about 50% of known pregnancies were terminated by abortion in Bulgaria, Romania, and Yugoslavia and about 30% were aborted in the other countries. The GDR was an exception with its lower level. Blayo (1993) cites more data towards the end of the 80s. The total abortion rate (interpreted as the number of abortions per woman) was 0.6 in Albania and below 1 in the GDR; between 1.2 and 1.8 in Bulgaria, Hungary, the Slovak Republic, the Czech Republic, and most of the republics of former Yugoslavia except Serbia where it was 3.5. The average number of abortions per woman in the ex-USSR European republics was between 2 and 3, 3.3 in Belarus, and 4.0 in the Russian Federation. The highest level was observed in Romania - 5.7. Blayo (1993) cites that the total abortion rate in the western European countries was much lower - between 0.15 and 0.63.

These high levels of induced abortions were the result of the low level of usage of modern contraceptives. Traditional methods of birth control are unreliable and need to be backed up by abortion. Where and when abortions were prohibited, criminal abortion rate was high. This was an additional reason for the liberalisation of the legal system in most of the countries. Stloukal (2000) finds this explanation insufficient. He adds the significance of changes in the social value system during the socialist regime that favoured abortion.

Blayo (1993) and David (ed., 1999) indicate that induced abortion started declining towards the end of the 80s in some of the central and eastern European countries. One cause for that decline was the initial spread of modern contraceptives. Table 2.5.4 exemplifies this decline with the general abortion rate (GAR - number of abortions per thousand women aged 15-44).

**Table 2.5.4 – Abortion rate, 1980-1999, per thousand women aged 15-44**

|  | 1980 | 1990 | 1996 | 1999 |
|---|---|---|---|---|
| Albania | - | 28.4 | 35.8 | 25.0 |
| Belarus | 94.0 | 116.9 | 73.6 | 59.6 |
| Bulgaria | 76.7 | 67.8 | 51.3 | 42.2 |
| Czech Republic | 32.2 | 49.3 | 20.6 | 17.8 |
| Croatia | - | 25.8 [3] | 12.4 | 8.2 |
| Estonia | 110.7 | 87.9 | 53.6 | 46.6 |
| GDR | 25.3 | 20.4 | 10.1 | - |
| Hungary | 36.3 | 41.2 | 34.5 | 30.9 |
| Latvia | 107.8 | 87.2 | 46.1 | 35.0 |
| Lithuania | 59.3 | 61.7 | 34.0 | 22.9 |
| Moldova | 101.2 | 83.1 | 45.8 | 38.8 [5] |
| Poland | 16.7 | 7.0 | 0.06 | - |
| Romania | 90.2 | 199.3 | 90.2 | 51.7 |
| Russian Fed. | 140.2 | 125.6 | 79.8 | 70.1 [5] |
| Slovak Republic | 28.7 | 40.9 | 17.2 | 16.1 |
| Slovenia | - | 27.4 [4] | 22.7 | 19.8 |
| Ukraine | 106.8 | 96.5 | 62.3 | - |
| F.R.Yugoslavia | - | 70.7 [1] | 44.9 [2] | 26.2 [5] |

(1) in 1991; (2) in 1995; (3) in 1992; (4) in 1993; (5) in 1998
Source: David, ed. (1999, p.14) for 1980, 1990, and 1996; estimations of the author based on data from the Council of Europe (2002), 1999.

The transition period saw the rise of new trends in the level of abortions (table 2.5.4). The GAR decreased significantly in all countries from 1990 to 1999, with the decrease being modest in Albania. The liberalisation introduced in 1990 in Romania contributed to a sudden rise of the abortion rate followed by a significant fall towards the end of the 90s. The decrease is particularly evident where the level was very high, namely in the ex-USSR countries. Notably the decrease was stronger in the Baltic than in the CIS countries. The fall in the abortion rate is due to the rise in the availability and usage of modern contraceptives.

Consider as a reference the GAR in three western countries: Austria, 1.4 per thousand; Finland 10.3 per thousand, and Italy 10.2 per thousand. The level observed in 1999 in Croatia was of this magnitude, but in all other countries abortions were still high as compared to the west. The continuation of the tendency of a fall in abortions may soon bring about their equalisation to a low level among most of the European countries.

The higher level of abortions in the central and eastern European countries as compared to the West in the end of the 90s is an issue of debate. Modern contraceptives are available and hence other reasons operate that keep the incidence of abortions high. Recent studies indicate that knowledge of modern methods of birth control is widespread and therefore its lack can explain only a small share of the abortions. Although modern contraceptive methods are known they are often considered as dangerous to health. In some cases the modern devices are expensive. Here the lack of information on the availability of devices and services for their usage at Family Planning clinics also counts.

The transition brought up a new issue for debate on abortions. Some civil and religious organisations saw it as a murder, analogously to what has been the case in some western countries. They insisted on the prohibition of abortion. Opponents of this view are liberal movements who insist on the right of the individual to shape his/her destiny. Gal (1994) discusses the debate in Hungary and Kulczynski (1995) and Githens (1996) discuss it in Poland.

### 2.5.4 Unmet needs for family planning

The high level of abortion indicates the existence of a large number of undesired pregnancies. It is reasonable therefore to deliberate on the level of unmet needs of family planning.

The FFS and RHS surveys carried out during the 90s give relevant information for the estimation of indicators on unmet needs for family planning. Klijzing (2000) provides estimates based on the FFS data, and the RHS-based estimates are provided by the relevant country-specific publications (table 2.5.5). As usual, the latter includes some western European countries for comparative purposes.

Consider the minimum estimate (ratio of fecund women who have sex, do not want a pregnancy and do not use any contraceptive method). Hungary and Slovenia are the only central and eastern European countries where this ratio is at the level observed in the western countries. Romania joined this group towards 1999. In the remaining central and eastern European countries the higher ratio is known to be due to disapproval of the usage of methods. The disapproval can be due to diverse factors such as disbelief in the functioning of the methods, religiousness, fatalism and a specific value system (Stloukal 1999). The impact of no knowledge of contraceptive methods has been found to be insignificant: nearly all women are acquainted with at least some modern methods.

## Table 2.5.5 – Unmet needs for family planning, women

| Country and year of survey | minimum[1] | maximum[2] |
|---|---|---|
| FFS data [3], central and eastern European countries: | | |
| Czech Republic 1997 | 8.0 | 15.4 |
| Hungary 1992/93 | 4.2 | 11.9 |
| Latvia 1995 | 10.6 | 17.0 |
| Lithuania 1994/95 | 12.1 | 23.3 |
| Slovenia 1994/95 | 6.6 | 18.9 |
| RHS data [4], central and eastern European countries: | | |
| Czech Republic 1993 | 9.8 | 30.6 |
| Romania 1993 | 8.5 | 39.1 |
| Romania 1999 | 4.5 | 28.7 |
| Russian F. 1996 (6) | 13 | 26 |
| Ukraine 1999 | 14.2 | 35.2 |
| WIN Project | | |
| Russian Fed. [5] | 8.3 | 29.3 |
| FFS data [3], western countries | | |
| Belgium 1991/92 | 2.1 | 5.6 |
| France 1994 | 5.7 | 9.8 |
| Italy 1995/96 | 7.4 | 22.8 |
| Spain 1994/95 | 3.0 | 12.3 |

[1] Minimum estimate: ratio of women with unwanted current pregnancy or fecund sexually active women not using a contraceptive method and wanting no (or no more) births, to all women.

[2] Maximum estimate: the above ratio is enlarged to include fecund women who use traditional methods and want no (or no more) births.

[3] Source: Klijzing (2000), table 1.

[4] Sources: RHS in the Czech Republic (1995), p.86; RHS in Romania (1995), p.94 and RHS in Romania (2000), table 5.6.1; RHS in the Russian Federation (1997); RHS in the Ukraine (2000), table 26.

[5] Source: David et al. (2000) and estimations of the author. The data refer to women in union only.

[6] The ratios are approximated.

The maximum level indicator calls for slightly different inferences. Women in Italy use traditional methods extensively and for this reason the maximum level of unmet needs of family planning is high in this country: much higher than the other religious countries, Spain and Belgium. Taking Spain as a benchmark, it can be seen that Hungary is the only country where these unmet needs are around the levels observed in the West. If Italy were the benchmark, we would add the other central European countries in the list as well as Latvia.

Romania and the Czech Republic are represented twice in the table because of the availability of two sets of data. In both countries the two indicators reveal a significant drop in the levels for unmet needs of family planning. This decrease is the result of the spread of modern methods as discussed above.

The high level of unmet needs for family planning explains the high prevalence of abortion. Women tend to avoid births more than they avoid pregnancies. There is an underlying trend of change in this behaviour, towards the substitution of prevention of pregnancies for the prevention of births.

### 2.5.5 Reproductive health

Reproductive health is an issue of family planning whose importance rose with the Cairo Population Conference in 1994. The topic was stated as of particular concern in the central and eastern European countries. Indeed, in the 90s attention was brought to the low prevalence of contraception and high prevalence of abortion and of maternal morbidity and mortality, the epidemic growth of sexually transmitted diseases (STD) in some of the countries and the relatively high prevalence of infertility. Lindmark *et al.* (1999) discuss these issues.

A comparative study of changes in reproductive health is difficult because of the scarce data, particularly where data for the construction of time series are necessary. For this purpose we focus only on the period during the transition.

Prevalence of contraceptives and abortions were discussed above and it was seen that their trends develop in a positive direction, i.e. a rise in the prevalence of contraceptives and a fall in abortion rates and ratios. The levels are still inappropriate from the point of view of requirements for reproductive health that can be set in these countries.

Maternal morbidity and mortality is high in the central and eastern European countries mainly because of the widespread use of abortion. While in western Europe maternal mortality is below 10 per 100,000 births, in most of the central and eastern European countries it is considerably higher. WHO and UNPF (1995) inform that during the first years of the transition Slovenia was the only country in the region where maternal mortality was as low as in western Europe. In Croatia, the Slovak Republic, the Czech Republic, and Poland, the level is slightly above 10 per 100,000 births; 20 to 30 per 100,000 in "The former Yugoslav Republic of Macedonia", the Federal Republic of Yugoslavia, Bulgaria, Georgia, and Belarus, and considerably higher in the remaining countries from the region. Romania topped the list with a level of app. 60 per 100,000, followed by Moldova and the Russian Federation with levels around 50 per 100,000. In general the level of maternal mortality is higher than that observed in western Europe although Zalanyi et al. (1996) found that it was falling. This could be expected with the fall of abortions because post-abortion infections as well as criminal abortions are among the main causes of maternal mortality.

The spread of certain STD increased drastically during the 90s in the ex-USSR countries. The highest level of new registered cases per 100,000 persons was observed around 1996-97, followed by a rapid drop. For example, the incidence rate in the Russian Federation was 277 per 100,000 in 1997, and 187 in 1999. Incidence rates of a close magnitude to this one were observed also in Belarus, Moldova and Ukraine. In the Baltic countries it was between 70 and 130 per 100,000. In the other central and eastern European countries the incidence of syphilis remained close to the level observed before the start of the transition. A certain increase was noted in Bulgaria and Romania. In the latter country there was a tendency of an increase all throughout the decade and in 2000 the incidence reached a level of 45 per 100,000. The Czech Republic and Hungary noted a slight increase while in Poland there was a decrease, but the incidence rate in these countries was below 10 per 100,000. In western Europe the spread of the disease is at a level of 2 per 100,000, and a similarly low level was observed in the central and eastern European countries before the start of the transition. Gromyko (1999) refers to the 30-40-fold rise in the incidence of syphilis in the ex-Soviet countries as epidemic. Similar inferences can be made where gonorrhea is considered.

Major reasons for the rise of this epidemic are the deterioration of health services within the context of overall social and economic crises as well as inadequate sexual behaviour, especially among adolescents.

Involuntary infertility (excluding voluntary childlessness) is a significant aspect of reproductive health whose importance has risen during recent years in the central and eastern European countries. Before the start of the transition infertility in central and eastern Europe was close to the average level observed in western Europe, around 6 per cent. During the 90s it has increased in many countries in the region. A specialised study conducted by Philipov et al. (1998) indicates that in western Siberia, 16.7% of the couples could not achieve a desired pregnancy for at least 12 months (i.e.

were infertile). 3.8% of the couples suffered from primary infertility (never had pregnancy before) and 12.9% from secondary infertility (has ever had a pregnancy before). The Bulgarian Association of Sterility and Reproductive Health states that infertility is between 9 and 15.3 per cent. The Reproductive and Health Surveys provide information on the basis of interviews and considers as infertile a couple who attempted a pregnancy unsuccessfully for at least two years, while other data consider a period of at least one year. The Czech RHS from 1993 found a prevalence of infertility of 12.9 among the responding women. In the Romanian RHS in 1993 the prevalence rate was 12.0 and in 1999 it was 11.1. The Ukrainian RHS gives a value of 10.6 for infertility. In all these cases the prevalence of infertility is significantly higher than the 10% prevailing in western Europe, considering the difference in the waiting time for achieving a pregnancy.

Infertility is one of the negative consequences of the spread of STDs. Another reason is the high post-abortion infection rate. The latter increased during the 90s and thus has offset the impact of the decline in abortions to infertility.

The rise in infertility accounts for some part in the decrease in fertility. The data are insufficient in order to carry out any estimates. It may be expected that the fertility level has dropped by some 5% as a result of the rise in infertility, were the latter around 10%.

## 2.6 Mortality

Reported research on mortality and morbidity in central and eastern European countries exceeds significantly the one in the field of fertility and family formation. WHO is among the leading international organisations where such research is being done and data are being collected. The WHO database "Health for all" gives diverse information, used extensively here. Articles on the topics can be found in demographic, medical, health and other journals, as well as in the region-specific "Central European Journal of Public Health". Among related books one can find useful reports in those edited by Cornia and Paniccià (2000), and Hertzman, Kelly and Bobak (1996), as well as in the study due to Cockerham (1999).

The Council of Europe recently published an extended study on mortality in Europe from 1950 to 1996 (Vallin and Meslé; Valkonen 2001). These studies give detailed information on mortality trends in European regions, including the central and eastern European countries. For this purpose the presentation here is restricted to a general outline of the major trends.

As we have shown in this report the populations in central and eastern European countries have been subject to a rapid ageing process and therefore the crude death rate will indicate trends in mortality changes biased by changes in the population age structure. We will therefore not use it. Crude rates were not used for the same reason in the study of nuptiality and fertility. Instead, we use such well-known indicators as the life expectancy at birth and the infant mortality rate, as well as the standardised death rate (SDR) estimated by WHO using the standard European population age distribution. The discussion also includes changes in age-specific mortality and causes of death.

### 2.6.1 Life expectancy at birth

The life expectancy (at birth) is a concise indicator of the overall level of mortality. Demographic research has outlined two major periods in its change during the few decades preceding the transition. The first one started after the Second World War and lasted up to the mid-60s. The life expectancy marked a rapid increase, mainly because of the steep decline in infant mortality and mortality due to contagious diseases. During the second period: after the mid-60s and up to the end of the 80s, its rise declined considerably. In many central and eastern European countries it remained about constant or even decreased for the males and increased very slowly for the females. Table 2.6.1 illustrates the second period with data for 1980 and 1990, and figure 2.6.1 gives a visual impression for the same decade. This stagnation covers significant changes in the causes of mortality. Thus while infant mortality and mortality due to contagious diseases continued to decrease, there was a rise due to heart and cerebro-vascular diseases as well as to malignant neoplasms.

The differences in life expectancies observed in eastern and western Europe during this second period are termed the "East-West life expectancy gap" (Hertzman et al. (1996) or the "life expectancy crisis" (Meslé 1996). The reasons for this crisis have been the topic of extensive scientific discussions. For example, the chapters in Hertzman *et al.* (1996) focus on reasons such as socio-economic change, quality of medical care, environmental pollution, lifestyle and behaviour differences (order follows chapters and not necessarily importance). While these reasons are generally accepted as significant, the debate as to which ones were the most significant remains open. The lack of data for a foregone period remains an unsurpassed obstacle.

The transition period brought about a new phase in the trends of life expectancy at birth. Figure 2.6.1 and table 2.6.1 give the relevant information, separately for males and females. They complement the data presented by Vallin and Meslé; Valkonen (2001) with data up to 1999.

## Table 2.6.1 – Male and female life expectancy at age zero

| | Males | | | | | | | Females | | | | | | |
|---|---|---|---|---|---|---|---|---|---|---|---|---|---|---|
| | 1980 | 1990 | 1995 | 1997 | 1998 | 1999 | 2000 | 1980 | 1990 | 1995 | 1997 | 1998 | 1999 | 2000 |
| Albania | 67..7 | 69.6 | 71.5 | 70.8 | 71.5 | 71.7 | - | 72.2 | 75.8 | 78.4 | 79.5 | 78.7 | - | - |
| Armenia | 69.9 | 68.6 | 69.7 | 71.3 | 72.5 | 72.6 | 73.5 | 76.2 | 75.4 | 76.2 | 76.8 | 77.3 | 77.2 | - |
| Belarus | 65.9 | 66.3 | 62.9 | 62.9 | 62.7 | 62.3 | - | 75.5 | 75.8 | 74.4 | 74.4 | 74.6 | 74.0 | 78.1 |
| Bulgaria | 68.4 | 68.3 | 67.4 | 67.0 | 67.4 | 68.4 | 68.5 | 73.8 | 75.0 | 74.9 | 73.8 | 74.7 | 75.1 | 75.1 |
| Croatia | 66.6 | 68.7 | 69.3 | 68.6 | 68.6 | 68.9 | 69.1 | 74.2 | 76.4 | 77.2 | 76.5 | 76.2 | 76.6 | 76.7 |
| Czech Rep. | 66.8 | 67.6 | 69.8 | 70.6 | 71.2 | 71.5 | 71.8 | 73.9 | 75.5 | 76.8 | 77.6 | 78.2 | 78.3 | 78.6 |
| Estonia | 64.1 | 64.8 | 61.9 | 64.9 | 64.6 | 65.5 | - | 74.1 | 75.0 | 74.5 | 76.1 | 75.7 | 76.4 | - |
| Macedonia | 68.3 | 70.3 | 70.0 | 70.5 | - | - | 71.2 | 72.0 | 74.5 | 74.5 | 75.1 | - | - | - |
| Georgia | 67.1 | 69.0 | 65.9 | 69.4 | 70.3 | 70.2 | 71.9 | 74.8 | 76.6 | 74.9 | 76.6 | 78.5 | 77.9 | 77.4 |
| Hungary | 65.5 | 65.2 | 65.3 | 66.4 | 66.1 | 66.4 | 67.2 | 72.7 | 73.9 | 74.7 | 75.3 | 75.3 | 75.2 | 75.8 |
| Latvia | 63.6 | 64.3 | 60.2 | 63.9 | 63.5 | 64.8 | 64.9 | 74.2 | 74.6 | 73.0 | 74.8 | 74.6 | 75.4 | 76.2 |
| Lithuania | 65.5. | 66.6 | 63.6 | 66.0 | 66.7 | 67.1 | 67.6 | 75.4 | 76.4 | 75.3 | 77.0 | 77.0 | 77.5 | 78.0 |
| Moldova | 62.6 | 65.1 | 62.0 | 63.3 | 64.2 | 63.8 | 64.0 | 69.3 | 72.0 | 69.7 | 70.6 | 71.6 | 71.4 | 71.4 |
| Poland | 66.0 | 66.6 | 67.7 | 68.5 | 68.9 | 68.9 | 69.8 | 74.4 | 75.6 | 76.5 | 77.1 | 77.4 | 77.5 | 78.1 |
| Romania | 66.6 | 66.6 | 65.5 | 65.3 | 66.3 | 67.2 | 67.8 | 71.8 | 73.1 | 73.5 | 73.4 | 73.8 | 74.2 | 74.8 |
| Russian F. | 61.5 | 63.8 | 58.3 | 61.0 | 61.4 | 60.0 | 59.2 | 73.1 | 74.4 | 71.7 | 73.0 | 73.3 | 72.5 | 72.4 |
| Slovak Rep. | 66.8 | 66.8 | 68.4 | 68.9 | 68.7 | 67.4 | 69.3 | 74.3 | 75.8 | 76.5 | 77.0 | 77.0 | 76.9 | 77.6 |
| Slovenia | 67.3 | 70.0 | 70.9 | 71.2 | 71.3 | 71.8 | - | 75.2 | 78.0 | 78.7 | 79.2 | 79.2 | 79.5 | - |
| Ukraine | 64.6 | 65.7 | 61.3 | 62.4 | 63.3 | 62.8 | 62.3 | 74.0 | 75.0 | 72.6 | 73.3 | 73.9 | 73.7 | 73.6 |
| EU average | 70.7 | 73.1 | 74.2 | 74.9 | 75.0 | - | - | 77.5 | 79.8 | 80.8 | 81.2 | 81.3 | - | - |
| WHO'CE | 66.8 | 67.1 | 67.6 | 68.0 | 68.4 | 68.6 | 69.3 | 73.8 | 75.0 | 75.7 | 76.0 | 76.3 | 76.4 | 76.9 |

Source: Health for all Database, WHO, January 2002.

## Figure 2.6.1 – Expectation of life at age 0: left males, right females

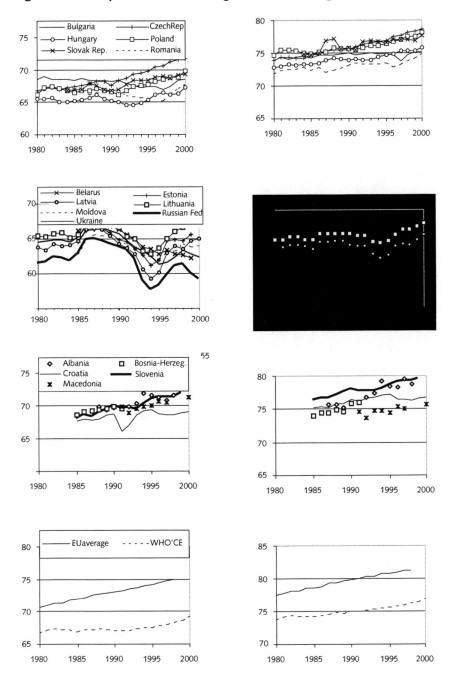

The lowest two plots on the figure represent weighted averages of the life expectancy in two European regions: the European Union with its 15 member-countries, and the central and eastern European region with 12 central European countries[5]. They exhibit a clear difference in levels and trends. The life expectancy was considerably higher in the EU countries than in WHO'CE, and it increased rapidly during the whole period from 1980 to 1998, with these countries' populations gaining nearly 5 years of additional life as compared to 1980. The life expectancy was also increasing in the WHO'CE region, but this increase was slower than the one in the EU region, and where males are considered there was no increase before 1990. The last years of the 90s reveal a rising rate of increase. The period is too short to assess whether this increase represents a new trend or is the result of fluctuations.

The first through the third plot from the top of figure 2.6.1 exhibit trends of change in separate countries: the first one for countries from central Europe, the second one for ex-USSR countries, and the third one for the ex-Yugoslav countries and their neighbour Albania. All plots are visually comparable insofar as the width of change in the life expectancy is 15 years.

Consider the first plot to the left (males). It can be seen that up to 1990 the life expectancy was around constant in all countries, except for minor fluctuations. The start of the transition initiated an immediate increase in some countries, particularly vivid for the Czech Republic and Poland. An increase was observed also in the Slovak Republic. In Hungary there was a drop in the beginning of the 90s, followed by a rapid increase. The same trend developed in Bulgaria and Romania, except that the initial drop lasted longer than in Hungary. In both countries the increase after 1996 is notable.

Where females are considered, nearly the same picture was observed up to 1990, except for a temporary increase in the Slovak Republic in 1986 and 1987. During the 90s the changes are similar to those for the males. The rise is again significant in the Czech and Slovak Republics and Poland. Notably the Hungarian males and females have a lower life expectancy than the Czech and Slovak Republics and Poland. This difference is traditional.

The third plot on figure 2.6.1 gives the trends observed in the ex-Yugoslav countries and Albania. Some of these countries have experienced the effect of wars. The analyses of the effect of these wars on mortality in general

---

[5] The central and eastern European region defined by WHO does not coincide with ours. It excludes the ex-USSR countries and comprises altogether 12 countries. We refer in the text to the WHO central and eastern European region as to the WHO'CE region. The group provided by WHO for the ex-USSR countries includes the ex-Soviet Asian republics. For this reason the grouping is not discussed here.

requires a special study and is out of the scope of this paper. For this purpose we mark trends that do not refer to years of war. We consider first the males. During the 80s (since 1985) the trends exhibit an increase. During the 90s the life expectancy for males increased altogether, and the increase in Slovenia is profound. The level of life expectancy is in general higher than in the other WHO'CE countries. Where females are considered, approximately the same picture can be observed. Slovenia is the only country from the whole region that has a life expectancy close to the EU level. The same is observed for Albania and "The former Yugoslav Republic of Macedonia" where males are considered.

The life expectancy in the ex-Soviet countries was considerably below that in the WHO'CE region. It went up from the mid-80s and then fell abruptly during the middle of the 90s. A similar but softer fluctuation was observed during the second half of the decade, except for the Baltic countries where the life expectancy rose towards the end of the 90s. Where males are considered the lowest level of life expectancy was observed in the Russian Federation. In 1994 it went down as low as 57.6 years. This is the only country among all the central and eastern European countries where the life expectancy for males has not been higher than 65 years during the period 1980-1999.

There is a debate in the literature where the explanation of these fluctuations is considered. The dominating opinion is that there is a common effect of two groups of factors. The first one is due to the anti-alcohol campaign that was carried out by the Gorbachov regime from the middle of the 80s. The decrease in alcohol consumption led to the postponement of mortality for some people. Therefore there is a "postponement" effect that is similar to the tempo and quantum effect discussed in section 2.4 above: people that would have died because of alcohol related causes of death have died later as a result of a temporary reduction of alcohol consumption. The other group of explanatory factors refers mainly to the drop in life expectancy during the transition period connected to the deteriorating health care system and the worsened conditions of life, impoverishment, malnutrition and spread of diseases that increased with the start of the transition. Both groups of factors complement each other. The fluctuations in mortality in the ex-Soviet countries have been extensively studied; see for example Meslé, Vallin and Shkolnikov (1998).

The next description relates to changes in the inter-country differences in life expectancy for males and females from 1990 to 2000, i.e. during the transition. The first plot on figure 2.6.1 shows that it increased to more than 5 years for the males in 2000, while in 1990 it was around three years. There is some increase for the females as well. The major reason for the increase in the differences seem to be the retarded growth of the expectation of life in Bulgaria and Romania compared to the Czech Republic.

The third plot does not reveal much more than the delineation of the life expectancy in Croatia where males are considered, and the relative increase in the differences between the female life expectancy in "the former Yugoslav Republic of Macedonia" and the other countries in this group. As it was noted, additional studies are necessary for the explanation of these differences.

The inter-country differences in life expectancies are particularly pronounced for the ex-USSR countries. While it was around three years for males and less than that for females in 1990, it went up to nearly eight years for males and about five years for females (excluding Moldovian females). The growth in this difference is mainly due to the rapid increase in the life expectancy during the second half of the 90s in the Baltic countries and its decrease during the same period in the other ex-USSR countries. This difference can be considered as a significant indicator of the way conditions of life are changing in these groups of ex-USSR countries.

Figure 2.6.1 and table 2.6.1 make possible a comparison of the life expectancy of males and females. Towards 1998 the difference between the two sexes for the EU region was around six years, while in the WHO'CE region it was nearly eight years. The larger difference in the WHO'CE region is due to the lower male life expectancy. Towards the end of the 90s females in the ex-Soviet European states lived longer than males by 10 to 12 years, and somewhat less in Moldova, Armenia, Georgia and the countries of central Europe (first plot). The life expectancy for the females in the WHO'CE and in the ex-USSR countries is closer to the one observed in the EU region.

In general, relative to females, males in the central and eastern European countries are in a position of considerable disadvantage where length of life is considered. The only exceptions are Armenia (difference of less than five years), the Czech Republic and Belarus (app. six years), Bulgaria, Romania, and Albania (app. seven years). Males are also significantly disadvantaged when their length of life is compared to that observed in the EU countries.

### 2.6.2 Age and mortality

The level of mortality differs significantly for different ages. We turn to a brief description of this type of structural change.

### Infant mortality

This is defined as the number of deaths of babies less than one year old to 1000 live births.

Note should be taken with the definition of a live birth that affects infant mortality. The definition used before the start of the transition in some central and eastern European countries did not conform to the one recommended by WHO. This refers to the birth of a foetus that is less than 1000 g in weight and before the completion of 28 weeks of pregnancy. In case the foetus survived for more than seven days it would be registered as a live birth; if it survived less than seven days it would be registered as a (spontaneous) abortion. The WHO definition would register such a birth as a live birth independently of the length of survival, provided the conventional signs of life at the moment of birth were present (such as breathing and pulse). At the beginning of the 90s the Baltic countries adopted the WHO definition, while the other ex-Soviet countries and Bulgaria still use the Soviet-type of definition. This difference in definitions hinders international comparisons of infant mortality. It brings about an underestimation of the real level of infant mortality. Kingkade and Sawyer (2001) suggest that after a change in the definition infant mortality could rise significantly, as high as 40-50 per cent as compared to the levels observed now in some countries using the old definition.

Table 2.6.2 and figure 2.6.2 inform about the trends in infant mortality during the last two decades. We discuss first the comparison of the EU and WHO'CE countries.

The lower right panel on figure 2.6.2 shows that infant mortality in the WHO'CE region has been decreasing all throughout the 80s and the 90s and this decrease was a little faster than the one observed in the EU region. The transition period does not differ significantly from the previous period. There is hardly any other demographic process where this inference could be equally valid.

Country-specific trends reveal significant diversity in the level and change of infant mortality. Bulgaria is the only country among those included in the upper left panel on figure 2.6.2 where the level of infant mortality remained around constant during the 90s, while in all other countries it dropped significantly. The figure shows though that towards the end of the 90s there has been some retardation in the decrease of infant mortality in some countries.

In the ex-USSR countries (upper right panel) infant mortality rose considerably immediately after the start of the transition. In the Baltic countries its rise began in 1990-1991. Probably the change in the definition discussed above has contributed significantly. Indeed, the increase in the other countries where the definition was not changed was smaller. Impoverishment and worsening of health care are among the most cited reasons for this rise. During the second half of the decade infant mortality began declining again.

The lower left panel informs about the ex-Yugoslav countries. Time series was available for only three of them. Infant mortality in Slovenia and Croatia was only slightly higher than that observed in the EU countries, while the rate in "The former Yugoslav Republic of Macedonia" noted a rapid decline.

131

The Czech Republic and Slovenia reached a level of infant mortality as low as that in the EU countries towards the end of the 90s. This level was below 10 per thousand in several other countries. It remains high as judged by European standards in Romania, Bulgaria, Moldova and the Russian Federation. A definitional change in these countries would reveal an even more unfavourable level of infant mortality.

**Table 2.6.2 – Infant mortality in the central and eastern European countries**

| | 1980 | 1990 | 1995 | 1996 | 1997 | 1998 | 1999 | 2000 |
|---|---|---|---|---|---|---|---|---|
| Albania | - | - | 23.3 | 20.2 | 15.6 | 14.7 | - | - |
| Armenia | 23.4 | 18.3 | 14.2 | 15.5 | 15.4 | 14.7 | 15.7 | 15.8 |
| Belarus | 16.6 | 12.1 | 13.5 | 12.5 | 12.6 | 11.2 | 11.4 | - |
| Bulgaria | 20.2 | 14.8 | 14.8 | 15.6 | 17.5 | 14.4 | 14.6 | 13.3 |
| Croatia | 20.6 | 10.7 | 9.0 | 8.1 | 8.2 | 8.2 | 7.8 | 7.4 |
| Czech Rep. | 16.9 | 10.8 | 7.7 | 6.1 | 5.9 | 5.2 | 4.6 | 4.1 |
| Estonia | 17.0 | 12.4 | 14.8 | 10.4 | 10.1 | 9.3 | 9.5 | - |
| Georgia | 29.4 | 15.8 | 13.1 | 17.3 | 16.1 | 14.3 | 15.3 | 12.2 |
| Hungary | 23.2 | 14.8 | 10.7 | 10.9 | 9.9 | 9.7 | 8.4 | 9.2 |
| Latvia | 15.3 | 13.7 | 18.9 | 15.9 | 15.4 | 15.0 | 11.3 | 10.4 |
| Lithuania | 16.5 | 10.2 | 12.5 | 10.1 | 10.3 | 9.3 | 8.6 | 8.6 |
| Moldova | 34.4 | 19.2 | 21.5 | 20.7 | 19.6 | 17.9 | 18.5 | 18.4 |
| Poland | 21.2 | 16.0 | 13.6 | 12.2 | 10.2 | 9.5 | 8.9 | 8.1 |
| Romania | 29.3 | 26.9 | 21.2 | 22.3 | 22.0 | 20.5 | 18.6 | 18.6 |
| Russian Fed. | 22.0 | 17.6 | 18.2 | 17.5 | 17.3 | 16.4 | 17.1 | 15.2 |
| Slovak Rep. | - | 12.0 | 11.0 | 10.2 | 8.7 | 8.7 | 8.3 | 8.6 |
| Slovenia | - | 8.3 | 5.6 | 4.8 | 5.2 | 5.2 | 4.6 | - |
| Macedonia | 54.2 | 31.6 | 22.7 | 16.4 | 15.7 | 15.3 | 14.9 | 11.8 |
| Ukraine | 16.2 | 13.0 | 14.8 | 14.5 | 14.2 | 12.9 | 13.0 | 12.0 |
| EU average | 12.4 | 7.6 | 5.6 | 5.5 | 5.2 | 5.1 | - | - |
| WHO'CE | 23.5 | 18.2 | 14.8 | 14.0 | 13.0 | 12.3 | 11.4 | 11.1 |

Source: Health for all Database, WHO, January 2002.

**Figure 2.6.2 – Infant mortality: number of deaths per 1000 live births**

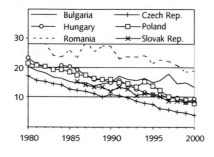

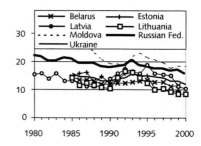

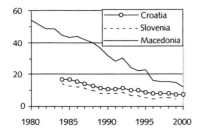 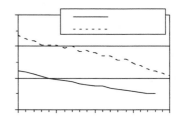

The fall in infant mortality is observed equally well for its main constituents: neonatal and post-neonatal infant mortality. The neonatal part refers to deaths that occurred during the first 28 days after the birth, and the post-neonatal part comprises the remaining period up to age 1. The WHO data reveal an approximately proportional decrease for both parts. Thus neonatal mortality decreased from 1990 to 1998 in the EU countries from 4.5 to 3.2 per thousand; in the WHO'CE countries from 10.0 to 7.2, and in the NIS countries from 10.3 in 1991 to 9.1 per thousand in 1998. Post-neonatal mortality decreased correspondingly from 3.0 to 1.7 per thousand in the EU, from 8.9 to 5.6 in the WHO'CE, and from 10.7 in 1991 to 8.6 in 1998 in the NIS countries.

The rapid fall of infant mortality to low levels achieved in most of the central and eastern European countries had an effect on the overall level of life expectancy at birth: the increase in the latter was due to a certain extent to the decrease in the former. This can be illustrated by making use of life expectancy estimated at age 1, i.e. for the persons who have survived to age 1. The WHO data for males reveal that in the EU the life expectancy at age 0 increased from 1990 to 1998 with 1.9 years, while at age 1 it increased with 1.7 years. The small difference of 0.2 years is due to the elimination of the effect of infant mortality. In the WHO'CE region these number are correspondingly 1.3 and 0.9, that is, about one third of the increase in life expectancy at birth was due to the decrease in infant mortality. In the NIS countries the situation is reversed: the life expectancy at birth dropped by 1.4 years, and without the effect of infant mortality it would have been larger, 1.8 years.

The high level of infant mortality in the central and eastern European countries (excluding the Czech Republic and Slovenia) as compared to the EU countries is a general indicator of less favourable conditions of life.

## Mortality of the adult population

During the 80s mortality of the adult population marked a significant increase in many central and eastern European countries. That is, the age-specific death rates for the age interval 20-60 increased considerably. The rise was higher for the males and less significant for the females. Carlson (1989) discusses in particular the increase in mortality among manual workers in Hungary and Carlson and Tzvetarski (1992) describe this in Bulgaria. Analogous rises were observed in the ex-USSR countries. Meslé et al. (1998) describe it in the Russian Federation.

During the middle of the 90s mortality of the adult population, and specifically of the males, increased considerably in the ex-USSR countries. However, in the other countries in the region it decreased. Mc Kee and Shkolnikov (2001) show that, relative to the EU, the countries from central Europe had a relatively higher mortality in the age interval 35-54. For the males it was some 2.5 times higher and for the females 1.6 times. In the ex-USSR countries the difference was much larger. The mortality of males aged 35-44 was 4 times higher, while the largest difference for the females was observed for the ages 25-34 where it was 2.8 higher.

Figure 2.6.3 describes age-specific mortality changes relative to 1980 in two countries: Lithuania and Hungary. In the case of Lithuanian males the figure illustrates the rapid decline in infant mortality and reveals the decline in all ages up to 20 up to 1999. The males aged between 40 and 60 had a higher mortality than in 1980 all throughout the two decades and the rise was considerable in 1995. The data for 1994, not shown on the figure, would reveal an even higher rise. Recalling that life expectancy dropped considerably around 1995, it can be inferred that this drop was primarily the effect of the rise in mortality of adult males in this country. Towards the end of the decade the excess adult mortality lessened considerably and was offset by the fall in mortality of the younger males. Hence life expectancy increased. The same inferences are valid for the other ex-USSR countries.

Where Lithuanian females are considered the inferences are similar except that the relative changes in the age-specific mortality rates were considerably softer than those observed for the males.

The mortality of the Hungarian males and females changed in a similar way. Again the mortality of the adult males was lowest in 1980 and the maximum was observed in 1995 among the years shown on the graph.

Excess mortality of adults is the main reason for the decrease in the life expectancy observed in the ex-Soviet countries in the middle of the 90s. It is also the main reason for the slowdown of the mortality decline observed in some central European countries during the 90s.

### 2.6.3 Causes of deaths

We mentioned briefly above the major changes in causes of death observed before the start of the transition. More details concerning this period can be found for example in Vallin and Meslé; Valkonen (2001), and Meslé (1996).

This sub-chapter briefly summarises changes in causes of death that dominated during the 90s. Detailed information is provided again by Vallin and Meslé; Valkonen (2001) as well as by Mc Kee and Shkolnikov (2001) and the citations therein.

There exist definitional problems where causes of death are considered. In the past the central and eastern European countries have used a specific classification of diseases that did not coincide with the international ones. Whilst the central European countrieshave adopted the recommended ninth International Classification of diseases (ICD-9), most of the ex-USSR countries have not changed to this as yet. These definitional differences hinder international comparative analyses. For this reason we only give a general description of research findings.

Table 2.6.3 gives the standardised death rates (SDR) for selected causes of death for the age interval 0-64, because it was adult mortality that had a specific unfavourable trend in the region of interest. The SDR are estimated using a standard European population age distribution, applying a direct standardisation method. Thus the effect of the age distribution is controlled, because all countries and regions are assumed to have a population with one and the same age distribution. The SDR gives the number of deaths per 100,000 persons. The table includes NIS, a region comprising all ex-Soviet countries. This region includes Asian countries as well.

The high level of deaths due to cardiovascular diseases and injuries had the greatest impact on the slowdown of mortality decline in some countries and its reverse to a rise in others. In the WHO'CE deaths due to these causes remained high, although a decline was observed during the 90s. In the NIS countries these deaths increased considerably during the period. In both regions these levels are two-three times as high or more as compared to the EU.

Malignant neoplasms are also among the leading causes of death but it did not show a significant change during the 90s (table 2.6.3). A significant rise was registered in deaths due to sexually transmitted diseases and tuberculosis in the Russian Federation and other ex-USSR countries.

Cardiovascular diseases are attributed to a number of reasons. Unhealthy diet dominates many central and eastern European populations. It is characterised by a high level of fat intake and low consumption of fruits and vegetables. Increased cardiac diseases are also due to high consumption of alcohol and smoking. Lifestyle contributes to their rise as well, and the deficiency of physical exercise in particular.

Table 2.6.3 illustrates the impact of alcohol intake and smoking on mortality. This impact is measured indirectly, insofar as alcohol and tobacco have an effect through causes of death that can appear for other reasons as well. Nevertheless the methodology developed at WHO permits a useful comparison. The data illustrate that the effect of alcohol intake and smoking is much higher for males than for the females. This is an important reason for the male over-mortality. The data also show that the level of death due to these causes has been falling during the 90s in the EU but has increased in the WHO'CE and NIS, except for the decrease in alcohol-induced deaths in the WHO'CE countries.

**Table 2.6.3 – Standardised death rates (number of deaths per 100,000 persons) for selected causes of death, ages 0-64, and all ages**

|  | EU | | Central and eastern Europe | | NIS | |
|---|---|---|---|---|---|---|
|  | 1990 | 1998 | 1990 | 1998 | 1990 | 1998 |
| **Ages 0-64** |  |  |  |  |  |  |
| Diseases of circulatory system | 64 | 49 | 148 | 132 | 166 | 206 |
| Ischeamic heart disease | 34 | 25 | 63 | 56 | 91 | 108 |
| Cerebrovascular diseases | 12 | 9 | 34 | 34 | 49 | 56 |
| Malignant neoplasms | 88 | 79 | 108 | 106 | 114 | 100 |
| External causes: injury and poison | 38 | 31 | 66 | 57 | 116 | 143 |
| Other external causes[2] | 13 | 10 | 31 | 28 | 60 | 85 |
| **All ages** |  |  |  |  |  |  |
| Selected alcohol related causes, |  |  |  |  |  |  |
| - males | 149 | 97 | 234 | 196 | 233 [1] | 247 |
| - females | 53 | 35 | 70 | 57 | 70 [1] | 74 |
| Selected smoking related causes, |  |  |  |  |  |  |
| - males | 421 | 358 | 560 | 574 | 861 [1] | 919 |
| - females | 196 | 168 | 287 | 306 | 498 [1] | 550 |
| All causes | 780 | 687 | 1134 | 1065 | 1168 | 1292 |

(1) In 1991.
(2) Does not include motor vehicle traffic accidents.
Source: Health for all Database, WHO, January 2002.

Deaths due to injuries and violence remained at high levels during the 90s. The table lists external causes such as injuries and poisons. Other related causes, not included in the table are motor vehicle traffic accidents, homicide and suicide. The table indicates a high level of external causes in the WHO'CE countries, although a moderate decrease is evident. However, in the NIS countries there was a significant increase. These causes of death are often the result of high alcohol consumption. An important reason in some of the NIS countries is also the increased difficulty in receiving urgent health care, particularly in remote rural areas.

Hence the rise in cardiovascular diseases, injuries and violence is due to factors that are linked to lifestyle. Indeed, unhealthy diet, lack of exercising, alcoholism and smoking are factors whose influence depends on the choice of the people. Information about the negative impact of these factors on health is available and widely distributed so it remains to be clarified why people willingly make the wrong choice.

Answers to such a question can be sought in two directions. The first one is the direct impact of impoverishment. It relates primarily to unhealthy diets and malnutrition. Impoverishment may cause the consumption of low quality alcohol and tobacco that is most dangerous to the health. Stress-related factors form the other major group that may provide an explanation for a preference for an unhealthy lifestyle. The difficult times of the transition bring tension and anxiety in the life of many. One way to overcome stress is by drinking and smoking. Bobak *et al.* (1998) found that lack of control over one's life is closely linked to the level of mortality among adult men.

These findings are closely related to the discussion of social anomie and social exclusion in Chapter 3. The disruption of the paternalistic state and of the social support provided by the communist regimes left people alone in their struggle for survival. It is logical to expect that the number of those that do not survive will increase.

Note should be taken that the impact of social anomie and exclusion is much lower in the central European countries. The Baltic countries do not belong to this group where mortality is considered.

**Figure 2.6.3 – Age-specific mortality in Lithuania and Hungary, relative to 1980**
*(The age-specific mortality rates in each one of the selected years were divided by those observed in 1980; the results are plotted on the figures. Hence the rates in 1980 are all equal to unity.)*

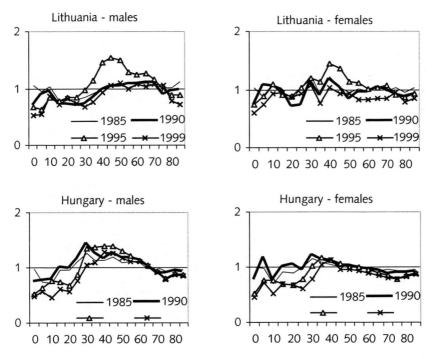

The impact of the transition on mortality is certainly not uniform over the total population within any single country. Those that suffer most from the transition are also the most affected by rising mortality. They are the people with lower income, low education, as well as the unemployed. Mc Kee and Shkolnikov provide a review of the literature. They also refer to a study (Leon 2001) which shows that the «east-west gradients in mortality from different causes and the social class gradient in the United Kingdom are strikingly similar» (p. 1054). Social exclusion seems uniform over Europe where the direction of mortality differences are considered. Where level of mortality differentials are considered, countries can be significantly different. This holds true for the central and eastern European countries too. The description in the above paragraphs may relate to a smaller part of the populations in central Europe than in NIS countries.

## 2.7 Migration[6]

With the end of Socialism, and from the point of view in particular of migration following the disappearance of the Iron Curtain, the conditions for international migration in the former Socialist countries underwent a fundamental change. Various aspects of this change are especially identifiable:

• democratisation with an increase in individual freedom, including with regard to the choice of country of residence;

• the introduction of a free market economy with growing international links, reorganisation of the international markets, and hence offers of work abroad;

• the necessary economic restructuring which is concomitant with the development of unemployment and the opening up of international labour markets;

• the continuing gap in the standard of living between western and eastern Europe, as well as between the former Socialist countries;

---

[6] Unless otherwise stated, the data used as a basis in this chapter are taken from the annual publications of the Council of Europe (Recent demographic developments in Europe). The analyses use only the data contained in the national reports (Tab. 6 in each case). According to information provided by various country representatives in the group of experts of the Council of Europe commissioned with drafting this research report, the data contained in the section relating to the overview of countries (Table 1.4 – rate of net migration) are imprecise. The migration balance shown there does not correspond to the information provided by the countries, but is calculated by using the difference between the population number on 1 January and 31 December and the balance of live births and deaths. The migration balance thus calculated does not correspond with the information contained in the national reports, which can also be interpreted as an indicator that the data are generally insecure. Only for a small number of countries do closed time series exist for the nineties. The information shows gaps, in particular for the first half of the nineties. Much better data are available for the second half of the nineties.

- the abolition of the previous strict control of migration by the Communist regimes;

- the collapse of multinational states such as the former Soviet Union and the former Yugoslavia.

After decades of political isolation these changes meant that in the nineties migration once more became a relevant topic in central and eastern Europe. Specific migration systems had previously existed in the former Socialist countries for quite some time. These were primarily characterised by restricting access to the West. Only the formerYugoslavia, Poland and Hungary permitted limited migration for work. This does not mean that no international migration took place in central and eastern Europe since the post-war period. There were some specific migration flows, the most important of which are briefly mentioned below:

1. the emigration of ethnic Germans from the Czech Republic, Poland, Romania, the Soviet Union and Yugoslavia;

2. the settlement of eastern Germans in western Germany, in particular up to 1961, and the exodus from the GDR between 1989 and 1991;

3. the emigration of the Jewish population – largely from Romania and the former Soviet Union – to Israel or the USA;

4. the work-motivated migration of Yugoslavs and their families to western Europe in the sixties;

5. the mostly illegal emigration of Poles to western Europe hoping to find work there.

Normal East-West migration was virtually impossible in the sixties, with the exception of Yugoslavia. Nevertheless, a total of between 12 and 13 million people emigrated from the former Socialist countries.

The situation was different where it concerned migration between the former Socialist countries, which was also strictly regulated, but for which there was a higher degree of freedom of movement. This migration was mostly pure migration for work, based on the issuance of time-limited residence permits. This migration system united all the former Socialist countries, including those such as Cuba, Nicaragua, Mozambique and Vietnam which are geographically very far removed from central and eastern Europe. When the border from Hungary to Austria was opened in the autumn of 1989 and the exodus of eastern Germans to the Federal Republic of Germany began this migration system collapsed and was replaced by new migration flows which were the result of fundamentally altered political and economic conditions.

## 2.7.1  Trends and situations in the individual countries

### Net migration

A view of the total migration balance for the former Socialist countries over the nineties cannot be provided since the available data are not cohesive.[7] It is therefore only possible to observe the situations in the individual countries.

These vary widely (Figure 2.7.1 and Table 2.7.1). Countries with mostly a strong negative migration balance (Azerbaijan, Estonia, Latvia, Moldova, Poland and Romania) contrast with countries with almost constant migration gains (Belarus, Croatia, the Czech Republic, Hungary, "The former Yugoslav Republic of Macedonia", the Russian Federation and the Slovak Republic). There is no uniform trend in Lithuania and Slovenia, there being years with both migration gains and with migration losses. No information can be provided for Bulgaria and Ukraine because of the lack of data. One finds particularly noticeable situations with very high migration gains in the Russian Federation and Croatia, and very high migration losses in Poland, Romania and presumably Ukraine. The country-specific analyses show that very specific causes are responsible for the differing trends.

**Table 2.7.1 – Migration balance of former Socialist countries, 1990 up to 2000 (in 1000)**

| Countries | Migration balance | Countries | Migration balance |
|---|---|---|---|
| Croatia[1] | 256 | Moldova | -  74 |
| Czech Rep. | 72 | Poland | -  125 |
| Estonia | - 40 | Romania | -  99 |
| Hungary | 79 | Russian Fed. | 3123 |
| Latvia | - 78 | Slovak Rep. | 18 |
| Lithuania | - 17 | Slovenia | 17 |

| Countries | Migration balance |
|---|---|
| Macedonia | 14 |
| Ukraine[2] | - 188 |
| Azerbaijan[3] | -  40 |
| Belarus[4] | 94 |

Source: Council of Europe, Recent demographic developments in Europe, different years
[1] not incl. 1990 – 1992, [2] 1993 – 1995, [3] not incl. 1993 and 1994, [4] not incl. 1990 and 1991

---

[7] If one adds the balances shown in Tab. 2.7.1 a positive balance of 3 million people emerges over the nineties for the countries included in the analysis. This picture is deceptive, however, since such a balance largely arises because of Russia's high migration gains caused by the remigration of ethnic Russians from the former Republics of the Soviet Union. Since data are only available for a small number of these countries, the negative migration balances are not included in the calculation.

Fig. 2.7.1 shows the trend in net migration over the nineties in the individual countries. In order to make the situations easier to compare, the migration balances have been referred to 1,000 of the population. This benchmark is not an official rough net migration figure for the transition countries, but is only intended to indicate differences and make trends visible. It is not identical with the net migration rates published by the Council of Europe in "Recent demographic developments in Europe".

It can be observed in general terms that, on the one hand, the intensity of migration decreased over the nineties. The respective negative or positive balances are no longer so pronounced in the second half of the nineties as they were in the first half. On the other hand, one can see that negative migration balances are more frequent in the first half of the nineties than in the second half.

The collapse of the Eastern Bloc initially set off stronger migration flows at the start of the nineties. This was caused to a considerable extent by the collapse of the former Soviet Union, the crisis in the former Yugoslavia and – if one includes the former GDR – an increase in intra-German east-west migration.

The situations around the former Soviet Union and the former Yugoslavia, where migration was caused by ethnic tension and armed conflicts, are particularly noticeable. The disintegration of Communist authoritarian rule throughout central and eastern Europe and the CIS countries brought to the surface suppressed nationalist feelings and movements, some erupted into civil wars or armed conflicts. Many of these armed conflicts started as civil wars in the Soviet Union and Yugoslavia prior to their dissolution and, with the establishment of independent successor states, they became international conflicts.

This is clearly proven by data for the former Soviet Union, the collapse of which caused the re-migration of the Russian population from the Republics to the Russian Federation. Up to 1994, the Russian Federation's migration gains had increased to 800,000 persons per year. After this time, a fall to values around 300,000 occurred. Accordingly, countries such as Estonia, Latvia, Lithuania or Azerbaijan experienced considerable migration losses at this time (cf. the individual national sections). These countries are now recording much more stable migration balances.

A similar trend can be observed for Romania. There too, considerable migration losses occurred, caused by the emigration of ethnic Germans in the first half of the nineties, but this is no longer the case. The emigration of the ethnic German population is also the cause of a negative migration balance in Poland during the nineties.

Countries which were not or which were less exposed to crises hardly show caesuras in their trends and generally demonstrate less intensive migration movements. These include Hungary, the Czech Republic, the Slovak Republic, Slovenia and "The former Yugoslav Republic of Macedonia".

**Figure 2.7.1 – Net migration rates for selected transformation countries, 1990 up to 2000**

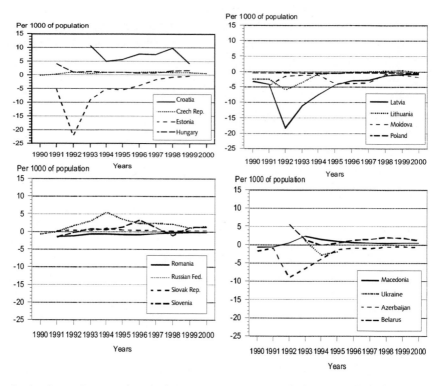

Source: Recent Demographic Developments in Europe, Council of Europe, different years, own calculations

Measured against our own calculation of the net migration rate, noticeable migration movements occur exclusively in the first half of the nineties. Compared with the population size, only Croatia showed very high migration gains. The migration gains of the Russian Federation, which were high in absolute terms, can be put into perspective in this comparison. A noticeably high number is shown only around 1994. In addition, the migration losses of the Baltic Republics and Azerbaijan between 1992 and 1995 are also noticeable. All other year-specific national results are in a framework which is typical of the migration situation in Europe.

*The situation in the transition countries*

The migration flows and their causes are so differentiated that it appears necessary to discuss the individual countries in greater detail in order to see which immigration and emigration flows are behind the net balance, and to see where the immigrants come from and where the emigrants go to.

## Croatia

Migration data for Croatia are only available from 1993 onwards. From a relative point of view, it is the country with the highest migration gains of all the transformation countries. The net migration balance is clearly positive over the entire period of observation.

Information on the migrants' territories of origin and their destination countries are only available for the second half of the nineties. Immigration and emigration are restricted to a small number of countries, whilst Bosnia-Herzegovina plays the most important role in terms of both immigration and emigration. In 1999, of some 32,000 immigrants, 22,000 were from Bosnia-Herzegovina. The other countries with large shares in immigration and emigration are the Federal Republic of Yugoslavia and Germany. We therefore largely observe short-haul migration or the return of asylum-seekers from Germany.

## Czech Republic and Slovak Republic

The migration intensity between the Czech Republic and the Slovak Republic, and to and from other countries, remained relatively low over the nineties. Both countries record migration gains during the nineties and both are linked by migration. The lion's share of immigrants to the Czech Republic comes from the Slovak Republic, and most immigrants to the Slovak Republic come from the Czech Republic. In the statistics, each country has a positive migration balance in relation to the other. This situation occurs since the migration statistics in the Czech Republic and the Slovak Republic are based only on registrations in the immigration country (no deregistration in the country of origin). In 'Population development of the Slovak Republic 1999', estimates of the actual net migration rate are provided. Based on this, in the period between 1995 and 1999 there was a negative net migration rate of roughly 2,300 persons per year.

Other important countries of origin and destination include Ukraine, Germany, the Russian Federation and, for the Slovak Republic, Austria. The shares of these countries in flows of immigration and emigration are however relatively small in comparison with the migration taking place with one another.

## Hungary

With the exception of 1991, for which there are no data regarding the migrants' countries of destination and origin, the migration intensity with other countries is also relatively low in Hungary. The migration balance is positive over the nineties, especially as a result of immigration from Romania, which clearly dominates the migration balance. A relatively large number of immigrants also come from the Federal Republic of Yugoslavia and Ukraine. Emigration from Hungary is virtually non-existent.

### Estonia, Latvia, Lithuania

The Baltic Republics are characterised, in particular in the first half of the nineties, by strong emigration losses. Only Latvia shows slight migration gains in the second half of the nineties. The lion's share of emigration is of ethnic Russians to the Russian Federation. Ukraine and Belarus are in particular the dominant emigration destinations in the first half of the nineties, in addition to the Russian Federation. In Estonia, Finland takes on increasing significance in the second half of the nineties. For Latvia and Lithuania, the United States, Israel and Germany also play a certain role as migration destinations. Immigration to the Baltic Republics has remained limited, restricted to a few hundred individuals per year. Immigrants mainly come from the Russian Federation, Belarus and Ukraine. Migration in the Baltic region is likely to be ethnically motivated. The migration flows lead to Russia and come from Russia. Migration between the Baltic Republics themselves is very rare.

### Moldova

Moldova has a constantly negative migration balance. Detailed information is only available for 1993/94 and 1999/2000. When considering the destination countries and countries of origin, there is a specific pattern for Moldova. The Russian Federation is not the only area of origin and destination for migration, emigration also takes place to a considerable degree to Israel, Germany and the United States. The immigrants' main countries of origin are Syria and Turkey, in addition to the Russian Federation and Ukraine. Moldova is one of the few exceptions among the transition countries, where migration is characterised not only by short-haul migration between neighbouring countries but also by migration flows to and from western Europe and overseas.

### Poland

Poland, too is characterised over the whole nineties by a negative migration balance, masking the relatively high emigration and immigration figures. The migration flows are completely different in nature than those in the Baltic States and in the former Soviet Union. They are largely turned towards western Europe and the USA and Canada. The vast majority of emigration takes place to Germany, followed by the USA. Equally, the lion's share of immigrants comes from these two countries. The special role played by Germany is explained by the fact that visa-free entry into Germany has been possible since 8 April 1991.

## Romania

Romania also has a negative migration balance over the entire period under observation and this was particularly large in the first half of the nineties. During this period emigration mostly took place to Germany and Hungary. In the second half of the nineties, in addition to Germany the USA, Canada and Italy took on greater significance. Seen over the nineties, most immigrants also come from Germany. Here too, shifts in proportions took effect after 1995; Moldova and Ukraine have become more significant than Germany as migrants' countries of origin.

## The Russian Federation

With the exception of 1990 the Russian Federation has always had positive migration balances due to the return of Russian populations from the former Republics of the Soviet Union. The absolute migration flows are much higher than in the other transition countries, but are only average in nature when considered in relation to the size of the population. The vast majority of immigrants come from the former Republics of the Soviet Union, in particular from Kazakhstan, Ukraine and Uzbekistan. Emigration takes place especially to Ukraine, then to Germany and to Kazakhstan. One of the five most important emigration countries in the second half of the nineties is Israel.

## Slovenia

Data are only available for Slovenia for 1991 and the second half of the nineties. Slovenia had a positive migration balance in these years except in 1991 and 1998.

## "The former Yugoslav Republic of Macedonia"

"The former Yugoslav Republic of Macedonia" has had a positive migration balance with a low migration intensity since 1992. The vast majority of immigrants come from the Balkan region, in particular from Croatia, Bosnia-Herzegovina and the Federal Republic of Yugoslavia. There is virtually no immigration (1999: 141, 2000: 172). Countries of origin for immigration also include Croatia, Bosnia-Herzegovina and the Fedral Republic of Yugoslavia.

## Ukraine

Information on migration is only available for 1994 and 1995. Pronounced migration losses are characteristic of these two years with 143,000 and 94,000 persons respectively. Large numbers of immigrants (1995: 902,000) contrast with even higher numbers of emigrants (1995: 997,000). The Russian Federation is primarily the territory of origin and destination of the immigrants and emigrants. Israel, USA and Germany also play a role as emigrants' destination areas.

## Azerbaijan

Azerbaijan epitomises the typical migration situation of a former Republic of the Soviet Union. There are relatively high migration losses which become smaller in the second half of the nineties. The emigrants primarily go to the Russian Federation, the immigrants primarily come from there. The destination and origin territories also include Georgia and Ukraine. In the second half of the nineties emigration also went to Israel, with a slight upwards trend.

## Belarus

Belarus has a positive migration balance, a situation which contrasts with the majority of the former Soviet Republics. This arises primarily from the positive balance with the Russian Federation, which is the main territory of origin and destination of the migration flows. The immigrants come exclusively from the territory of the former Soviet Union. Emigration in the first half of the nineties was almost exclusively to the Republics of the former Soviet Union. This changed in the second half of the nineties, when Israel, the USA and Germany became more significant as destination countries.

### 2.7.2 Types of migration and causes of migration flows

The nationality of the migrants, and their motives, are even more difficult to ascertain on the basis of the data than a description of the migration flows. This section will therefore not attempt to quantify the migration flows by migration types. The estimates that exist are based on the various annual reports of the OECD on trends in international migration and on data analyses carried out in the previous sections.

There is no dispute that ethnic conflicts, including wars, clear gaps in the standard of living, earning potential and the economic transformation crises have provided a wide variety of motivations for migration.

A distinction is made between three types of migration which at the same time indicate the causes of the migration flows without achieving a general overview in this context: flows of refugees and migration of ethnic minorities, temporary migration for work and permanent migration. The causes of the migration flows are to be discussed in two sections:

1. east-west migration
2. migration between the countries of central and eastern Europe.

### East-west migration

East-west migration took place even before the borders were opened, such as the immigration of ethnic German populations from eastern Europe to Germany or the emigration of Poles to the USA. The opening of the borders to western Europe could therefore only intensify east-west migration. This intensification is caused by each of the three types of migration.

On the basis of its Constitution, Germany is obliged to accept German-origin populations from abroad. The number of those immigrating for this reason had considerably increased at the start of the nineties. Emigration took place not only to Germany. Finland took ethnic Fins from the Russian Federation and the Baltic, and the population of Turkish origin migrated from Bulgaria to Turkey. These migration flows have an ethnic background – minorities returning to their countries of origin - and take place with the aim of permanent immigration in mind.

Conflicts between the countries of the former Yugoslavia and the former Soviet Union have also caused ethnic migration flows which were created as asylum-seekers moved towards western Europe. This reason for migration was particularly pronounced in the first half of the nineties. Now, the number of asylum-seekers from eastern Europe has been considerably reduced as the countries were categorised as 'safe states'. The number of return migrations of ethnic minorities is also falling since the migration potential has become smaller in this sense.

By contrast, temporary migration for work is gaining significance. This is connected with the fact that residence permits are not required if the stay is shorter than three months. Temporary migration for work is clearly focussed on east-west neighbouring countries. Thus, intensive temporary migration for work takes place between Poland and Germany, as well as between the Czech Republic, the Slovak Republic and Austria.

Other causes of migration, such as family reunification, play a subordinate role.

In comparison to east-west migration, migration flows in the other direction have remained low. Where such migration takes place, it is expressly directed at those countries which are enjoying success on the path towards economic transformation – Poland, Hungary and the Czech Republic. As a rule, the causes of this are economic in nature, and are connected with the growing together of markets. The immigrants are entrepreneurs, managers or highly-qualified workers. It should be noted that permanent immigration by western Europeans is becoming more common although the size of the foreign population in the countries of central and eastern Europe is still very low and the number of western Europeans among the foreigners is negligible. In 1997, for instance, Hungary stated a proportion of foreigners among the population of 1.4 % (144,000 persons). Of these, Germans (8,400) and Greeks (2,000) were the only western European minorities stated. Comparable situations exist in the other countries.

*Migration between the countries of central and eastern Europe*

The vast majority of migrations in central and eastern Europe are the result of so-called intra-regional migration between the countries in this region. Because of the sometimes vast differences in the migration situation, it is difficult to provide a compact overview of this. As mentioned above, two large migration centres have formed; these are the country groups of the former Soviet Union and of the former Yugoslavia. Smaller centres of intra-regional migration are Hungary-Romania and the Czech Republic-Slovak Republic, Poland-Ukraine and Bulgaria-Russia.

Ethnic migration, in other words the migration of ethnic minorities returning to their countries of origin, epitomised the picture that formed in the first half of the nineties. The goal of this migration was to settle in the accepting 'home countries'. The migration of ethnic minorities and return migration became less intensive in the second half of the nineties.

By contrast, with the reorganisation of the markets in central and eastern Europe (CEFTA – central European Trade Area) temporary migration for work has also increased between the former Socialist countries. There are no overview data here either. Examples from Hungary, the Czech Republic and Poland, the pioneers in economic transformation, prove the increasing trend.

A special group which should not remain unmentioned has arisen in central and eastern Europe in the shape of transit migrants. These come as tourists, students and business people with the goal of reaching western Europe or the USA. This type of migration is naturally concentrated on those countries which share borders with western European countries. Poland and the Czech Republic are transit countries on the way to Germany. Bulgaria, Hungary, and increasingly, the Slovak Republic, are used as stop-overs for transit migrants wishing to reach Greece or Austria. The Baltic Republics are a springboard for migration to northern Europe. Attempted transit migration is illegal and consequently only sometimes successful. "Only a fraction of the transit migrants succeed in reaching the west (principally Germany, Austria, the Nordic countries and, to a lesser extent, Switzerland and Italy); others remain in the transit country or return to their country of origin." (OECD 2000:68).

## 2.7.3 Summary

The opening of the borders in central and eastern Europe towards the west and the facilitation of migration between the former Socialist countries led initially to the presumption of a massive migration potential aimed towards western Europe. The end of the former Socialist community of states did indeed set off migration flows, but these were less intensive than anticipated, and did not lead solely to western Europe. "The political and economic changes as well as the manifestation of social and ethnic tensions which followed the opening of the borders in central and eastern Europe led to sizeable migration movements and to concerns regarding the possibility of large-scale population transfers. These concerns have not been realised." (OECD, 2000:61). Migration in central and eastern Europe is hence primarily migration between the former Socialist countries. The migration distances are thus relatively small, and restricted to neighbouring countries. East-west migration within Europe, by contrast, is relatively rare. East-west migration overseas is even less common.

Two centres of higher migration intensity have come about within eastern Europe. These are the countries of the former Soviet Union and of the former Yugoslavia, between which a lively exchange of populations took place, especially in the first half of the nineties. The migration balance, which was positive during the nineties in the Russian Federation, is the result of the remigration to the Russian Federation of ethnic Russians from the former Republics of the Soviet Union. Because of this fact, the migration intensity was generally higher in the first half of the nineties than in the second half.

The country situations are very different in individual cases. There are more countries with a negative than with a positive migration balance. Negative balances are especially typical for the countries of the former Soviet Union grouped around the Russian Federation. The data for the former Yugoslavia are insufficient, so that generalised statements are not possible. Croatia, Slovenia and "The former Yugoslav Republic of Macedonia" have positive migration balances. The immigrants come mainly from the Balkan region. This also applies to Hungary, whose migration gains are based on immigration from Romania. Poland is in an exceptional situation among the former Socialist countries. The most characteristic migration patterns are west-east or east-west migration from and to Germany and the USA.

Migration to western Europe is primarily targeted towards Germany. This can be explained by the acceptance of ethnic Germans from eastern Europe. Migration over longer distances leads first and foremost to the USA and to Israel. Migration from eastern to western Europe retains its negative reputation. The talk is about new mass migration, of a flood of immigrants from eastern Europe. This has not happened in most cases since the collapse of the "Iron Curtain". The migration potential will remain high as long as socio-economic differences and ethnic conflicts remain. However, there are doubts that it will actually occur.

In general terms, the statistical information and the state of research on the complex and very differentiated picture offered by migration in, from and to eastern and central Europe, is to be categorised as insufficient. There is an urgent need for further work on this.

# Chapter 3

## Possible explanations of demographic changes in central and eastern Europe

*Dimiter Philipov*

The descriptive analysis in the previous chapter showed that before the start of the transition the demographic trends of family formation more or less converged among the ex-socialist countries. The transition was paralleled by unprecedented demographic changes. The demographic trends developed speedily towards patterns typical for western countries. This chapter suggests possible explanations to the pre-transitional and transitional demographic trends. We first note in brief the explanations given to the demographic change in the west, then those that refer to the demographic trends of the socialist period, and finally possible explanations of the recent demographic trends.

A vast body of demographic literature discusses diverse theoretical considerations that link numerous explanatory factors to indicators of nuptiality and fertility. The theoretical background of the discussion is usually supported by empirical data from western countries. The central and eastern European countries have been rarely mentioned, possibly because of the lack of data. Therefore it remains unclear whether the available theoretical approaches have a satisfactory explanatory power in these countries, particularly for the period before the transition.

It is not the purpose of this chapter to expose a rigid theoretical discussion of an academic field. It provides highlights that could help the reader get a deeper understanding of a complex, multifaceted, matter.

### 3.1 Western Europe

The demographic changes that occurred in the western European countries since the middle of the 60s are studied by referring to diverse and numerous aspects of cultural, economic, and societal change. These aspects have a combined effect and may reinforce each other (Lesthaeghe and Surkin 1988, Pollack and Watkins 1993). For the purposes of the brief description here we consider the diverse explanations grouped into two main theoretical approaches: ideational and economic.

Ideational changes that spread after the Second World War and particularly after the mid-60s form a central line of social development, composed of important transformations in social norms and values. Enduring rise in democracy made possible the expansion of individual autonomy. Increased freedom of personal choice was accompanied by enlarging tolerance to others' choices. Individuals became less dependent on social norms when taking decisions directly relevant to their personal life.

Ideational changes of this kind are considered as a group of factors that have caused the appearance of the new demographic trends (Lesthaeghe 1983, Lesthaeghe and van de Kaa 1986, van de Kaa 1987). Consider just one example: ideational change leads to the weakening of norms related to family life so the external pressure on unmarried women to enter into marriage is released. In addition, the rise in tolerance eased the spread of non-marital unions and extra-marital childbearing.

Through work women became able to rely on their own earnings and not, as it was traditionally, rely mainly on their husband's earnings. Working women were therefore not pressed by the necessity to enter into an early marriage for the purpose of ensuring their well being. They could postpone marriage until they were able to find a suitable partner and a proper moment in their personal career. Such behaviour is in line with the release of prescriptions set by traditional norms that has resulted by ideational changes. An increasing number of women rejected entry into a marriage at all.

The higher education raised women's human capital and hence their earnings. The opportunity costs of time spent for the family and for rearing children were raised and so births decreased. The contemporary division of household labour where both partners share most of the household activities brought only partial relief to working women.

Cohabitation is a less binding partnership than marriage because of the lower risk in the formation of the union. It could be viewed as a temporary situation that can be reversed easier than a marriage. Given that changed social norms would now sanction cohabitation, the latter rose. Gradually cohabitants started having their children within the non-marital union. Thus extra-marital fertility increased. The non-marital status was found satisfactory by couples who decided to reject its later transformation into a marriage. Finally, the achieved economic independence enabled women to initiate dissolution or divorce in case the partnership was found unsatisfactory. Thus divorces increased.

There exists an abundant demographic literature on the economic aspects of family changes, known as the "new home economics". Becker (1981 and a series of other publications) provided the theoretical background. A recent general description can be found in Ermisch (1996).

The impact of education so far was considered from the point of view of level of education. In addition people spend more time in education. Prolonged education, aside of the achieved level, impedes early family formation because women are usually economically dependent on their parents whilst their education continues and family life conflicts with educational occupations where time and labour are considered. Hence they would postpone the creation of a new family until the end of education, independently of whether a higher level was achieved or not. Thus postponement of unions and births extended (Hoem 1985, Blossfeld and Huinink 1991, Blossfeld 1992 are among the first to provide empirical evidences).

## 3.2 Eastern Europe before the start of the transition

The explanations to the pre-transition trends in the central and eastern European countries are considered below. Most of them are hypotheses that are difficult to prove because of the lack of adequate data and studies due to restrictions on this kind of research set by the totalitarian regime. As a result it is impossible to make sound conclusions on the proper impact of each one of them. The hypotheses are scattered around research publications of demographers predominantly from the central and eastern European countries, and usually refer to a single country. This complicates the citation of relevant literature. Demographic research on the region as a whole was rare and usually descriptive. Interest in this part of Europe raised significantly with the start of the transition. Monnier and Rychtaříková (1991) provide a concise description of both demographic trends and causes for their appearance. Ni Brochlain (1993) gives a systematic generalisation of papers presented at a specialised session on nuptiality in central and eastern European countries at the European Population conference held in Paris in 1991.

### 3.2.1 Preservation of cultural traditions

Hajnal (1965) outlined two marriage patterns that historically prevailed in Europe, geographically delineated by an imaginary line connecting Saint-Petersburg and Trieste (referred to also as Hajnal's line). He found that to the west of this line there dominated a pattern characterised by a late entry into marriage and non-universal marriages, while to the east of the line marriages were early and nearly universal. A woman who lived to the west of the line would be expected to enter into first marriage not earlier than around age 23 on average, while a woman who lived to the east of the line would have married by that age. At age 50 some 70-80% of a female population that is to the west of the line would have ever been married, while this proportion would be over 90% for 50-year old females found to the east. The differences between the two patterns were the result of deep-rooted cultural features. While Hajnal's line referred to marriages only, it is extendable to include birth of the first child. Traditionally the first child is born within a period of 1-2 years after the marriage. This is a reason for considering the patterns of marriage described above as broader patterns of family formation.

Our previous discussion in chapter 2 indicated that these differences between the western and eastern family formation patterns could be observed during the 80s as well. One can argue that cultural traditions were indirectly preserved by the totalitarian regime. Indeed, a repressive regime would hardly tolerate ideational changes such as individual autonomy and tolerance of individual behaviour. Value shifts like the latter were namely the cause of a new demographic behaviour in the western European countries.

Hajnal's line does not coincide exactly with the political line that delineates the central and eastern European countries where totalitarian regimes prevailed. Some of these countries had a demographic regime typical for the west of the line, such as the GDR, the Baltic countries, the Czech Republic, and Poland. The descriptive analyses in the previous chapter showed that the demographic patterns in these countries during the 80s were non-traditional, i.e. like those observed in the east. Therefore the totalitarian regime had some inherent effect on the demographic behaviour that made the latter similar to the one traditionally observed to the east of Hajnal's line. The text in sub-chapter 3.2.4 below is relevant to this topic.

Ni Brochlain (1993) provides a discussion on this topic, with citations to related country-specific research.

### 3.2.2 Population policy effects

Population policies were conducted in most of the central and eastern European countries. They were centred on pronatalism. Pronatalist policies were adopted for example in Bulgaria, Hungary and Romania since the end of the 60s, Czechoslovakia, GDR and Hungary since the first half of the 70s, and the USSR since the early 80s, with the aim of reaching a temperate and steady population increase. They were carried out with instruments such as child allowances, maternity leave, preferential loans and preferential housing supply. In some countries the regime made use of this or restrictive instruments such as the ban on abortion, introduction of a bachelor's tax, restriction to the supply of modern contraceptives. David (1988) named their effect "compulsive childbearing". Keil and Andreescu (1999) discuss the Romanian case.

It is generally considered that the pronatal polices were successful in reaching their aim. Support is found for example in the trends of change in the TFR, in that the downward trends observed during the 60s turned upwards and remained around replacement level. The people accepted positively policy instruments such as child allowances and extended mother's leave and the effect of such instruments was positive. The quantitative effect of the policy has been a subject of scientific debate. Studies have established that they invoked a temperate and stable increase in fertility (see Buettner and Lutz 1989, and Monnier 1990, for the GDR; Philipov 1992, for Bulgaria; Stloukal 1998, for the Czech and Slovak Republic; Kamarás 2000 discusses the case for Hungary). Keil and Andreescu (1999) found a significant policy impact in the case of Romania. It has also been well documented that policies cause an initial, short-term, high increase in fertility that is followed by a decrease, known as a compensatory effect (numerous publications; see for example Debroy 1988). This increase has been accompanied by a fall in the mean age of order-specific childbearing and therefore it was by and large due to a tempo, rather than quantum, effect[1]. It was the quantum and not tempo that was the aim of the population policies (Philipov and Kohler 2000) and the above-mentioned publications refer to quantum effect.

### 3.2.3 Social and economic explanations

Female labour-force participation rates were very high in all central and eastern European countries. Therefore child rearing confronted high opportunity costs for working mothers. The conflicting role of women as workers and mothers was eased by the state through the development of a wide and inexpensive child-care system.

The slow growth of income in a changing society would mean a relative decrease in income. Hence direct costs of children rose. The socialist state counteracted this tendency by imposing low prices on child goods and services.

Housing is often cited as a major difficulty for young families. In some of the central and eastern European countries it remained private and the high prices were a significant obstacle. In other countries it was supplied by the state. The small living space rather than availability was the problem young people in these countries faced. Housing was a problem mainly in the urban areas and larger cities in particular.

These considerations show that social and economic conditions of life were favourable for the early formation of a family with a limited number of children. Thus arose the prevalence of the two-child family pattern.

Carlson (1992) found a link between a sociological and an economic argument. He applied the Easterlin's hypothesis to fertility in central and eastern European countries during the period after the Second World War and until 1989. The Easterlin's hypothesis (Easterlin 1987) focuses on consumption aspirations and preferences for the number of children within the framework of changing macro-social and economic environment. These aspirations and preferences are formed during adolescence in the parents' family. Later in life individuals face changed social and economic conditions of living that cause their confrontation. Individuals may therefore postpone childbearing or reject having (more) children in their wish to keep their level of consumption closer to the desirable one. Conditions of living change when young cohorts of different size than the adult ones enter the labour market and cause corresponding changes in the supply of labour on the labour market. For example, when the younger cohorts are larger in size, supply of labour increases and earnings fall relatively to rising consumer aspirations. Hence fertility would decrease. Carlson found the inverse link: shrinking young cohorts entered the labour market and therefore could not maintain the growth of a labour-intensive economy (a typical feature of planned economies). Hence fertility decreased.

### 3.2.4 Sociological explanations

The totalitarian regime restricted freedom and individual autonomy both ideologically and through the constraints set by a planned economy. The latter for example restricted the possibilities of a choice of education and of a profession, or of a place of living. The uniformity of labour income restricted alternatives for getting higher income. From the point of view of the individual life course restricted autonomy resulted in a constricted set of alternatives for decision making. In a constrained set of alternatives of the life course it becomes more probable to select those that refer to family formation. Hence mean ages were low and universality of marriages and first births could be maintained. This fundamental inference, referred to as the "restricted choice hypothesis", is helpful for the better understanding of other hypotheses.

The shrinkage of possibilities for decision making for one's own life, reduced possibilities for higher income or for a choice of a profession affected men more than it did women, hence male autonomy decreased more than female autonomy.

Another hypothesis refers to the rising value of the family. Family was considered in reality, not only ideologically, as the "basic cell of society". The social family policy was rich and assured many advantages to the family as compared to single individuals. Hence the choice for family formation was by itself a competing alternative for decisions related to the life course.

The constrained set of alternatives has a different side, namely, that choices are more certain than those made out of a richer set. In addition, the socialist regime contributed a high certainty to a number of crucial life events, for example through the assurance of education and the full employment policy. Given a relatively high certainty of the future life, individuals could take the risk for irreversible,or difficult to reverse, events such as marriage and birth. This "high certainty" hypothesis has been the basis for conclusions that the socialist regime has created conditions that were favourable for family formation. In fact certainty increased because the set of decision-taking alternatives decreased, and thus the number of competitive options to family formation decreased. High certainty was the result of restricted choice. Better conditions for family formation existed as a result of decreased individual freedoms. Mozny and Rabušic (1992) provide a discussion on this topic.

## 3.3 Eastern Europe during the transition

The new conditions of life in the central and eastern European countries during the 90s swept away the pre-transition demographic trends and engendered new, entirely different ones. They invalidated most of the justifications that were relevant to the trends observed during the pre-transition period and therefore it is natural to search for a radical change in the explanations.

Consider first the preservation of cultural traditions as a feature of the totalitarian regime. The appearance of new trends such as the rise in cohabitation, extra-marital births and divorce rates, contradicts historically set cultural norms throughout the entire region. These particular trends are the result therefore of a new behaviour. Other trends, such as the fall in the levels of marriage and childbearing and the rise in their mean ages are historically untypical for the countries lying to the east of Hajnal's line. Therefore the contemporary demographic trends in these countries have hardly any basis in traditional norms.

Where the central and eastern European countries situated to the west of Hajnal's line are considered, there remains the question as to whether the latter trends represent a return to traditional behaviour or are the result of a new behaviour. One is tempted to conclude that the division of trends like the one above is artificial and that all trends are part of a whole; therefore the contemporary demographic behaviour is the result of new factors that have arisen with the new conditions of life. Another view could rest on the assumption that the population is heterogeneous, in that some people form demographic decisions influenced by the new conditions while others may pertain to the traditional norms. There is insufficient research that could help disentangle the two alternatives.

Consider the population policy. It collapsed with the start of the transition. The state-based care for children crashed: child and other allowances became minimal because of high inflation, and although maternity leave remained guaranteed it was not as attractive as in the past. In addition, the employers became reluctant to employ pregnant women because of maternity leave and women were thus forced to minimise their absence from work. Kindergartens became more expensive. The introduction of a market economy ruled out the effectiveness of measures such as reduced interest rates or preferential housing supply. (A detailed discussion can be found in: United Nations 1999, 2000.)

Equally inapplicable are the social and economic explanations, as they were formulated with respect to the pre-transition trends. The crash of state-based subsidies for the child-care system made the latter unable to keep low the opportunity costs of children. Hence women faced sharply the conflict between motherhood and work. Income diversified considerably without any constraints. Guaranteed labour disappeared and unemployment rose significantly. Housing turned into a significant problem after the liberation of prices, particularly for young families. A simple extension of the trends used by Carlson (1992) beyond 1989 indicates that his conclusions do not apply to the transition period. This could be expected with the abolition of the planned economy.

The sociological argumentation was characteristic for a totalitarian regime only. The collapse of the latter removed the restrictions to freedom and individual autonomy. Thus the "restricted choice" hypothesis lost its validity. The transition to a democratic society is not a change that appears overnight, it is now known to be a slow process that takes years and decades until the central and eastern European societies achieve freedom and equality such as those achieved in the west. This topic is debated again below.

Analogously to the situation in western Europe, contemporary demographic literature discusses two main groups of explanations that are relevant to the demographic changes in the central and eastern European countries. One is based on the impact of social and economic factors, and the other on ideational change. We delineate separately an additional group of factors, connected to specifics of the societal transition, such as disorderliness and social anomie.

### 3.3.1 The impact of social and economic factors

The rise in unemployment and impoverishment and the overall fall in income are the popular principal factors that caused the abrupt drop in nuptiality and fertility, particularly in presentations in the mass media. Many demographers emphasise their prevalence over other factors. Cornia and Paniccià 1995a and 1995b, Rychtaříková 1999, Ellman 2000, are examples where the region is considered; United Nations (1999 and 2000) display a more temperate stance. The sudden drop in income puts people in a position to think more of their own survival than of creating a family or having a baby. For some people, particularly in the better-off countries, income did not fall drastically but they feel the burden of relative deprivation, in that income is insufficient to ensure satisfying standard needs. In either case people will postpone or reject irreversible events such as marriage and births.

The fall in income resulted in a sudden rise in the direct costs of children, reinforced by the ending of subsidies for child goods. Opportunity costs of children changed in diverse directions. These costs decreased for unemployed females where the husband's income suffices for the support of the family. Such a situation is rare. A more frequent situation is where the husband's income dropped far below the level necessary for the maintenance of the family well-being. Given therefore a low level of family income, any additional income or benefit that the woman could bring in the family, however small, would be of importance. From this point of view her economic time would be valuable and could bring about a relative significant rise in the opportunity costs of children, although her income may have significantly decreased. The "new home economics" approach (Becker 1991) argues that rising costs of children bring about a decrease in natality, and that is what was observed.

The transition to a market economy caused a rise in the economic uncertainty of the individuals and their families. Employed workers may fear losing their jobs. Unemployed ones may fear long-term unemployment. Those with higher income may feel uncertain of it lasting. Considerations like these are typical for a market economy. In addition, the new economic situation in the central and eastern European countries is under development. The markets are still immature and the legal and the institutional systems are rapidly changing. In general, the process of transition makes economic uncertainty stronger than in an established market economy. Ranjan (1999) discusses the demographic impact of economic uncertainty in the central and eastern European countries.

The emergence of a market economy made it possible for people with initiative to start their own business. Others preferred to leave the secure state jobs and move to better paid but less secure private ones. Such people may increase their income and attribute a significant rise in the value of their time. Reallocating time to family matters became expensive. Hence such people would postpone or refuse entering into marriage or having a baby. Time allocation considerations are in line with the "new home economics" as debated for western countries with established market economies.

The transition brought about a substantial rise in the opportunities for acquiring a higher and more desirable education. This is a significant social change. On the one hand, the process of education was prolonged; on the other, more people entered higher levels of education. It is known from demographic theory that people tend to postpone family formation until the completion of education (Blossfeld and Huinink 1991). Billari and Philipov (2002) proved its validity for central and eastern European countries. Thus mean ages of marriage and childbearing rose.

The emergence of a housing market made housing available but the high prices made it unreachable. Housing might have an even greater effect on marriages and births than before the start of the transition. Unfortunately no sound inferences on this topic are at hand, although it looks very likely.

Economies of scale of the family can bring about some relaxation in the income situation, for example by sharing expenses for the maintenance of one dwelling. One would expect it could stimulate early marriages. This has not been observed because this factor, when combined with those listed above, and particularly insecurity in the future, could stimulate a different alternative: extra-marital unions that are not binding as marriages are. Moreover the restrictions to non-marital cohabitation imposed by the past repressive regime not longer exist. No data are available to prove or disprove this conjecture.

The discussion on the validity of the socio-economic approach is based on inferences done at the macro level, while it needs a rigid support on the micro level. Indeed, the theories considered above are microeconomic and their implementation should be carried out at the micro level. So far only two studies exist at the micro level. One is by Kohler and Kohler (2001) who find that uncertainty does not have the expected impact on fertility. They consider as a dependent variable the births that have appeared between two consecutive rounds of the Russian Longitudinal Monitoring Survey (RLMS). Their inference is expected given that nearly all women would like to have at least one child. The question is whether families would like to have a second or higher order births. The small number of observations does not allow for a detailed discussion. The second available study is by Philipov and Shkolnikov (2001). They use the RLMS too and find that intentions for second or higher-order births are linked to the exchange of help with friends or relatives. This topic is considered in details below in this section. Micro-level research is hindered by the unavailability of adequate data.

The socio-economic approach fails to explain why similar demographic trends developed in countries with dissimilar social and economic situations. The central European countries are doing considerably better economically and impoverishment is not observed at the level it appears in the eastern European countries. Analogous arguments can be raised with respect to other aspects of social and economic development beside impoverishment.

### 3.3.2 Ideational changes of the western European type

Ideational changes, referred to as the basis of the second demographic transition, were discussed as factors of primary importance to the demo-graphic changes observed in western Europe since the middle of the 60s. One can reason that the collapse of the totalitarian regime has opened the way for analogous changes in the central and eastern European countries. Hence the newly observed demographic trends can be seen as results of factors similar to those that emerged in western Europe around three decades earlier. The totalitarian regime has only slowed down this demographic development; or inversely, the transition has only stimulated them. This topic is debated among demographers from central and eastern European countries. Vishnevskii (1999) and Zakharov and Ivanova (1996) argue that sources of the demographic upturn in Russia could be found in changes before the start of the transition, while Elizarov (1999) reflects on the primacy of economic factors. Rabušic (1996) supports the significance of ideational changes in the Czech Republic and Rychtaříková (2000) argues on the presence of demographic crisis. A monograph edited by Kotowska (1999) includes debates of Polish demographers on demographic changes during the 90s in the light of the second demographic transition.

Demographers support their preference towards the role of ideational changes with the observation that the new demographic trends are about the same as those observed earlier in western Europe, except that the rate of change is higher. It seems natural to suppose that similar trends would be the outcome of similar reasons. In addition some ideational changes, such as secularisation, rise in female labour force participation rates and increase in female autonomy were observed in the central and eastern European countries before the start of the transition. The expansion of freedom and individual autonomy achieved with the overthrow of the suppressive totalitarian regime just fill the picture.

Where ideational changes before the transition are considered, it is necessary to explain how they could emerge and diffuse through the fearful restrictions of the political regime. It can be argued that some value changes were imposed by the socialist ideology. For example, secularisation was nearly forced in some of the countries. Female autonomy was a direct outcome of the large-scale women's inclusion in the labour force and therefore relates much more to economic autonomy than to the new gender roles of equal positions of men and women in society and in the family. Some social norms did change in a different way. For example changes in sexual behaviour were similar to those in western Europe.

Where ideational changes after the start of the transition are considered, one may enquire how new trends could emerge and diffuse in society virtually immediately, and also immediately influence the demographic behaviour.

### 3.3.3 The impact of disorderliness and social anomie

The application of the socio-economic and the ideational approaches provide a basis for the explanation of recent demographic trends. While being necessary for such explanations they are insufficient, as has been shown with the last paragraphs of the corresponding subsections above. Their insufficiency is an outcome of a sketchy understanding of the societal transformation in the central and eastern European countries.

In the beginning of the 90s the central and eastern European countries started a conversion from a socialist, repressive, regime to a democratic society. Conversion was observed in all spheres of society, including an entire change of state institutions and the legal system and laws. Such a change consisted in an abolition of the old institutions and laws and the establishment of new ones. The new ones needed a period of adjustment. Laws had to be amended and institutions reorganised. In between the abolition of the old institutional system and the appearance of a new sound one there was a period of adjustment when laws and institutions were ineffective. The state was weak, the law was eroded. A state of *disorderliness* in society arose (Arms *et al.*, 1995; Sztompka 1996). Extensive corruption appeared. Disbelief in such institutions as the judicial system, police and government rose to high levels. The same was true for new private and privatised institutions and particularly banks. People were forced sometimes to take care of their well being without full reliance on institutions. In some of the countries the former state paternalism was suddenly replaced by a "wild" market society, where families and individuals should rely on themselves without much hope for support by state institutions.

A drastic transformation of society like this would disrupt diverse social norms. This led to the weakening of the normative self-regulation of society. Corruption, theft and cheating rose to unprecedented levels. In addition, individuals faced enormous divergence in values among their friends and relatives. Differences in economic status and political preferences put an end to long-lasting personal ties but may have enforced new ones. Social ties and social networks transformed substantially. Such a societal status is known as the state of *anomie*, i.e. lack of rules. Its study is connected to the Durkheimian fundaments in sociology. Social anomie during the transition has been widely studied in the transition countries; for example see Arms *et al.* (1995), Sztompka (1996), Rabušic and Mareš (1996), Genov (1998), Spéder *et al.* (1999), Andorka (1999).

Social norms and values provide guidance or an orientation for individuals' choices. Anomie destroys the possibilities for orientation and therefore brings about an increase in uncertainty. Uncertainty encompasses not only the economic aspects as discussed above, but also the overall well being of the individual. Disorderliness as discussed above has a similar impact on the individual in that it reinforces uncertainty.

Anomie and disorderliness mean that individuals confront a situation where they have to take decisions for their life on their own, without reliance on society or state. Thus "individual autonomy" arose. This type of individual autonomy was not the result of an evolutionary achievement of freedom of choice that took place in democratic societies. Its appearance was enforced by the societal transformation.

When confronted with a sudden rise in anomie and disorderliness and the resulting uncertainty, people will tend to postpone and reject crucial irreversible events, such as births and marriage, or will make them reversible where possible, so will prefer cohabitation to marriage. The lack of social norms does not prevent the spread of extra-marital cohabitation and extra-marital births. Therefore anomie and disorderliness provoke a fall in nuptiality and fertility, and a rise in extra-marital unions. Thus the demographic picture of the 90s is accomplished.

### 3.3.4 Assessment of the explanations

The above explanations do not necessarily exclude each other. For example, rising education can be the result of a social change or of an ideational change, but it is also a way of escaping uncertainty through the acquirement of higher human capital. Cohabitation could be the result of softening of norms and increased individual autonomy, or a way to use economies of scale when living with a partner, or as the outcome of the neglect of existing norms characteristic for a state of social anomie. In general, the demographic trends described in the previous chapter could be the result either of the economic pressure on the individuals, or of the ideational changes, or of the most recent institutional changes, or their combinations. The macro-level demographic data stemming from vital statistics along with the macro-level social and economic data do not provide sufficient information for the prefer-.ence of a specific set of explanations. The information is insufficient also with respect to checking hypotheses regarding combinations of the explanations, such as supposing the validity of one set for a specific sub-population, or supposing the validity of more than one set for one and the same population.

Yet the literature and the overall political, social, and economic development in cultural-specific societies allow making some general reflections. Philipov (2001) provides a discussion, considering an abstract geographical line that unites Saint-Petersburg with Dubrovnik. The central and eastern European countries situated to the west of the line experience a quicker transition in all spheres of life: political, social, and economic, with the Baltic countries having joined the group recently. In these countries impoverishment is not as widespread, income is higher, educational enrolment increased faster - to mention but a few economic and social differences. Ideational changes in these countries are faster (Philipov 2001 found differences in the value systems using the WVS.) Therefore it may be concluded that the impact of social and economic factors on demographic behaviour is more pronounced than ideational changes in the countries situated to the east of the line. In the countries situated to the west it is ideational changes that matter more than the economic factors do. Care should be taken that these reflections represent more a hypothesis than final findings. Care should also be taken with the interpretation of the line. Huntington (1998) has considered an approximate line in a political treatise that does not necessarily connect with demographic behaviour.

# Chapter 4

## Population change

*Jürgen Dorbritz*

### 4.1 The population size

A total of 3.7 billion people live in the reforming states of eastern and central Europe that are included in the study. The size of the population has increased by more than 60 million in comparison with 1960. The population sizes and trends of these countries differ massively (Tab. 4. 1, Figure 4.1). The similar positive trends up to 1990 have changed now into different situations.

Table 4.1 – Population on 1 January, 1960 up to 2001 or latest available year (in thousands)

| Countries | Years | | | | | | |
|---|---|---|---|---|---|---|---|
| | 1960 | 1970 | 1980 | 1990 | 1995 | 2000 | 2001 |
| Albania | ... | 2110.6 | 2645.2 | 3286.5 | 3248.8 | 3401.2 | ... |
| Bulgaria** | 7829.2 | 8464.3 | 8846.4 | 8767.3 | 8427.4 | 8190.9 | 8149.5 |
| Croatia** | 4127.4 | 4403.4 | 4598.1 | 4687.5 | 4776.5 | 4567.5 | 4381.0 |
| Czech Rep. | 9637.8 | 9789.5 | 10272.6 | 10362.1 | 10333.2 | 10278.1 | 10266.5 |
| Estonia | 1209.1 | 1351.6 | 1472.2 | 1571.6 | 1491.6 | 1371.8 | 1366.7 |
| Georgia | 4129.2 | 4686.4 | 5041.0 | 5421.7 | 4499.5 | 4071.3 | 3916.4 |
| Former GDR** | 17285.9 | 17074.5 | 16740.3 | 16433.8 | 15531.4 | 15217.3 | ... |
| Hungary** | 9961.0 | 10322.1 | 10709.5 | 10374.8 | 10245.7 | 10043.2 | 10005.2 |
| Latvia | 2104.1 | 2351.9 | 2508.8 | 2667.9 | 2499.3 | 2379.9 | 2366.1 |
| Lithuania | 2755.6 | 3118.9 | 3404.2 | 3708.3 | 3717.7 | 3698.5 | 3692.6 |
| Moldova | 2967.7 | 3568.9 | 3987.2 | 4361.6 | 4347.9 | 4281.5 | 4271.9 |
| Poland | 29479.9 | 32670.6 | 35413.4 | 38038.4 | 38580.6 | 38653.6 | 38644.2 |
| Romania | 18319.2 | 20139.6 | 22132.7 | 23211.4 | 22712.4 | 22455.5 | 22430.5 |
| Russian Fed. | 119045.8 | 129941.1 | 138126.6 | 147662.1 | 147938.5 | 145559.2 | 144819.1 |
| Slovak Rep. | 3969.7 | 4536.6 | 4963.3 | 5287.7 | 5356.2 | 5398.7 | 5402.5 |
| Slovenia** | 1580.5 | 1719.9 | 1893.1 | 1996.4 | 1989.5 | 1987.8 | 1990.1 |
| Macedonia | 1384.5 | 1616.8 | 1878.1 | 2121.4 | 1957.3 | 2021.6 | 2031.1 |
| Ukraine | 42468.6 | 47118.2 | 49952.5 | 51838.5 | 51473.7 | 49456.1 | 49036.5 |
| Armenia** | 1829.5 | 2488.9 | 3073.9 | 3514.9 | 3753.5 | 3803.4 | 3802.4 |
| Azerbaijan | 3815.7 | 5117.1 | 6114.3 | 7131.9 | 7643.5 | 8016.2 | 8081.0 |
| Belarus | 8147.4 | 8992.2 | 9591.8 | 10188.9 | 10210.4 | 10019.5 | 9990.4 |
| Bosnia and Herzegovina | 3212.3 | 3685.7 | 4136.9 | 4499.2 | ... | ... | ... |
| F.R. Yugoslavia | 8006.4 | 8877.9 | 9792.7 | 10343.8 | 10535.3 | 10637.4 | 10645.3 |

Council of Europe, Recent demographic developments in Europe, 2001
** De facto population

Figure 4.1 provides an overview of the trends since 1960. Whilst in the sixties, seventies and eighties, considerable increases took place in the population numbers in all countries of central and eastern Europe, with the exception of the former GDR, a diverging development took place in the nineties. Some countries had undergone considerable growth up until the start of the transformation process. The population had almost doubled in Armenia and Azerbaijan. Increases of approx. 50 % had been recorded in "The former Yugoslav Republic of Macedonia" and Moldova. The populations of Bosnia and Herzegovina, Lithuania, the Slovak Republic and the Federal Republic of Yugoslavia had increased by roughly one-third. Relatively small increases were recorded in Hungary (+ 4.1 %) and the Czech Republic (+ 7.5 %). The former GDR was the only country which experienced a negative trend (- 3.6 %) between 1960 and 1990.

**Figure 4.1 – Trends in population sizes between 1960 and 2000 (1960 = 100 %)**

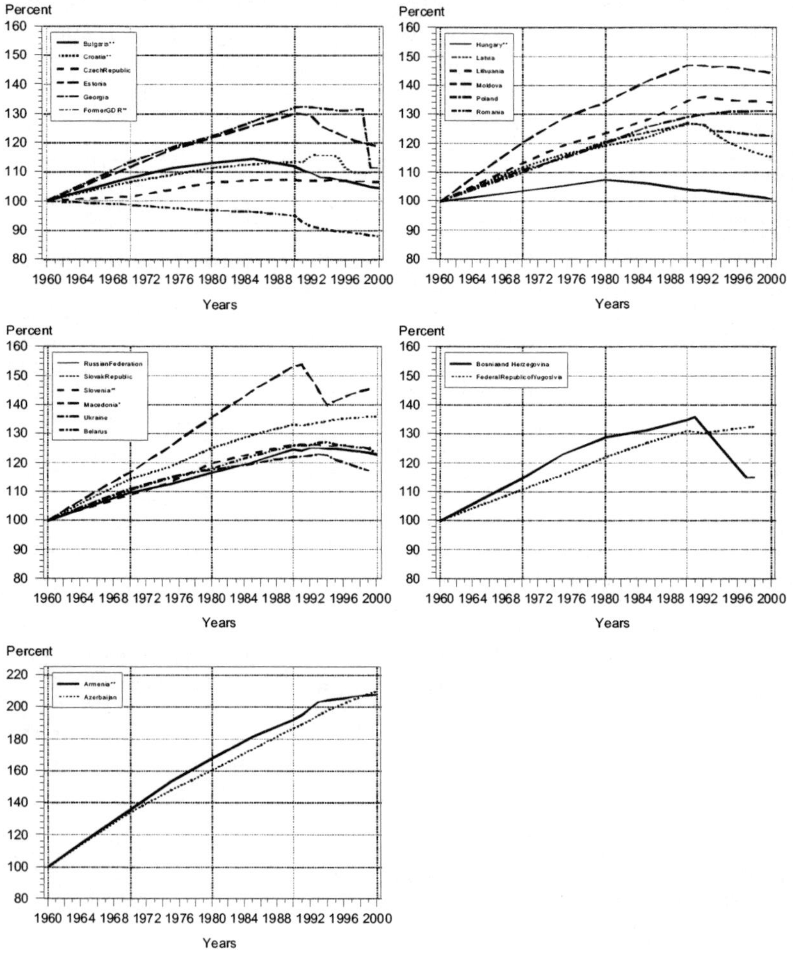

In the nineties the population numbers fell (Fig. 4.1 and 4.2) with a few exceptions (Albania, Poland, the Slovak Republic, Armenia, Azerbaijan and the Federal Republic of Yugoslavia). If one compares figures from 1990 up to 2001, one finds that these are disproportionate in Georgia, Latvia, Estonia , Bulgaria and eastern Germany. Noticeably positive population balances were registered in Azerbaijan (+ 11.5 %) and Armenia (+ 8.1 %).

Obvious changes, both positive and negative, occurred primarily at the start of the nineties. In general, population growth rates were higher in the seventies and eighties than in the nineties. In some of the former Socialist countries the nineties started with more considerable variations as to their population number. Some of the countries with obvious drops in population at the beginning of the nineties were Albania, Bulgaria, Croatia, Estonia, eastern Germany, Latvia and Romania. Stronger growth was registered in "The former Yugoslav Republic of Macedonia", Armenia and Azerbaijan. Slight upward or downward trends were typical in the majority of the other countries.

**Figure 4.2 – Population growth rate, 1990 up to 2000/2001**

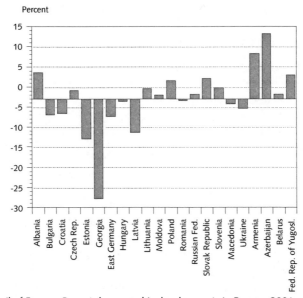

Source: Council of Europe, Recent demographic developments in Europe, 2001

Table 4.2 provides an overview of the actual situation with the growth rates in 2000 or the latest available year. The countries are sub-divided into those with a positive growth rate and those with a negative growth rate. Declines in population are typical of the majority of countries at the end of the nineties. An upward trend is noticeable in only seven countries. Relatively clear growth, at more than 0.8 %, is now only registered in Croatia, Albania and Azerbaijan.

**Table 4.2 – Population growth rates in the countries of central and eastern Europe in 2000 or latest available year (in %)**

| Positive growth rate | Negative growth rate |
| --- | --- |
| Albania (0.82) | Armenia (-0.03) |
| Azerbaijan (0.81) | Bulgaria (0.51 |
| Croatia (0.88) | Czech Republic (-0.11) |
| Slovak Republic (0.07) | Estonia (-0.37) |
| Slovenia (0.12) | Georgia (-3.88) |
| Macedonia(0.02) | Former GDR (-0.47) |
| Federal Republic of Yugoslavia (0.07) | Hungary (-0.38) |
| | Latvia (-0.58) |
| | Lithuania (-0.16) |
| | Moldova (-0.22) |
| | Poland (-0.02) |
| | Romania (-0.11) |
| | Russian Federation (-0.52) |
| | Ukraine (-0.85) |
| | Belarus (-0.29 |

Source: Council of Europe, Recent demographic developments in Europe, 2001

## 4.2 Natural increase and net migration

It is difficult to ascertain the causes of the change in population size, in inter-play between the natural population balance and net migration. The group of experts repeatedly emphasised that net migration, especially, is highly uncertain. For this reason, the figures below only show fertility and mortality for the individual countries.

The changes in population numbers in the countries of central and eastern Europe have been caused since the sixties by the relationship between births and deaths in particular (figure 4.3). In the majority of countries, the migration balance has revolved around zero from 1960 up to the present day. One exception is the years around 1990. The variations in the population growth rates are caused by fluctuations in immigration and emigration figures. The disintegration of the former Socialist states, linked to the opening of the borders, led to short-term negative net migration in a large number of countries. However, some states, in particular those in the former Soviet Union and the former Yugoslavia also had positive net migration for a time. These countries include Albania, Croatia, Slovenia, "The former Yugoslav Republic of Macedonia", Ukraine, Armenia and Belarus. The disintegration of these countries also led to considerable flows of migrants for a restricted time.

The change in the population number has however been influenced in a more sustained manner by the natural population balance. The sometimes considerable population growth in the former Socialist countries in the sixties, seventies and eighties occurred because of high birth surpluses. The only exceptions are east Germany and Hungary. In east Germany, a negative natural population balance had already occurred in the first half of the seventies, which was followed in the eighties by slightly positive balances. A surplus of deaths has been registered in Hungary since the start of the eighties. In almost all other countries there was a positive natural population balance until the end of the eighties. These surpluses had however already reduced in the eighties and reversed in most cases in the nineties. Only Albania, Armenia and Azerbaijan have a considerable birth surplus. In some of the other countries the figures almost balanced out in the nineties. This group of countries is formed by Croatia, Georgia, Poland, the Slovak Republic and Slovenia. In the other group of countries, the natural population balances reversed and then became negative. In the nineties a surplus of deaths is characteristic of Bulgaria, the Czech Republic, eastern Germany, Estonia, Hungary, Latvia, Lithuania, Moldova, Romania, the Russian Federation, Ukraine and Belarus. Considerable falls in the birth rates were typical of the former Socialist countries in the nineties. In many countries these have led to a surplus of deaths as against births, and hence to a fall in population numbers, if the net migration is balanced.

## Figure 4.3 – Crude births and deaths rates, 1960-2001

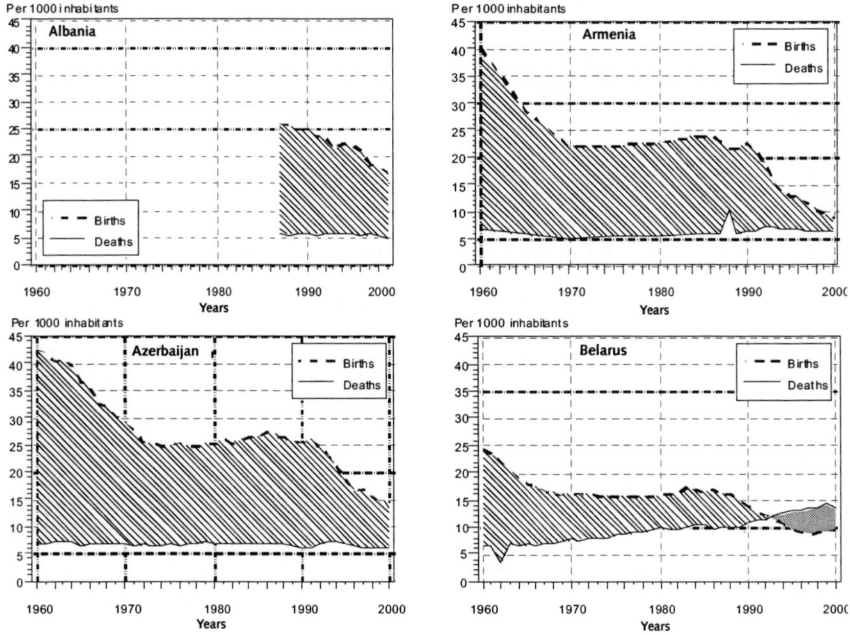

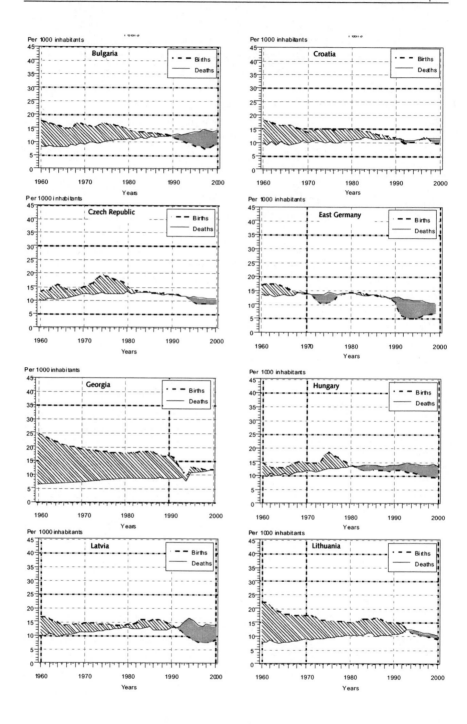

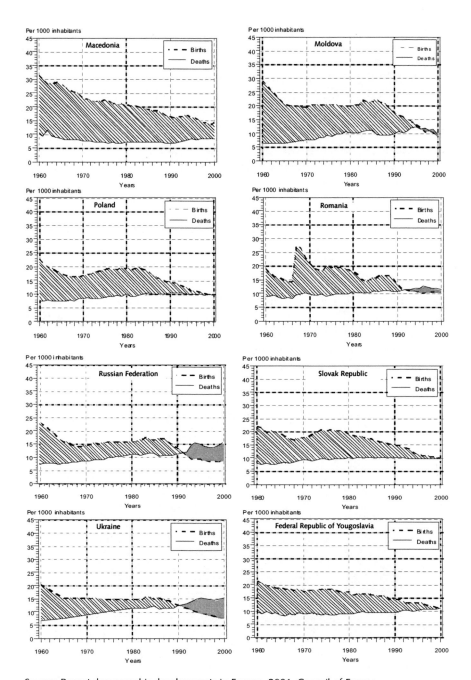

Source: Recent demographic developments in Europe, 2001, Council of Europe

## 4.3 Age structure of the population

The high birth level, in comparison to the western welfare states – the considerable fall in the birth rate in western Europe in the time of "Europe's second demographic transition" was much less significant in the former Socialist countries – and a lower average life expectancy meant that the ageing of the population in central and eastern Europe was much less advanced.

The differences in the age structure prior to the start of the social transformation process will be described, taking as an example the 1990 age structures in Austria and Hungary (figure 4.4). The different shares taken up by the individual age groups among the population are obvious. The higher birth rate in Hungary led to larger shares being accounted for by children and juveniles. The larger shares accounted for by 25- to 30-year-olds shows that the age structure in Austria was characterised by in-migration, in contrast to that of Hungary. Furthermore, the higher life expectancy led to larger shares of the over-sixties.

An overview of the age structure at the end of the nineties is contained in fig. 4.5. According to this, at the end of the nineties, too, various types of population can be identified, as revealed by the interplay between the birth rate and mortality in the course of the demographic transition. Here, it is possible to distinguish between four types of age structure among the population:

**Figure 4.4 – Population by gender and age in Austria and Hungary, 1990**

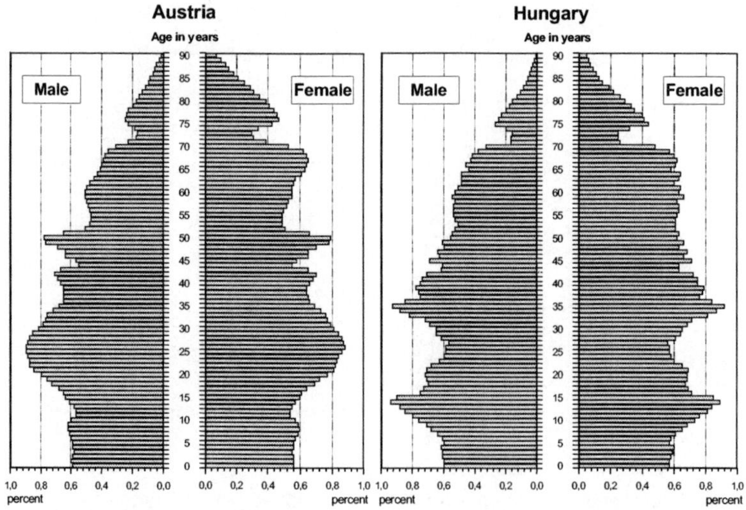

Source: Statistiches Handbuch für die Republik Österreich 1991

Source: Hungarian Statistical Yearbook 1990

1. The pretransitional type arising on the basis of a stable balance of high mortality and a high birth rate. The result is a population that is stationary, but very young. Such an age structure is typical of none of the former Socialist countries.

2. A second type of population structure arises as a result of a mortality-led juvenation of the population in the first phase of the demographic transition. Through a fall in child and juvenile mortality the population number grows because of juvenation from below. The age structure of the population looks like a pyramid. This type is now only represented by a small number of countries, in particular by Albania and Azerbaijan, and to a certain degree also by Armenia and Georgia.

3. As the fall in the birth rate starts, what we see is demographic ageing which is fertility-led. Initially, the population grows more slowly, and then starts to shrink. The age structure of the population takes on the shape of a bell. This bell shape is also relatively rare. The age structures of the populations in Croatia, "the former Yugoslav Republic of Macedonia" and the Federal Republic of Yugoslavia have taken on this shape.

4. The fourth age structure shape is created when a population reaches and exceeds a life expectancy of roughly 70 years, whilst demonstrating a sustained low birth rate. Fertility- and mortality-led ageing and a shrinking of the population take place in such populations. The pyramid shape becomes increasingly narrow from below in such cases. This type of age structure is only pronounced in eastern Germany. In all other countries, there are indications of a transition to the pyramid shape becoming narrower from below.

One of the most noticeable characteristics of the demographic change in central and eastern Europe is the drop in the birth rate, which has already made its mark on in the age structure of the population. Since, however, with the exception of eastern Germany, movement in this variable only became pronounced in the second half of the nineties, the impact on the age structure is only now becoming apparent.

Figure 4.5 – Age structure of the population, around 2000 (in %, 5-year age groups)

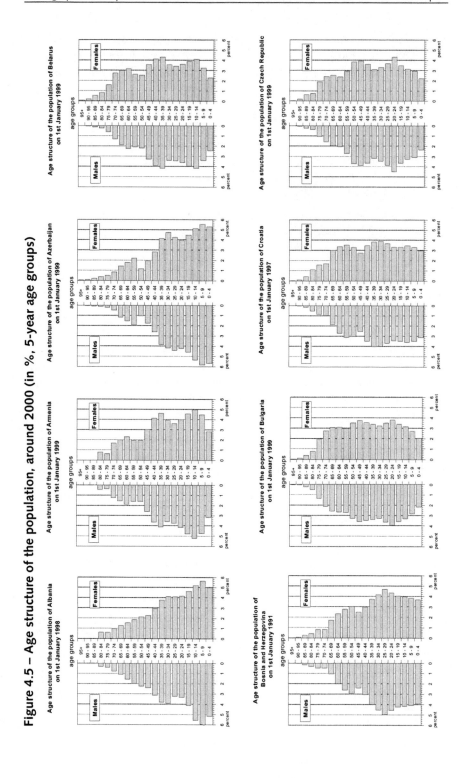

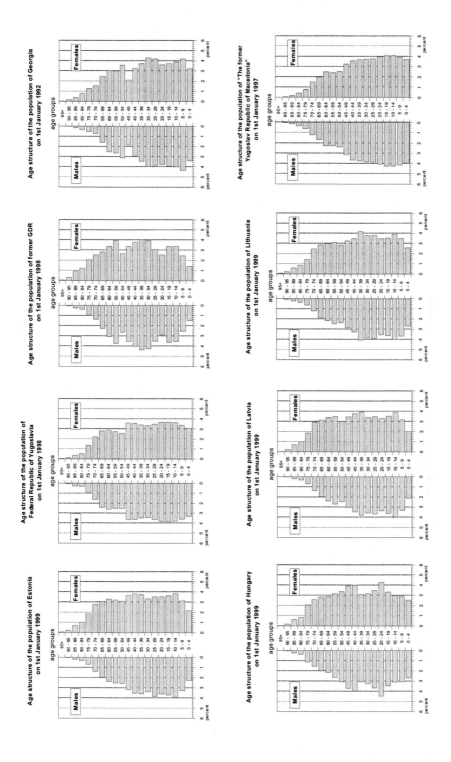

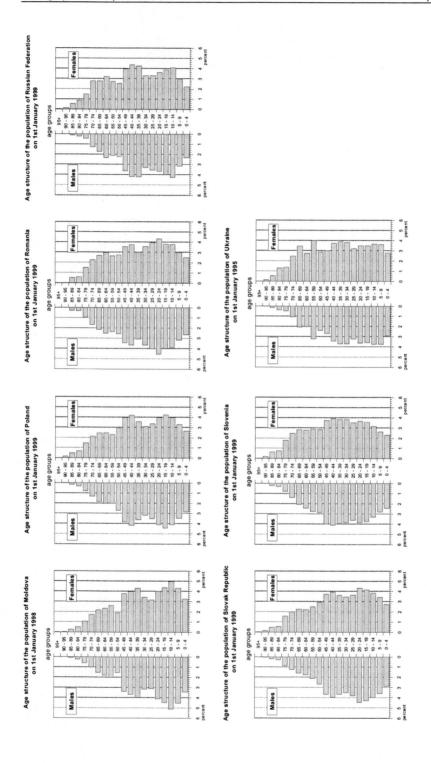

At the end of the nineties, the age structure took on a transitory shape in the majority of countries of central and eastern Europe. It is possible to distinguish between two groups.

*Firstly:* In the majority of countries the bell shape was the characteristic population structure in the eighties. In these countries, the transition from the third to the fourth type of age structure was caused by the fall in the birth rate. This was however accompanied by the particularity of being largely related to fertility-led ageing of the population. Life expectancy is just reaching the level from which mortality-led ageing is caused. Belarus, Bulgaria, the Czech Republic, Estonia, Hungary, Poland, Romania, the Russian Federation, theSlovak Republic, Slovenia and Ukraine belong to this group of countries.

*Secondly:* The birth rate started to fall in some countries when the age structure still showed the triangle shape. These countries might move from Type 2 to Type 4 if the low birth rates continue in the long term. This group of countries is made up of Armenia, Bosnia-Herzegovina and Moldova. The demographic ageing process has started in these countries too. It is also overwhelmingly fertility-led. Life expectancy is not yet so high that it is possible to speak of mortality-led ageing.

Detailed information relating to the particularities of the age structure can also be obtained from the proportions accounted for by individual age groups among the population contained in table 4.3.

**Table 4.3 – Population structure by major age groups in the countries of central and eastern Europe, 1999**

| Countries | Age groups | | | |
|---|---|---|---|---|
| | 0-14 | 15-44 | 45-64 | 65+ |
| Albania | 32.6 | 45.2 | 16.0 | 6.1 |
| Bulgaria | 16.2 | 41.9 | 25.5 | 15.8 |
| Croatia | 19.9 | 43.6 | 24.3 | 12.3 |
| Czech Republic | 17.0 | 43.8 | 25.5 | 13.7 |
| Estonia | 18.6 | 43.2 | 23.9 | 14.3 |
| Georgia | 24.2 | 43.8 | 21.4 | 9.9 |
| Former GDR | 14.8 | 43.5 | 26.4 | 15.3 |
| Hungary | 17.3 | 43.2 | 24.9 | 14.5 |
| Latvia | 18.5 | 43.0 | 24.0 | 14.5 |
| Lithuania | 20.4 | 44.5 | 22.1 | 13.1 |
| Moldova | 21.7 | 38.7 | 16.5 | 7.9 |
| Poland | 20.3 | 45.5 | 22.3 | 11.9 |
| Romania | 19.0 | 45.3 | 22.8 | 13.0 |
| Russian Federation | 19.0 | 45.7 | 22.8 | 12.5 |
| Slovak Republic | 20.4 | 46.7 | 21.6 | 11.3 |

| Countries | Age groups | | | |
|---|---|---|---|---|
| | 0-14 | 15-44 | 45-64 | 65+ |
| Slovenia | 16.6 | 45.5 | 24.4 | 13.6 |
| "The former Yugoslav Republic of Macedonia" | 24.1 | 46.2 | 20.7 | 9.1 |
| Ukraine | 20.4 | 42.7 | 22.9 | 13.5 |
| Armenia | 25.4 | 48.9 | 17.0 | 8.7 |
| Azerbaijan | 32.8 | 48.2 | 13.3 | 5.7 |
| Belarus | 19.6 | 45.2 | 21.6 | 13.1 |
| Bosnia and Herzegovina | 23.6 | 49.1 | 20.6 | 6.7 |
| Federal Republic of Yugoslavia | 20.8 | 43.1 | 23.1 | 13.0 |

Source: Council of Europe. Recent demographic developments in Europe. 1999

The following groups were found:

*Group 1* consists of Albania and Azerbaijan, with extraordinarily high proportions of children, namely higher than 30 %, and extremely low proportions accounted for by the age groups 45 to 64 (16 and 13.3 %) and 65 and older (roughly 6 %). The demographic ageing process has progressed least in these two countries.

*Group 2* brings together the countries (Georgia, "The former Yugoslav Republic of Macedonia" and Armenia, as well as Bosnia and Herzegovina) in which the shares of children, at about 25 %, are also very high, and the shares of 65-year-olds and older are very low, at less than 10 %.

*Group 3* consists of the countries with average proportions of children (around 20 %) and of the elderly (about 10 %). This group brings together Croatia, Lithuania, Poland, Romania, the Russian Federation, the Slovak Republic, Ukraine, Belarus and the Federal Republic of Yugoslavia.

*Group 4* encompasses Bulgaria, the Czech Republic, Estonia, eastern Germany, Hungary, Latvia, and Slovenia. Demographic ageing has progressed furthest in this group. The share of children amongst the population is 15 to 18 % as a rule, and the share accounted for by the elderly population is the highest, at 14 to 15 %.

The dependency ratios provide information on the relation between the main age groups of a population. For the depiction in fig. 4.6, 0- to 14-year-olds and 65-year-olds and older were related to the 15- to 64-year-old population. The data gained in this way are referred to as the youth and elderly quotients.

The various demographic situations of the populations in central and eastern Europe also become visible on the basis of the youth and elderly quotients. Albania and Azerbaijan are two countries with very many children and few elderly people in relation to the number of the population in gainful employment. Similarly, low elderly quotients can be found in Bosnia-Herzegovina, but with much lower youth quotients. A uniform group is formed by "The former Yugoslav Republic of Macedonia", Georgia, Moldova and Armenia with still relatively high youth quotients and already average elderly quotients. A relatively harmonic group is formed by most other countries in central and eastern Europe, where the ageing process has progressed further. The youth quotients are low, at 20 – 33 %, and the elderly quotients, with values around 20 %, are high in relation to the standard in this group of countries.

**Figure 4.6 – Dependency ratios in countries of central and eastern Europe. 1999 or latest available year**

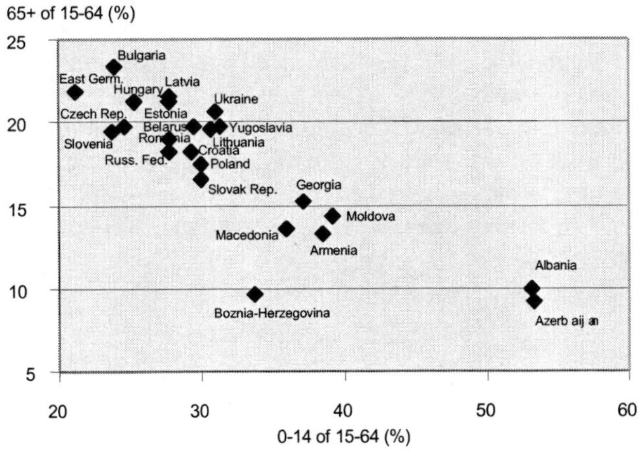

Source: Council of Europe. Recent demographic developments in Europe. 1999

## 4.4 Foreign population

Information relating to the share taken up by the foreign population is available only for a small number of countries (eastern Germany, Hungary, Latvia, Poland, Romania, the Slovak Republic, Slovenia and Azerbaijan). It is characteristic of these that the shares are very low in comparison to the other European countries. The highest shares of foreigners are to be found in eastern Germany (1.9 %), Slovenia (1.7 %) and Hungary (1.5 %). In the other countries, the shares are lower than one percent. Latvia states its share of foreigners to be 0.7 %, Poland 0.1% and Romania and Azerbaijan near zero. The foreign population is 1,400 in Romania and 500 in Azerbaijan. This reveals that the former Socialist countries have not been open to migrants. These countries are not the only ones in Europe with low shares of the foreign population. Europe diverges highly in this respect. Thus, similarly low figures are to be found in Finland (1.6 %), Italy (1.7 %) or Spain (1.5 %). In other countries, such as Switzerland (19.4 %), Austria (9.1 %) or Belgium (8.9 %) the proportions accounted for by foreigners are much larger.

## 4.5 Population projection

In order to gain an impression of the possible future directions in population trends until 2050, the medium variable of the 2000 UN population projections (UN Population Division, 2000) will be shown. In order to be able to evaluate the occurring trends, it is first necessary to show the projection assumptions concerning fertility, mortality and migration.

### Fertility assumptions

With the exception of Albania, the transformation states are now so-called low fertility countries in which the combined birth rates are lower than the replacement level for the parents' generations. The following assumptions have been reached for this: "Fertility in low-fertility countries is generally assumed to remain below the replacement level during most of the projection period, reaching by 2045-2050 the fertility of the cohort of women born in the early 1960s or, if that information is lacking, reaching 1.7 children per woman if current fertility is below 1.5 children per woman or 1.9 children per woman if current fertility is equal to or higher than 1.5 children per woman" (UN Population Division, Highlights, 2000: 17). This means de facto that a new increase in fertility is assumed for the transformation countries, in some cases of considerable proportions, although again with the exception of Albania (Tab. 4.4). However, such an increase cannot be taken for granted. This implies for the projection calculation that highly favourable assumptions have been used for the main result, namely demographic ageing. For instance, in Estonia, where a TFR of 1.10 is assumed in the period 2000–2005, an increase to 2.0 is anticipated by 2045-2050. An increase from 1.1 to 1.7 is presumed in the same period for Ukraine. Only for Albania is a decline from 2.27 to 2.10 assumed (replacement level of the parents' generation). In spite of the considerable increases in fertility expected, it is not projected for any of the other countries that simple population reproduction will be regained, so that in these countries in the long term a state of demographic ageing continues under the TFR value of 2.10.

**Table 4.4 – Projection assumptions, 2000 and 2050**

| Countries | Total fertility rate | | Life expectancy (both genders) | | Net migration per year (per 1,000 population) | |
|---|---|---|---|---|---|---|
| | 2000-2005 | 2045-2050 | 2000-2005 | 2045-2050 | 2000-2005 | 2045-2050 |
| Albania | 2.27 | 2.10 | 73.7 | 79.9 | -6.3 | -2.6 |
| Bulgaria | 1.10 | 1.89 | 70.9 | 78.3 | -2.6 | -4.3 |
| Croatia | 1.70 | 1.90 | 74.2 | 79.6 | 0.0 | 0.0 |
| Czech Rep. | 1.16 | 1.97 | 75.4 | 81.4 | 1.0 | 1.2 |
| Estonia | 1.20 | 2.00 | 71.2 | 78.2 | -6.8 | -9.0 |
| Georgia | 1.39 | 1.90 | 73.6 | 79.3 | -5.8 | -9.0 |
| Hungary | 1.20 | 1.97 | 72.0 | 79.4 | -0.4 | 0.0 |
| Latvia | 1.10 | 2.00 | 71.2 | 78.0 | 0.0 | 0.0 |
| Lithuania | 1.20 | 2.00 | 72.7 | 79.6 | 0.0 | 0.0 |
| Poland | 1.26 | 2.10 | 73.9 | 80.1 | -0.5 | -0.6 |
| Moldova | 1.40 | 1.90 | 66.6 | 77.2 | -1.9 | -2.2 |
| Romania | 1.32 | 2.05 | 69.8 | 76.9 | -0.2 | -0.3 |
| Russian Fed. | 1.14 | 1.75 | 66.0 | 76.9 | 0.3 | 0.5 |
| Slovak Rep. | 1.28 | 1.70 | 73.7 | 79.5 | 0.4 | 0.4 |
| Slovenia | 1.14 | 1.83 | 76.1 | 81.8 | 0.5 | 0.6 |
| Macedonia | 1.48 | 1.90 | 73.6 | 79.5 | 0.0 | 0.0 |
| Ukraine | 1.10 | 1.70 | 68.1 | 77.5 | -2.1 | -3.2 |
| Armenia | 1.10 | 1.70 | 73.4 | 79.3 | -1.3 | -1.5 |
| Azerbaijan | 1.51 | 1.90 | 72.2 | 79.0 | -0.6 | -0.6 |
| Belarus | 1.20 | 1.86 | 68.5 | 77.9 | 1.0 | 1.2 |
| Bosnia and Herzegovina | 1.30 | 1.70 | 74.0 | 78.9 | 9.8 | 0.0 |
| F.R.Yugoslavia | 1.55 | 1.90 | 73.2 | 79.1 | -1.9 | -0.7 |

Source: United Nations, Population Division, World Population Prospects, The 2000 Revision, Volume1

*Mortality assumptions*

"Mortality is projected on the basis of the models of change in life expectancy produced by the United Nations" (UN Population Division, Highlights, 2000: 17). This presumes a continuous increase in life expectancy. Life expectancy for both genders is stated. Life expectancy increases in the transformation countries by amounts between 4.9 years (Bosnia and Herzegovina) and 10.9 years (Russian Federation). Lower increases are assumed for those countries where the level is already high. Relatively high increases in life expectancy are assumed by 2050 in countries where life expectancy is low, as for example in Russia or Moldova. For the majority of countries, life expectancy increases by between six and seven years in the UN population projections (Table 4.4).

*Migration assumptions*

The migration assumptions stem from a combination of two approaches: the normal migration assumption and the zero-migration assumption. The past situation is taken as the basis for the normal migration assumption. "The future path of international migration is set on the basis of past international migration estimates and an assessment of the policy stance of countries with regard to future international migration flows" (UN Population Division, Highlights, 2000: 18). In the zero-migration assumptions "for each country, international migration is set to zero for the period 2000-2050. These two assumptions make it possible to sub-divide the countries into four groups:

*Firstly, countries for which zero migration was assumed:*
Croatia, Latvia, Lithuania, "The former Yugoslav Republic of Macedonia"

*Secondly, countries for which negative net migration was assumed over the entire projection period:*
Albania, Bulgaria, Estonia, Georgia, Poland, Moldova, Romania, Ukraine, Armenia, Azerbaijan, Federal Republic of Yugoslavia

*Thirdly, countries for which positive net migration was assumed over the entire projection period:*
Czech Republic, Russian Federation, Slovak Republic, Slovenia, Belarus.

*Fourthly, countries in which zero migration follows positive or negative net migration:*
Hungary, Bosnia and Herzegovina.

The results of the medium variable below are based on the medium fertility assumption, the normal mortality assumption and the respective zero or normal migration assumption.

The main results of the 2000 UN population projections for the transformation states of eastern and central Europe can be combined in two statements:

*1. By 2050, in some cases, considerable demographic declines are recorded (Fig. 4.7 / Tab. 4.5)*

A consistently negative trend can be observed in the majority of countries (Belarus, Bulgaria, Czech Republic, Hungary, Poland, Moldova, Romania, Russian Federation, Ukraine, Estonia, Latvia, Lithuania, Slovenia, Federal Republic of Yugoslavia). The most obvious reductions can be found in Bulgaria and Estonia, where the population will almost halve, and in Ukraine, where a reduction to 61 % may take place. This is caused by the fact that for these countries, considerable migration losses are projected over quite a long period. Declines to values of between 86.5 % (Poland) and 72.1 % (Russian Federation) are expected for the other countries.

The population size is expected to increase at first. In a small number of countries this trend should then reverse to become a demographic decline (Slovak Republic: start of the population decline 2013, Bosnia and Herzegovina: 2015, Croatia: 2008, "The former Yugoslav Republic of Macedonia": 2021). For these countries, too, the population size will fall to values of around 90 %.

An exception is Albania once again. The comparatively high fertility over the entire projection period, in combination with a favourable age structure, lead to the population size exceeding that of 2000 by almost one-quarter at the end of the projection period. In the case of Albania one should take account of the fact that an increase from 3.1 to 3.9 is completed.

**Figure 4. 7 – UN Population projection, 2001-2050**

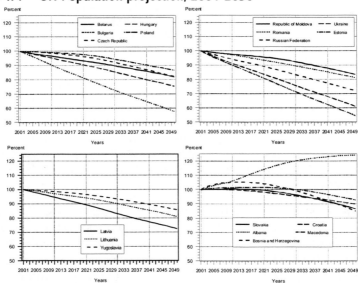

Source: United Nations, Population Division, World Population Prospects, 2000 Revision, Volume 1

**Table 4.5 – Total population by countries, 2000-2050 (in 1000)**

| Countries | Years | | | |
|---|---|---|---|---|
| | 2000 | 2015 | 2025 | 2050 |
| Albania | 3.134 | 3.439 | 3.676 | 3.905 |
| Belarus | 10.187 | 9.964 | 9.335 | 8.305 |
| Bosnia and Herzegov. | 3.977 | 4.279 | 4.165 | 3.458 |
| Bulgaria | 7.949 | 6.816 | 6.125 | 4.531 |
| Czech Republic | 10.272 | 10.028 | 9.727 | 8.429 |
| Croatia | 4.654 | 4.622 | 4.519 | 4.179 |
| Estonia | 1.393 | 1.190 | 1.062 | 752 |
| Georgia | 5.262 | 4.775 | 4.377 | 3.219 |
| Hungary | 9.968 | 9.254 | 8.783 | 7.486 |
| Latvia | 2.421 | 2.225 | 2.090 | 1.744 |
| Lithuania | 3.696 | 3.538 | 3.418 | 2.989 |
| Macedonia | 2.034 | 2.075 | 2.067 | 1.894 |
| Moldova | 4.295 | 4.152 | 4.052 | 3.577 |
| Poland | 38.605 | 38.035 | 37.254 | 33.370 |
| Romania | 22.438 | 21.437 | 20.585 | 18.150 |
| Russia | 145.491 | 133.314 | 125.687 | 104.258 |
| Slovak Republic | 5.399 | 5.420 | 5.317 | 4.674 |
| Slovenia | 1.988 | 1.926 | 1.847 | 1.527 |
| Ukraine | 49.568 | 43.335 | 39.569 | 29.959 |
| F.R.Yugoslavia | 10.552 | 10.309 | 10.044 | 9.030 |

Source: UN Population Division, Highlights, 2000: 28 - 33

## 2. The process of demographic ageing will continue and become more dynamic

Demographic ageing will be experienced in all countries without exception. The scale shifts in the demographic age structure are just as evident as the declines in the population size. In all countries, the proportion of children and young people aged under 14 will fall by 2050 and the proportions of the population aged between 15 – 59 and of the over-sixties will be higher than in 2000 (Tab. 4.6).

A complex indicator of the ageing process lies in the increase in the median age. In 2000, only Bulgaria among the reforming states (place 7) was among the ten oldest populations in the world, having a median age of 39.1. The oldest population in this period lived in Japan (median age 41.2). By 2050, clear changes will have taken place both as to the ranking and the median age. In 2050, the oldest population in the world will be that of Spain (median age 55.2). And the situation in the reforming states will worsen. Then, three of the ten oldest populations will live in the reform states. Slovenia will have the second-oldest population, at 54.1, Armenia the fifth-oldest (53.4) and the Czech Republic the seventh-oldest (52.4). In the context of the transition states, Ukraine will then follow with 51.5, and Bulgaria with 51.3.

**Table 4.6 – Distribution of the population by major age groups, 2000 and 2050 (in %)**

| Countries | Years | | | | | |
|---|---|---|---|---|---|---|
| | 2000 | | | 2050 | | |
| | Age groups | | | | | |
| | 0-14 | 15-59 | 60+ | 0-14 | 15-59 | 60+ |
| Albania | 30.0 | 61.1 | 9.0 | 19.0 | 56.4 | 24.6 |
| Belarus | 18.7 | 62.4 | 18.9 | 14.6 | 49.6 | 35.8 |
| Bosnia & Herzegov. | 18.9 | 66.1 | 14.9 | 12.9 | 49.3 | 37.7 |
| Bulgaria | 15.7 | 62.6 | 21.7 | 13.8 | 47.6 | 38.6 |
| Czech Rep. | 16.4 | 65.2 | 18.4 | 13.6 | 46.3 | 40.1 |
| Croatia | 18.0 | 61.8 | 20.2 | 16.3 | 53.0 | 30.8 |
| Estonia | 17.7 | 62.1 | 20.2 | 15.6 | 48.5 | 35.9 |
| Georgia | 20.5 | 60.8 | 18.7 | 14.4 | 49.8 | 35.8 |
| Hungary | 16.9 | 63.3 | 19.7 | 14.4 | 49.4 | 36.2 |
| Latvia | 17.4 | 61.7 | 20.9 | 15.0 | 47.5 | 37.5 |
| Lithuania | 19.5 | 62.0 | 18.6 | 14.6 | 48.1 | 37.3 |
| Macedonia | 22.6 | 63.0 | 14.4 | 14.2 | 52.0 | 33.8 |
| Moldova | 23.1 | 63.2 | 13.7 | 15.3 | 52.2 | 32.5 |
| Poland | 19.2 | 64.3 | 16.6 | 15.7 | 48.7 | 35.6 |
| Romania | 18.3 | 62.9 | 18.8 | 15.9 | 50.0 | 34.2 |
| Russia | 18.0 | 63.5 | 18.5 | 13.5 | 49.3 | 37.2 |
| Slovak Rep. | 19.5 | 65.1 | 15.4 | 13.2 | 50.0 | 36.8 |
| Slovenia | 15.9 | 65.0 | 19.2 | 12.4 | 45.1 | 42.4 |
| Ukraine | 17.8 | 61.6 | 20.5 | 12.9 | 49.0 | 38.1 |
| F.R.Yugoslavia | 20.0 | 61.7 | 18.3 | 15.2 | 52.4 | 32.5 |

Source: UN Population Division, Highlights, 2000: 50 - 55

The most noticeable shifts according to the results of the projections (Tab. 4.7) will be in Azerbaijan and Armenia. There, the median ages of the population will increase by 23.0 and 20.5 respectively. The median ages of the populations in the transition countries will increase by an average of about 14 years.

**Table 4.7 – Transition countries by median age, 2000 and 2050 (in years)**

| Countries | Years 2000 | Years 2050 | Difference | Countries | Years 2000 | Years 2050 | Difference |
|---|---|---|---|---|---|---|---|
| Albania | 26.5 | 39.5 | 13.0 | Romania | 34.6 | 46.7 | 12.1 |
| Bulgaria | 39.1 | 51.3 | 12.2 | Russian Fed. | 36.8 | 50.0 | 13.2 |
| Croatia | 37.9 | 44.3 | 6.4 | Slovak Rep. | 34.0 | 50.2 | 16.2 |
| Czech Rep. | 37.6 | 52.4 | 14.8 | Slovenia | 38.1 | 54.1 | 16.0 |
| Estonia | 37.3 | 47.9 | 10.6 | Macedonia | 32.3 | 49.1 | 16.8 |
| Georgia | 34.8 | 49.2 | 14.4 | Ukraine | 37.3 | 51.5 | 14.2 |
| East Germany | 40.1 | 50.9 | 10.8 | Armenia | 30.4 | 53.4 | 23.0 |
| Hungary | 38.1 | 49.8 | 11.7 | Azerbaijan | 26.7 | 47.2 | 20.5 |
| Latvia | 37.8 | 49.8 | 12.0 | Belarus | 36.3 | 48.6 | 12.3 |
| Lithuania | 35.7 | 50.6 | 14.9 | Bosnia-Herzeg. | 35.1 | 50.7 | 15.6 |
| Moldova | 31.5 | 46.6 | 15.1 | F.R.Yugoslavia | 35.4 | 46.7 | 11.3 |
| Poland | 35.2 | 48.0 | 12.8 | | | | |

## 4.6 Summary

Because of the fall in the birth rate, social and economic change in the countries of central and eastern Europe has led to changed trends in demographic developments. Three facts should be emphasised:

*Firstly*, the growth in population numbers based on high birth surpluses has reversed into negative trends. Only Armenia and Azerbaijan have high population growth rates because of the continued high birth rate. The population number is falling in the majority of countries. Slow growth can still be observed in a few countries.

*Secondly*, it can be observed that migration has virtually no influence on the development of the population number, as was already the case in Socialist times. Only around 1990 was an influence exerted on demographic developments by considerable variations in migratory flows, both in positive and negative terms.

*Thirdly*, the fall in the birth rate has led to accelerated ageing amongst the population, although in comparison with western, northern or southern Europe the populations are still younger on average. The majority of European populations outside central and eastern Europe are ageing in terms of fertility and mortality. Because life expectancy remains lower in central and eastern Europe, the typical ageing of the population is largely a result of the low birth rate.

Fourthly, the UN projections show that ageing will accelerate considerably in the period up to 2050. The growth in the elderly population in comparison with that of children and young people and the working-age population will become clear in the projection period up to 2050.

# References

**Chapters 1 and 4, and sections 2.3 and 2.7 in chapter 2:**

Brezinski, Horst, 1996: "Der Stand der wirtschaftlichen Transformation". In: Brunner, Georg, 1996: *Politische und ökonomische Transformation in Osteuropa, Schriftenreihe der Deutschen Gesellschaft für Osteuropakunde*, Band 36, Berlin Verlag.

Brusis, Martin, Ochmann, Corneliius, 1996: "Mittel- und Osteuropa auf dem Weg in die Europäische Union". In: Weidenfeld, Werner (Hrsg.), *Mittel- und Osteuropa auf dem Weg in die Europäische Union*, Verlag Berteilsmann Stiftung, Gütersloh 1996.

Burchardt, Hans-Jürgen, 1995: "Wirtschaftsdynamik im Realsozialismus, Gründe eines Scheiterns". In: *Osteuropa*, Jg. 45, Nr. 2, p. 103 – 119.

Council of Europe, 2000: *Recent demographic developments in Europe*. Council of Europe Publishing, Strasbourg.

Dahrendorf, Ralph, 1990: *Betrachtungen über die Revolution in Europa in einem Brief, der an einen Herrn in Warschau gerichtet ist*, Deutsche Verlagsanstalt, Stuttgart.

EBRD: Transition Report 1999.

EBRD: Transition Report 2000.

Eger, Thomas, 2000: "Systemtransformation als umfassender institutioneller Wandel: Die fünf Dimensionen der Transformationsprozesse in Osteuropa", *Arbeitsbericht* No. 12/00, Frankfurter Institut für Transformationsstudien, Europa-Universität Viadrina, 44 pages.

Golinowska, Stanislawa, 1999: "Nedza, ubóstwo, niedostatek". In: Rzeczpospolita, 09.09. 1999.

Häder, Michael und Häder, Sabine, 1990: *Turbulenzen im Transformationsprozess, Individuelle Bewältigung des sozialen Wandels in Ostdeutschland* 1990-1992, Westdeutscher Verlag, 388 Seiten.

Höhmann, Hans-Hermann, 1995: "Marktwirtschaft ohne Alternative? Aspekte und Bewertungsmaßstäbe der osteuropäischen Wirtschaftstransformation". In: *Zwischen Krise und Konsolidierung, Gefährdeter Systemwandel im Osten Europpas, Carl Hanser Verlag, Münschen, Wien*.

Höpflinger, Francois, 1987: *Wandel der Familienbildung in Europa*, Campus Verlag, Frankfurt/New York, 295 p.

Lang, Kai-Olaf, 2001: "Systemtransformation in Ostmitteleuropa: Eine erste Erfolgsbilanz". In: *Aus Politik und Zeitgeschichte, Beilage zur Wochenzeitung Das Parlament*, 6. April 2001, p. 13 – 21.

Merkel, Wolfgang, 1995: "Theorien der Transformation: Die demokratische Konsolidierung postautoritärer Gesellschaften". In: *Politische Vierteljahresschrift*, 26, 1995.

Meuschel, Sigrid, 1990: "Revolution in der DDR. Versuch einer sozialwissenschaftlichen Interpretation". In: *Die Modernisierung moderner Gesellschaften, Verhandlungen des 25. Deutschen Soziologentages in Frankfurt am Main 1990*, Herausgegeben im Auftrag der Deutschen Gesellschaft für Soziologie von Wolfgang Zapf, Campus Verlag, Frankfurt/New York, S. 558 – 576.

Nikolic, Milos, 1995: "Fünf Jahre Transformation zu Demokratie und Marktwirtschaft in Mittel- und Osteuropa". In:Utopie kreativ: *Diskussion sozialistischer Alternativen*, Heft 59.

Pállinger, Zoltán Tibor, 1997: *Der Umbruch in Osteuropa und die Theorien des Systemwechsels*, Eidgenössische Technische Hochschule, Forschungsstelle für Internationale Beziehungen, Zürich, 38 p.

Piazolo, Daniel, 2002: "Entwicklungsunterschiede innerhalb einer erweiterten EU, Herausforderungen und Chancen". In: *Aus Politik und Zeitgeschichte*, Beilage zur Wochenzeitung Das Parlament, 4. Januar 2002.

Popov, V., 2000: "Shock Therapy versus Gradualism, The end of the debate". In: *Comparative economic studies*, 42, 57 pages.

Rothacher, Albrecht, 1999: "Wirtschaft, Politik und Gesellschaft in Tschechien, Polen, Ungarn, Slowenien, Kroatien und Litauen", *Schriftenreihe der Wirtschaftskammer Österreich*, Heft 82, Wien 1999, 142 p.

United Nations, Population Division, *World Population Prospects*, 2000 Revision, Highlights, New York, 2001.

United Nations, Population Division, *World Population Prospects*, 2000 Revision, Volume 1, New York, 2001.

United Nations, *Economic Survey of Europe, 2001*: New York and Geneva, 222 p.

Welfens, Paul J.J., 1999: "Staat und Transformation: Theoretische und konzeptionelle Aspekte von Systemwandel und wirtschaftspolitischer Neuorientierung". In: Höhmann, Hans-Hermann (Hrsg.), *Spontaner oder gestalteter Prozeß, Die Rolle des Staates in der Wirtschaftstransformation osteuropäischer Länder*, Nomos Verlagsgesellschaft, Baden-Baden.

Ziemer, Klaus, 1996: "Politischer Wandel in Osteuropa: Die maßgeblichen innenpolitischen Kräfte". In: Brunner, G. (Hrsg.), *Politische und ökonomische Transformation in Osteuropa, Schriftenreihe der Deutschen Gesellschaft für Osteuropakunde*, Band 36, Berlin 1996, p. 9 – 41.

**Chapters 2 and 3 (except sections 2.3 and 2.7 in chapter 2) :**

Andorka Rudolf (1999): "Dissatisfaction and alienation". In: Andorka, Kolosi, Rose and Vukovich, editors: *A Society Transformed*. Central European University Press, Budapest.

Arts W., P. Hermkens, P. Van Wijck (1995). *Anomie, distributive justice and dissatisfaction with material well-being in Eastern Europe*. IJCS 36,1-2: 1-16.

Becker, Gary S. (1991). *A Treatise on the Family. Enlarged Edition*. Cambridge, MA:Harvard University Press.

Billari, F. and D. Philipov (2002). *Interrelations between education and timing of first unions: the case of Central and Eastern Europe*. Paper prepared for presentation at the 2002 meeting of the Population Association of America.

Blayo C. (1993) "The role of abortion in the countries of Central and Eastern Europe". [Le role de l'avortement dans les pays d'Europe Centrale et .] In: *International Population Conference / Congres International de la Population, Montreal 1993, 24 August – 1st September. Volume 1*, International Union for the Scientific Study of Population; Liege, Belgium, IUSSP; pp. 235-52.

Blossfeld H.P. and J. Huinink (1991): "Human capital investments or norms of role transition? How women's schooling and career affect the process of family formation", *American Journal of Sociology*, 97(1): 143-168.

Blossfeld H.P. (1992): *Women's Increasing Educational Attainment and Changes in the Process of Family Formation in Europe*. Brussels: Commission of the European Community.

Büttner T. and W. Lutz (1990): "Estimating fertility responses to policy measures in the German democratic Republic". *Population and Development Review*, 3:539-555.

Carlson E. (1992:): "Inverted Easterlin fertility cycles and Kornai's 'soft' budget constraint". *Population and Development Review*, vol. 18, N.4, pp. 669-688.

Carlson E. and M. Omori (1998): "Fertility regulation in a declining state socialist economy: Bulgaria, 1976-1995". *International Family Planning Perspectives*, Vol. 24/4, pp.184-187.

Coleman D. (1991): "European demographic system of the future: convergence or diversity?" In: *Human resources in Europe at the dawn of the 21st Century*. Luxemburg: Eurostat.

Coleman D., editor (1996): *Europe's population in the 1990s*. Oxford University Press.

Cornia, G. and R. Paniccià (1995a): "The demographic impact of sudden impoverishment: Eastern Europe during the 1989-94 transition". UNICEFF, Florence, *Innocenti Occasional Papers* EPS 49.

Cornia, G. and R. Paniccià (1995b). "The transition's population crisis: An econometric investigation of nuptiality, fertility and mortality in severely distressed economies". *Most*, N.1.

Council of Europe (2000): *Recent Demographic Developments in Europe*. Council of Europe Publishing, Strasbourg.

David H. (1988): *Compulsory childbearing: perspectives from Czechoslovakia and Romania*. Presented at the Annual Meeting of the Population Association of America, New Orleans, Louisiana, April 21-23.

David H., editor (1999): *From Abortion to Contraception (A Resource to Public Policies and Reproductive Behavior in Central and Eastern Europe from 1917 to the Present)*. Greenwood Press, Wesport, Connecticut, London.

David P., V. Bodrova, A. Avdeev, I. Troitskaia, M. Boulay (2000): *Women and Infant Health Project Household Survey 2000*. (Unpublished manuscript).

Debroy B. (1989): "Fertility trends and population policies and programmes in Socialist Europe". *Social scientist*; 17(7-8): pp. 66-87.

Easterlin RA. (1987) *Birth and fortune: the impact of numbers on personal welfare*, second edition. Chicago, Illinois, University of Chicago Press.

Elizarov V. (1999): "The demographic situation and problems of family policy". *Sociological Research*, 38/1, pp. 79-90.

Ellman M. (2000): "The social costs and consequences of the transformation process". *Papers from the ECE Spring Seminar*, 2000. ECE, United Nations, Geneva.

Ermisch, John (1996): "The economic environment for family formation". In: Coleman D., ed. *Europe's population in the 1990s*. Oxford University Press.

Frejka T. (1983): "Induced abortion and fertility: a quarter century of experience in Eastern Europe". *Population and Development Review*; 9(3): pp. 494-520.

Genov, N. (1998). "Transformation and anomie: problems of quality of life in Bulgaria". *Social Indicators Research* 43: 197-209.

Githens M. (1996): "Reproductive rights and the struggle with change in Eastern Europe". In: *Abortion politics: public policy in cross-cultural perspective*, edited by Marianne Githens and Dorothy McBride Stetson.; New York, New York, Routledge; pp. 55-68.

Gromyko A. (1999): "The challenge of rising trends in the incidence of sexually transmitted diseases in Eastern Europe". In: Lindmark *et al.* editors.

Hajnal John (1965): "European marriage patterns in perspective". In: Glass DV, Eversley DE, eds. *Population in history: essays in historical demography*. Chicago, Illinois, Aldine Publishing Company, pp. 101-143.

Hoem, Jan M. 1986: "The impact of education on modern family-union initiation", *European Journal of Population,* 2: 113-133.

Huntington S. (1998): *The Clash of Civilizations and the Remaking of World Order*. Touchstone Books.

Inglehart, Ronald, et al. (2000): *World Values Surveys and European Values Surveys*, 1981-1984, 1990-1993, and 1995-1997 [Computer file]. ICPSR version. Ann Arbor, MI: Institute for Social Research [producer], 2000. Ann Arbor, MI: Inter-university Consortium for Political and Social Research [distributor], 2000.

Kamarás F. (2000) : « Les tendances de la fécondité en Hongrie et les facteurs qui les influencent ». *Cahiers québécois de démographie.* Vol.29, no 2, p. 255-285.

Keil, Thomas and Andreescu V. (1999): "Fertility policy in Ceausescu's Romania". *Journal of Family History*; 24(4): pp. 478-92.

Klijzing E. (2000): "Are there unmet needs for family planning in Europe?" *Family Planning Perspectives,* Vol.32/2, pp.74-81.

Kotowska I., editor (1999): *The Demographic Changs in Poland during the 90s in the Light of the conception of the Second Demographic Transition.* Szkoła Głowna Handlowa w Warrszawe. (in Polish).

Kučera T., Kučerová O., Opara O., Schaich E. (2000): *New Demographic Faces in Europe (The Changing Population Dynamics in Countries of Central and Eastern Europe).* Springer.

Kulczycki A. (1995): "Abortion policy in postcommunist Europe: the conflict in Poland". *Population and Development Review*; 21(3): pp. 471-505.

Lehmann S.G. (1992) *Contemporary Russian marriage and childbearing patterns: a challenge to low fertility theory*. Ann Arbor, Michigan, University Microfilms International, 1992.; [8], 228, 16 p. (not cited).

Lesthaeghe R. (1983): "A Century of demographic and cultural change in Western Europe: and exploration of underlying dimensions". *Population and Development Review*, vol. 9, N. 3, pp. 411-435.

Lesthaeghe R. and D. van de Kaa (1986): "Twee demografische transities", in Lesthaeghe and van de Kaa (eds.) *Bevolking, groei en krimp*. Deventer: Van Loghum Salerus, 19-68.

Lesthaeghe R. and J. Surkyn (1988): Cultural dynamics and economic theories of fertility change. *Population and Development Review*, vol.14, N.1, pp. 1-45.

Lindmark G., M. Horga, A. Campana, and J. Kasonde, editors (1999): *Towards Better Reproductive Health in Eastern Europe (concern, commitment, and Change)*. Central European Press and world Health Organization.

Monnier A. (1990): "The effects of family policies in the German Democratic Republic: a re-evaluation". *Population. English Selection*; 2: pp. 127-40.

Monnier A. and J. Rychtaříková (1991): "How Europe is divided into east and west". [Comment l'Europe s'est divisée entre l'est et l'ouest.] *Population*; 46(6): pp. 1, 617-650.

Mozny I. and L. Rabušic (1992): "Unmarried cohabitation in Czechoslovakia". *Czechoslovak Sociological Review, Special Issue*; 28: pp. 107-17.

Philipov D. (1993): "Period-Cohort Analysis of the Effectiveness of the Demographic Policy", *Statistika*, National statistical institute, Sofia, 2/1993, pp. 40-51.

Philipov D. (2001): *Low Fertility in Central and Eastern Europe: Culture or Economy?* Paper presented at the IUSSP Seminar on "International Perspectives on Low Fertility: trends, theories and policies", Tokyo, March 21-23, 2001.

Philipov D. and H.P. Kohler (2000): "Tempo and Quantum Effects on Fertility". *Statistika*, National Statistical Institute, Sofia, N.4, pp.3-18.

Philipov D. and V. Shkolnikov (2001): *Fertility intentions and social capital-based coping strategies: results from the 1998 round of the Russian Longitudinal Monitoring Survey*. Paper presented at the Meeting of the Population Association of America, Washington DC, March, 2001.

Philippov OS; Radionchenko AA; Bolotova VP; Voronovskaya NI; Potemkina TV. (1998): "Estimation of the prevalence and causes of infertility in Western Siberia". *Bulletin of the World Health Organization*; 76(2): pp. 183-7.

Pollack R. and S.C. Watkins (1993): "Cultural and economic approaches to fertility: proper marriage or Messaliance?" *Population and Development Review*, vol. 19 n.3, pp.467-496.

Rabušic, Ladislav (1996): "On marriage and family trends in the Czech Republic in the mid - 1990s". *Socialni Studia*. 38(1):29-42.

Rabušic, L. and P. Mareš (1996): "Is Czech Society Anomic?", *Sociologický časopis*, XXXII:2, 175-187 (in Czech).

Ranjan, Priya (1999): "Fertility Behaviour under Income Uncertainty", *European Jouranl of Population*, 15, pp.25-43.

RHS in the Czech Republic (1995): *Czech Republic Reproductive and Health Survey 1993. Final Report*. Czech Statistical Office, Factum non Fabula, Centers for Disease Control and Prevention, Atlanta, Georgia USA *et al.*

RHS in Romania (1995): *Romanian Reproductive and Health Survey 1993. Final Report*. Institute for Mother and Child Health Care Bucharest, Romania, Centers for Disease Control and Prevention, Atlanta, Georgia USA.

RHS in Romania (2000): *Romanian Reproductive and Health Survey 1999. Preliminary Report*. Institute for Mother and Child Health Care Bucharest, Romania, Centers for Disease Control and Prevention, Atlanta, Georgia USA.

RHS in the Ukraine (2000): *Ukrainian Reproductive and Health Survey 1999. Preliminary Report*. Kiev International Institute of Sociology, Ukraine; Centers for Disease Control and Prevention, Atlanta, Georgia USA.

Rychtaříková J. (1999): "Is Eastern Europe experiencing a Second Demographic Transition?" *Acta Universitatis Carolinae, Geographica*, N.1, pp. 19-44, Prague.

Rychtaříková J. (2000): "Demographic transition or demographic shock in recent population development in the Czech Republic?" *Acta Universitatis Carolinae, Geographica*, N.1, pp.89-102, Prague.

Spéder Zsolt, Paksi B., Elekes Z. (1999): Anomie and satisfaction at the beginning of the nineties. In: Kolosi, Tóth and Vukovich: *Social Report 1998*. Social Research Informatics Center, Budapest.

Stloukal L. (1998): "An APC analysis of demographic responses to population policy measures: the case of the Czech and the Slovak republics 1960-1990". *Genus*, 54, 87-121.

Stloukal L. (1999): *Understanding the "abortion culture" in Central and Eastern Europe*. In: David H. (ed., 1999).

Sztompka P. (1996): "Trust and emerging democracy". *International sociology*, 11(1):37-62.

United Nations (1999): "Fertility decline in the transition economies, 1982-1997: political, economic and social factors". Chapter 4 in: *Economic Survey in Europe*, 1999/1, pp. 181-194, UN ECE, Geneva.

United Nations (2000): "Fertility decline in the transition economies, 1989-1998: economic and social factors revisited". Chapter 6 in: *Economic Survey in Europe,* 2000/1, pp. 189-207, UN ECE, Geneva.

United Nations (2000b): *Levels and Trends in Contraceptive Use, 1998.* United Nations, New York.

van de Kaa, D. (1987): "Europe's second demographic transition". *Population Bulletin* 42,1.

Vishnevskii, A. (1999): "The demographic potential of Russia". *Russian Social Science Review*. 40(4):4-29.

WHO Regional office for Europe and United Nations Population Fund (1995): *Family Planning and reproductive health in CCEE/NIS*. Copenhagen: World Health Organization.

Zakharov, Sergei and E. Ivanova (1996): "Fertility Decline and Recent Changes in Russia: On the Threshold of the Second Demographic Transition". In: DaVanzo (ed., with the assistance of G. Farnsworth): *Russia's Demographic "Crisis"*. RAND Conference Proceedings.

Zalanyi S., G. Bartfai, G. Falkay (1996): Reproductive health in the formerly socialist countries in Eastern Europe. Advances in Contraception, 12(4), pp.275-279.

**Section 2.6 :**

Bobak M., H. Pickhart, C. Hertzman, R. Rose, M. Marmot (1998): "Socio-economic factors, perceived control and self-reported health in Russia. A cross-sectional study". *Social Science and Medicine*, 47:269-79.

Carlson, E. (1989): "Concentration of rising Hungarian mortality among manual workers". *SSR*, 73/3, S.119-128.

Carlson, E.; S. Tsvetarsky (1992): "Concentration of rising Bulgarian mortality among manual workers". *International family planning perspectives*, 76/2, S.81-84.

Cockerham (1999): *Health and social Change in Russia and Eastern Europe*. Routledge.

Cornia, G. A., and R. Paniccià (2000): *The Mortality Crisis in Transitional Economics*. Oxford University Press.

Hertzman C, S. Kelly and M. Bobak (1996): *East-West Life Expectancy Gap in Europe*. Kluwer Academic Publishers.

Kingkade, Ward and Cheryl Chriss Sawyer (2001): *Infant mortality in Eastern Europe and the former Soviet Union before and after the breakup*. Paper presented at the XXIV IUSSP General Population Conference, Salvador de Bahia, Brasil.

Leon D. (2001): "Common threads: underlying components of inequalities in mortality between and within countries". In: Leon D., Walt G. eds. *Poverty, inequality, and health*. Oxford, Oxford University Press, pp.58-87.

Mc Kee, M. and V. Shkolnikov (2001): "Understanding the toll of premature death among men in Eastern Europe". *British Medical Journal*, Vol.323, 3 November 2001, pp.1051-1055.

Meslé F. (1996): "Mortality in Eastern and Western Europe: A Widening Gap". In: *Europe's Population in the 1990s*. D. Coleman, editor, Oxford University Press.

Meslé F., J. Vallin and V. Shkolnikov (1998): "Reversal of mortality decline: the case of contemporary Russia". *World Health Statistics Quarterly*, Vol. 51, N.2/3/4., pp.191-206.

Vallin J. and F. Meslé; Valkonen T. (2001): "Trends in mortality and differential mortality". Council of Europe Publishing, *Population Studies* No. 36.

## List of figures

Figure 1.1 – Elements of system transformation in the post-Socialist countries

Figure 1.2 – Real GDP in the ECE transition economies, 1980-2000 (Indices, 1989 = 100 %)

Figure 1.3 – Registered unemployment in the ECE transition economies, 1990-2000 (percent of labour force)

Figure 1.4 – Phase-level model of social transformation

Figure 1.5 – Average gross monthly wages, real growth rate in selected Transformation Countries, 1990-2000 (in %)

Fig. 1.6 – Total Fertility Rate and Gross Domestic Product in the post-Socialist countries, 1989-1999

Fig. 1.7 – Unemployment rate and Total Fertility Rate 1990-1999 in Hungary, the Czech Republic, Russia and Ukraine

Figure 2.2.1 – Total first marriage rates (left panel) and mean ages at first marriage (right panel)

Figure 2.2.2 – Age-specific first-marriage rates in Hungary 1986, 1990, 1996: (a) observed values and (b) standardised values

Figure 2.2.3 – Proportion ever married women in cohorts born between 1947 and 1967 (thick line – left axis) and mean age at entry into first marriage of the same cohorts (dotted line – right axis)

Figure 2.3.1 – Total divorce rates in Estonia, Latvia and Lithuania, 1960-2000

Figure 2.3.2 – Total divorce rates in Czechiathe Czech Republic, Eastern Germany, Hungaryia and Slovakia, 1960-2000

Figure 2.3.3 – Total divorce rates in Bulgaria, Croatia, Poland and Romania, 1960-2000

Figure 2.3.4 – Total divorce rates in Slovenia, Macedonia, Bosnia-Herzegovina, Yugoslavia, 1960-2000

Figure 2.3.5 – Divorces by duration of marriage, selected countries in transition, 1990 and 1999

Figure 2.4.1 – TFR (left panel) and mean age at birth of first child (right panel)

Figure 2.4.2 – First-order TFR

## List of tables

## Group of specialists on the demographic consequences of economic transition in countries of central and eastern Europe (PO-S-TEC)

**List of members**

*Croatia*: **Ms Franka VOJNOVIC**, Ministry for Public Works, Reconstruction and Construction, Vlaska 108, 10000 ZAGREB, tel: +385.1.46.95.736, fax: +385.46.95.739, E-mail: franka.vojnovic@zg.tel.hr

*Czech Republic*: **Mr Zdenek PAVLIK**, Professor, Charles University, Faculty of Sciences, Albertov 6, CZ-128 43 PRAHA, tel: +420.2.2195.2423, fax: +420.2.24.92.06.57, E-mail: pavlik.@natur.cuni.cz (Chairman)

*Hungary*: **Mr Ferenc KAMARAS**, Hungarian Central Statistical Office, Population, Health and Social Statistics Department, Keleti Karoly u. 5-7, P.O. Box, 1024 BUDAPEST, tel: +36.1.345.6565, fax: +36.1.345.66.78, E-mail: ferenc.kamaras@office.ksh.hu

*Lithuania*: **Mrs Virginija EIDUKIENE**, Head, Demographic Statistics Division, Lithuanian Department of Statistics, Gedimino ave. 29, 2746 VILNIUS, tel: +370.2.364.770, fax: +370.2.364.666, E-mail: virginijae@mail.std.lt

*Poland*: **Mrs Lucyna NOWAK**, Director, Demographic Statistics Division, Central Statistical Office, Al. Niepodleglosci 208, 00-925 WARSZAWA, tel: +48.22.608.31.21

*Romania*: **Mrs Aura-Mihaela ZAMFIRESCU**, Director, Demographic Studies and Projection Unit, National Institute of Statistics and Economic Studies, 16, Libertatii Avenue, sect. 5, 70542 BUCHAREST, tel: +40.1.410.67.44/1079, fax: +40.1.312.48.73, E-mail: popcens@insee.ro

*Russian Federation*: **Mr Andrei G. VOLKOV**, Head, Department of Demography, Research Institute of Statistics, Goskomstat of Russia, 39, Myasnitskaya Str., 103450 MOSCOW, tel: +7.095.207.41.26, fax: +7.095.207.49.27; E-mail: stat@gks.ru

*Slovak Republic*: **Mr Boris VANO**, INFOSTAT, Vyskumne demograficke centrum, Dubravska 3, 842 21 BRATISLAVA, tel: +421.7.59.37.92.71, fax: +421.7.54.79.14.63, E-mail: vano@infostat.sk

*"The former Yugoslav Republic of Macedonia"*: **Mr Apostol SIMOVSKI**, Statistical Office, 4 Dame Gruev, P.O. Box 506, 91000 SKOPJE, tel: +389.2.259.726, fax: +389.91.111.336, E-mail: apostol@stat.gov.mk

*Ukraine*: **Mr Serhii I. PYROZHKOV**, Director, National Institute of Ukrainian-Russian Relations, 18/7 Kutuzova Street, 252133 KYIV, tel: +38.044.295.34.66, fax: +38.044.294.81.35, E-mail: psi@niisp.gov.ua

**Mrs Tatyana KREMEN**, Attaché of the Council of Europe Division, Ministry for Foreign Affairs, 1, Mykhaylivska sq., 01018 KYIV, tel: +380.44.226.33.79, fax: +380.44.212.22.12

**Consultants**

**Mr Jürgen DORBRITZ**, BIB, Federal Institute for Population Research, Friedrich-Ebert-Allee 4, Postfach 5528, 65180 WIESBADEN, tel: +49.611.75.20.62, fax: +49.611.75.39.60, E-mail: juergen.dorbritz@destatis.de

**Mr Dimiter PHILIPOV**, Vienna Institute for Demography, Prinz Eugen Strasse 8-10, 1040 WIEN, tel: +43.1.51581.7793, fax: +43.1.51581.7730.199, E-mail: dimiter.philipov@oeaw.ac.at

## Titles in the same collection:

24. **Information and education in demography**
    Rossella PALOMBA, Alessandra RIGHI (1993)
    (ISBN 92-871-2111-7)

25. **Political and demographic aspects of migration flows to Europe**
    Raimondo CAGIANO de AZEVEDO (editor) (1993)
    (ISBN 92-871-2360-8)

26. **The future of Europe's population**
    Robert CLIQUET (editor) (1993)
    (ISBN 92-871-2369-1)

27. **The demographic situation of Hungary in Europe**
    Andras KLINGER (1993)
    (ISBN 92-871-2352-7)

28. **Migration and development cooperation**
    Raimondo CAGIANO de AZEVEDO (editor) (1994)
    (ISBN 92-871-2611-9)

29. **Ageing and its consequences for the socio-medical system**
    Jenny DE JONG-GIERVELD, Hanna VAN SOLINGE (1995)
    (ISBN 92-871-2685-2)

30. **The demographic characteristics of national minorities in certain European States (Volume 1)**
    Werner HAUG, Youssef COURBAGE, Paul COMPTON (1998)
    (ISBN 92-871-3769-2)

31. **The demographic characteristics of national minorities in certain European States (Volume 2)**
    Various authors (2000)
    (ISBN 92-871-4159-2)

32. **International migration and regional population dynamics in Europe : a synthesis**
    Philip REES, Marek KUPISZEWSKI (1999)
    (ISBN 92-871-3923-7)

33. **Europe'population and labour market beyond 2000**
   (Volume 1 : An assessment of trends and policy issues)
   Aidan PUNCH, David L. PEARCE (editors) (2000)
   (ISBN 92-871-4273-4)

34. **Europe'population and labour market beyond 2000**
   (Volume 2 : Country case studies)
   Aidan PUNCH, David L. PEARCE (editors) (2000)
   (ISBN 92-871-4399-4)

35. **Fertility and new types of households and family formation in Europe**
   Antonella PINNELLI, Hans Joachim HOFFMANN-NOWOTNY and Beat
   FUX (2001)
   (ISBN 92-871-4698-5)

36. **Trends in mortality and differential mortality**
   Jacques VALLIN and France MESLE, Tapani VALKONEN (2001)
   (ISBN 92-871-4725-6)

37. **People, demography and social exclusion**
   Dragana AVRAMOV (2002)
   (ISBN 92-8715095-8)

38. **The demographic characteristics of immigrant populations**
   Werner HAUG, Paul COMPTON, Youssef COURBAGE (editors) (2002)
   (ISBN 92-871-4974-7)